YouTube Blueprint For Beginners

The Strategies & Secrets To Starting & Rapidly Growing Your Channel, Becoming A Video Influencer, Mastering Social Media Marketing, Advertising & SEO

Brandon's Business guides

Table of Contents

Introduction 1

Section 1: Exploring YouTube 3

Chapter 1 - How Much Do You Know About YouTube? 4

    YouTube, an Ongoing History of Videos and Comments 4

        Google Steps In 5

        Redesign and Growth 6

    Changing Your Perspective of YouTube 7

    The Inner Workings of YouTube 8

    More Than Leisure 9

Chapter 2 - What Makes YouTube Unique? 10

    YouTube vs. Other Social Media Platforms 11

        Facebook 11

        Twitter 13

        TikTok 14

        Instagram 14

        The Verdict 15

    Why is YouTube the Best Choice for You Right Now? 16

    Using YouTube to Grow Business 17

    Using YouTube for Fun 19

Section 2: Starting Your Channel 20

Chapter 3 - Choosing a Niche 21

    Identifying Your Goals 21

    Why Choose a Niche? 22

    Introducing the Various Worlds in YouTube 23

    How to Choose Your Niche? 25

Chapter 4 - Setting Up Your Account and Channel 27

    Branding Your Channel 27

    What You'll Be Up Against 29

        Expenses 29

Search Engine Optimization *30*
Competition *30*
Time *31*
Earnings *31*

The Process of Creating Your Channel 32
Step 1: Set up your account. *32*
Step 2: Create a channel. *32*
Step 3: Personalize your channel. *32*
Step 4: Art *33*
Step 5: Add a profile picture. *33*
Step 6: Optimize your channel description *33*
Step 7: Add relevant links to your channel. *34*
Step 8: Add a trailer to your channel. *34*

Exploring Your Channel 34

Section 3: Creating, Editing, and Posting Videos on YouTube 35

Chapter 5 - Creating Content 36

It Depends on Your Niche and How You Strategize 36
See What the Other YouTubers are Doing 38
The Win-Win Solution 39
Read This Whenever You're Lost on What to Create Next 40
Constructing Scripts Your Way 42

Chapter 6 - How to Create or Record Your Videos 45

Creating vs. Recording 45
Equipment for Recording Videos 46
Guide for Recording Videos 47
Creating Videos without Recording 49

Chapter 7 - Editing Videos Like a Pro 52

The Makings of a Great Video 52
Using Video Editing Tools 54
The Actual Process of Video Editing 55
The Preview *55*

  Planing *56*
  The Rough Cut *56*
  Scene Editing *56*
  Effects *56*
  Rendering *57*
 How to Add Music 57
 Tricks to the Trade 58

Chapter 8: You Don't Just Upload a Video **60**
 The Video Details 60
 Creating YouTube Thumbnails 62
 Setting an Upload Schedule 63
 How to Upload Your Videos 65

Section 4: Growing Your YouTube Channel **67**

Chapter 9: Your YouTube Audience **68**
 The YouTube Community 68
 Where Do Viewers Come From 69
 Getting People to Subscribe and Hit that Notification Icon 70
 Engaging with Your Audience 71
 Tinkering with the Community Settings 72
 Consider Doing a Livestream 73

Chapter 10: Managing Your Channel **75**
 Welcoming Your Audience to the Channel 75
 Make Use of Playlists 76
 Are You Properly Utilizing YouTube Stories? 77
 How YouTube Videos are Ranked 77
  Keywords *78*
  Video Title and Description *78*
  Video Tags *79*
  Video Quality *79*
  User Experience Metrics *80*
  Closed Captions *80*

Mastering YouTube Analytics 80
   Youtube metrics *81*
   Audience Metrics *81*
   Youtube Discovery Metrics *82*
   YouTube Video Metrics *82*
   YouTube Engagement Metrics *83*
   YouTube Revenue Metrics *83*
Let's Talk About Copyright 83

Chapter 11: YouTube and SEO in a Nutshell 86
SEO, in General 86
How SEO Works on YouTube 87
Applying & Improving SEO on Your Channel 88

Chapter 12: YouTube Marketing 90
The Basics of Marketing 90
Social Media Marketing (SMM) 91
   How SMM Works *92*
Marketing on YouTube 93
   Branding on YouTube *94*
Promoting on Other Social Media Platforms 95

Chapter 13: YouTube Advertising 97
What You Should Know About Advertising 97
Paid Advertising on YouTube 98
Launching a YouTube Ad Campaign 99
   Budget and Prices *99*
   Networks *100*
   Location, Language, and the Advanced Settings *100*
   Targeting and Advanced Targeting *101*
Don't Forget to Check the Results 101
Optimize Before You Launch a New One 102
   Evaluate CPV *102*
   Evaluate View Rate *102*

 Evaluate CTR *103*

Section 5: Aiming and Achieving Your Long-Term Goals 104

Chapter 14: Becoming an Influencer..105
 What it Means to Become an Influencer...105
 YouTube Influencers in Every Field..106
 Your Checklist to Becoming an Influencer 107
 The Things You Can Do as an Influencer 108

Chapter 15: Making Money on YouTube 110
 Earning a Living Through YouTube...110
 The YouTube Partner Program (YPP) 111
 Becoming an Affiliate 112
 Getting Sponsors 113
 Selling Merchandise of Your Brand 115
 Getting Funds...116
 Licensing Your Content 117

Conclusion 118

References 119

Introduction

Do you want to become the next YouTube sensation but don't know where to start? Or maybe you want to use YouTube to grow your business but don't know exactly what your options are? Even if you just want to share your views on various topics with other people, but don't know where to start, this book will help you. Whether you already have a YouTube channel that you're planning to grow, or you just want to start one, this book will provide you with the essential information that you need to succeed.

Some people find it difficult to get started because they lack ideas or knowledge. Others don't really understand how YouTube actually works. It is time to stop overthinking, and start doing. YouTube is a user-friendly social media platform, but it is understandable if you have some fears that can only be dispersed by the certainty that comes with knowledge. The tips and techniques included in this book will help you not only to get started, but to also develop your channel, gather subscribers, and become a YouTube star!

It might feel odd reading a book on YouTube when you can just watch a few YouTube videos about YouTube. There is loads of information on YouTube about YouTube itself. However, you already know you should not trust everything you see or read on the internet. I spent years researching, developing, and growing together with the YouTube platform. By following all the changes that YouTube went through, and learning how to adapt to the numerous updates, I gathered enough expertise to help work with other channels as their producer and adviser. And even though you can find various videos on YouTube on how to build your subscriber base, or how to produce a good video, get awesome ideas, you would have to spend hundreds of hours searching for quality material. This book gathers all that information in one place, allowing you to come back to it and easily find everything you need at any given moment.

Learn about the rich but brief history of YouTube, or what equipment you should invest in. See the changes the platform went through, how it developed from a place where people shared their videos, to a full-blown social media platform. Did you know YouTube is the second biggest search engine in the world? Right after Google! Billions of people browse through various videos each hour of the day. People use it to find entertainment, to listen to relaxing music while they work, or to learn new skills or acquire new knowledge. Even academics use YouTube platforms to upload their lectures and share them with students all around the world. The possibilities are endless and if you know how to take advantage of them, you will succeed.

Learn how to start your own channel, how to develop your art, produce your first video and find your own niche in which you will leave a part for yourself. Connect with other Youtubers and with the audience by learning how to properly use other social media platforms to drive traffic to your channel. In order to be found, you will also need to learn the tricks of the trade, such as SEO and the importance of keywords. YouTube is special when it comes to SEO because it relies more on community engagement than on backlinks and website crawling. Optimize your

YouTube channel in order to attract the right type of audience, and in order to let the internet know what your videos are about. Only this way you will ensure the visibility and reach of your videos.

Learn about recording your videos, how to compose the scenes, what background to use, and how it all comes down to the niche you are working in. Learn how to edit your videos and get them up on YouTube. Do you still lack ideas for your first video? Or maybe you are already famous and you feel like you exhausted all your inspiration? In this book, you will find a list of things you could do next and find that elusive inspiration instead of waiting for it to come to you.

If you own a business and you want to learn how to use YouTube as a marketing tool, there is something for you in this book too. Since YouTube is part of social network marketing, you will learn all about how advertising works, how to drive traffic to your business' website, how to brand your YouTube channel or promote your already existing brand. And finally, you'll learn how you can use other YouTubers who cater to wide audiences, as the face behind your brand, as promoters and influencers who can convince their audience to buy your product or service.

Finally, if you are a YouTuber who wants to start earning a living from his content, you'll learn how to properly monetize your channel. Whether through ads, by becoming an influencer, or by setting up your own merchandising store.

Television programming is history. YouTube is the place to be. Whether you just want to stand in front of the audience and show them what you got, want to grow your business, earn money through YouTube, or become a famous gamer, you should grasp the opportunity and join the millions of content creators already on YouTube.

You might have heard that the time of YouTube stars is passing and that it is impossible to become famous these days, but that's not true. Yes, the competition is fiercer than ever, and you need to be unique in some way to stand out in the sea of content creators, but it is still possible as long as you play your cards right. In some ways, it's actually easier nowadays to make it on YouTube than a decade ago. So, start today because the opportunity is right in front of you, all you need to do is seize it!

Section 1: Exploring YouTube

Chapter 1 - How Much Do You Know About YouTube?

Nowadays, YouTube is a part of everyday life and everyone knows what it is. It's a household name. It's hard to imagine that not that long ago we didn't have a massive online video platform where we could look up everything from funny cat videos to programming tutorials. During the dark ages of the 2000s, people used dial-up to connect to the Internet, and sharing videos was always a struggle. YouTube was revolutionary.

YouTube is a massive entertainment and advertising platform and a search engine in its own right, trailing behind only Google. But until 2005, nobody knew what they were missing. The platform started like most websites and online platforms: as an unknown startup somewhere in Silicon Valley.

YouTube, an Ongoing History of Videos and Comments

YouTube's humble beginnings can be traced back to February 2005 when three former PayPal employees, Chad Hurley, Steve Chen, and Jawed Karim, envisioned a new idea. That's when they registered the youtube.com domain. Their objective was to create an online video-sharing platform where users could upload their videos for others to watch. At that time, YouTube was a dream, Facebook didn't exist, and everyone relied on messenger apps for communication. But things were about to change faster than anyone could anticipate.

YouTube was up and running, but videos couldn't be uploaded to the platform until April 23rd. That's the day when Chad Hurley posted the first video in YouTube's history, and it was a short 18 seconds long clip of him visiting the zoo in San Diego. The video wasn't anything spectacular, but it marked the beginning of the Internet as we know it today.

Initially, the founders intended to allow users to share videos with their friends and family. The videos weren't supposed to be public. As a result, there were only 19 videos uploaded to YouTube during the first two months of its launch and they had gathered an insignificant number of views. That was all about to change when the 20th video was uploaded.

In May 2005, YouTube became accessible to a limited number of beta users. The platform started growing, hosting more videos with each passing day, and on June 26th the first viral video was uploaded. Two kids dubbing a song by the Backstreet Boys made history by recording themselves and uploading their video titled "Tow chinese boys: i want it that way". Their hit also made history by becoming one of YouTube's first videos with a typo in the title. By 2021 the video gathered around 7 million views, which doesn't sound like much for a viral video by today's standards. But back then social media was in its infancy and even a few thousand views was something big.

The website's official launch date was December 15, 2005, and by that time it was already registering roughly two million views per day. That number started growing exponentially as YouTube reached 25 million views in the next two months. By July, the platform reached a major milestone, registering 100 million daily views with over 60,000 videos being uploaded each day. However, rapid growth came with a new set of challenges for the founders.

As traffic demands increased, the company had to regularly upgrade its hardware. New equipment was purchased to keep up with the high influx of new users and the sheer number of videos that were being hosted. Nonetheless, upgrading computers and investing in more broadband connections wasn't the biggest concern. YouTube started attracting the eyes of the media and entertainment industry. Some of the videos the users were uploading contained copyrighted material and the companies weren't happy about that. YouTube had to prepare for potential lawsuits and funding a large team of lawyers and legal advisors was extremely costly.

YouTube was spiraling out of control and it was all due to rapid success. The growing traffic was countered by growing costs that were too difficult to manage in such a short period of time. As a result, the founders started looking to sell.

Google Steps In

Despite the resounding success YouTube enjoyed, the costs of maintaining a continually growing infrastructure and copyright infringement lawsuits were too much for a company that lacked income. Bankruptcy was on the horizon, but the platform's quick rise to fame had attracted Google's attention.

In 2005-2006 Google was a major player, dominating the Internet. The search engine company attempted to create its own video sharing platform called "Google Video", but it failed to gain any serious traction and it was discontinued. So when YouTube began looking for a buyer, Google rushed with an offer of $1,65 billion. This acquisition marked another major milestone in the history of the Internet, YouTube, and Google.

Once YouTube went under Google's control, the search engine giant continued investing and developing the platform instead of absorbing it. In retrospect, this was a great strategy as YouTube is now generating roughly 10% of Google's revenue. Google had the financial power to minimize the risk of lawsuits by negotiating with the entertainment industry to allow YouTube to host certain copyrighted material. Users could not use various songs and footage to create their videos without the risk of having their content removed. However, this came with the condition of Google removing thousands of copyrighted videos that didn't fall under the fair use agreement that was negotiated.

As Google continued their efforts in taking YouTube to the next level, the focus went on expansion. The year of 2007 represented a new beginning. YouTube was launched in nine other countries together and a mobile version of the site was created as well. Google introduced in-video ads, significantly increasing the income generated by the platform and they created a partner program to stimulate content creators.

Note: Did you know that the first Rickroll happened in 2007? And did you know that the Queen of England launched her own YouTube channel that same year? It was a crazy year!

YouTube was expanding faster than ever. In 2008 and 2009, a series of improvements were made to the platform. The analytics tool was launched, captions and annotations became available, and by December 2008 720p HD was enabled. As the quality of videos increased, and more quality of life features were introduced, YouTube began attracting the attention of entertainment giants like MGM, CBS, and Disney, as well as governments and state-run institutions.

Google signed deals with MGM and CBS to bring their full-length programming to YouTube. The US Congress and the Vatican were among the first governmental powers to launch their own channels. YouTube was becoming a true social media force. By the end of 2009, YouTube announced that the platform reached one billion views per day. This impressive rate would double by May 2010 as the video quality was raised further to 1080p and a new Individual Video Partnership was launched.

Redesign and Growth

The year of 2010 marked the beginning of a new age, as Chad Hurley, one of the original founders, decided to step down as YouTube's CEO and function only in an advisory capacity. Salar Kamangar became the new chief executive of the company in October.

But major changes were already happening in March 2010, as YouTube was relaunched with a new, simpler design. The goal was to improve user experience to increase the time spent on the platform by simplifying the interface and making it more user-friendly. The result was a 1 billion views per day increase every year. In 2010 YouTube recorded two billion daily views and that rate doubled by 2012. YouTube was the dominant video-sharing platform in the US.

In 2011, more design changes occurred and the logo was modified for the first time. However, it was 2012 that proved to be a big year. That's when the Gangnam Style music video broke the Internet by quickly gathering over a billion views. The view count was unprecedented on YouTube and it is partially responsible for the future change in how the view count algorithm works. Since then, Youtube started ranking videos based on how much time viewers spent watching them, instead of just counting views.

Until 2013, YouTube continued on its path to attract more users through its simplicity and by integrating itself with other social media platforms. Google's own Google+ social networking platform was a prime example of this trend. At the time, YouTube could be accessed from the Google+ interface that was also integrated into the Chrome browser.

With the upgraded interface and the changes made to the ranking algorithm, new types of videos started emerging around 2012-2014. Longer videos usually translated to better ranking because viewers spent significantly more time on them. This led to the rise of "top 10" video compilations and "let's play" videos. PewDiePie (Felix Kjellberg) started out in 2010 with horror games gameplay videos and by 2012 he gathered a following of one million subscribers. By 2013, his channel had the highest number of subscribers on YouTube.

In 2014, the feature expansion project continued with the launch of 60 frames per second videos. In addition, YouTube started taking a new turn by seeking new methods of monetization. As a result, YouTube RED was introduced, nowadays known as YouTube Premium, which was/is a paid version of the platform, but without any ads and the ability to access videos offline.

YouTube maintained this path until 2021 without making any more drastic changes. Nonetheless, the video-sharing platform is barely recognizable when comparing it to itself back in 2005. A great deal of today's traffic data is eaten up by YouTube and the millions of people who watch and upload videos. In 2020, due to the coronavirus pandemic, YouTube's traffic increased so much that the European Union had to ask the platform to cut back on its bandwidth to leave more room for medical services.

Changing Your Perspective of YouTube

YouTube is no longer just a video-sharing website. It is a social media platform and a search engine at the same time. Video content is one of the best methods of sending a message to your audience. Whether it's for entertainment purposes, company branding, advertising, or teaching, YouTube is a powerful way of delivering information.

The video format is increasingly more popular and it's becoming a favorite for Google's search engine algorithms. Because of how frequently quality video content is shared via social media, Google is taking notice of it. If one of your goals is to grow your presence on the Internet, you can use YouTube videos to improve your brand's search engine optimization (SEO). In other words, provided you create a video and share it through YouTube by using great titles, accurate descriptions, and appropriate tags, Google will boost your ranking. Therefore, setting up a YouTube channel isn't just for gamers and vloggers anymore. If you want to run a successful business in any field, you can show off your brand, services, or products by making and sharing YouTube videos.

In addition to marketing yourself or your business directly, YouTube is probably the best platform you can use to teach others how to solve a problem. By demonstrating certain concepts related to your business via YouTube videos, you can establish yourself as an authority on the subject. This might not boost your business from the start, but over time it will show potential customers that you know what you're talking about and you have a lot of value to offer. Some of that value is present in your free YouTube videos, which leads to branding.

Videos transmit a lot of information quickly. A few seconds of video content are often more valuable than a page of text. The same thing goes for branding. People like visuals. It's as simple as that. It's much harder to grab someone's attention or convey a specific emotion or mood through text. Whatever you're promoting, video is the right way to do it and with YouTube's smooth integration into other social media platforms it's easier than ever to build your brand. Once you create a video, you can spread it easily. It's not locked away on YouTube. You can add to your Facebook timeline, share it on Twitter, and even email it.

All of this is possible on a small budget. The main purpose of YouTube was always to allow users share their videos. It wasn't intended for professional actors and movie producers. You can create good-quality videos that offer a lot of value to the viewer with a minimal investment in some basic video equipment and editing software.

The Inner Workings of YouTube

YouTube's growth and popularity boils down to a user-friendly interface and powerful backend engineering. The platform accepts a variety of different video formats such as MP4, AVI, MOV, and WMV, making it easy for anyone to upload their content no matter what capturing and editing software they use. This advantage extends to the ability to embed the video content on your own website.

As mentioned earlier, YouTube is an excellent marketing and branding tool, but it doesn't have to be the only tool you use. You can spread your content throughout social media, but YouTube also allows you to easily embed and play it to your audience from the comfort of your website. By using some basic HTML code (that you can find and copy-paste), you can embed the video you uploaded to YouTube to your own website. This implies installing a YouTube player on your website, which is a process that doesn't take more than a couple of minutes. But why bother when you can simply host your own video? Hosting a video requires bandwidth and if you have more than a few videos, you're going to end up spending a lot of money, especially if you want to offer your audience full HD quality. By using this method, YouTube will handle the hard part of the job for you. All you need to do is link your website to the platform.

While embedding videos is a great way to spread your wings over the Internet, most people will come across your content by searching for it. Since YouTube is also a search engine like Google, it works in similar ways to connect the user to specific content. YouTube's search algorithms are certainly complex but know enough to make them work in our favor. Whenever you're searching for video content, the algorithms use a number of variables to decide what results to display for you. Those results are ranked based on those variables. It's impossible to manipulate all of them, but the most important ones are the title of the video, its description, tags, and thumbnail. Keep that in mind when you upload a video. Decide the title and the rest of the metadata based on the kind of content you're sharing. Make it as easy as possible for people to find your content by focusing on specific keywords they might use.

YouTube used to base its ranking system on the number of views a video had. However, that was changed due to a number of vulnerabilities. Nowadays, the quality of the content is determined based on how much time people spend watching the video. Therefore, if the majority of viewers stop watching a thirty-minute video after just one minute, the algorithm starts thinking that there's something wrong with the content. That simple metric suggests that the uploader titled the video inaccurately, failed to provide an adequate description, or that the content doesn't offer anything of value to most users. On the other hand, if the majority of viewers watch the video close to the end, it means the metadata is accurate and the content offers value. As a result, the video receives a high ranking. That being said, we assume there are other ranking factors at play, but the algorithm is complex, in constant change, and YouTube doesn't want to reveal its secrets.

Where does it all go? Is my content safe? These are some of the most common questions about all the data that goes to YouTube. Data security is a valid concern, but rest assured, all the videos you upload to YouTube are stored and protected for you. In essence, it's impossible to lose anything. Google is in charge of safely storing everything that's on YouTube by using their massive data centers. These data centers, which are spread around the world, house thousands of servers that store your content and manage everything that goes on on the search engine. A typical data center is strictly controlled to ensure optimal computer operating temperatures. The servers themselves are regularly maintained, and multiple ones are used to backing up your data. Even if something goes wrong with a server, your content won't be lost. Furthermore, data centers are connected to each other and they communicate with each other. Once you upload your video, it's actually sent to the closest data center. When someone clicks on it to watch it, the video is sent from that data center to the one that's closest to the user. This ensures rapid access to the content, but it also means your data is kept safe. If something goes wrong with the data center itself, like a fire breaking out, all of the data stored there is sent to other data centers.

That being said, YouTube takes care of your content, makes it easily accessible if you satisfy the search engine's requirements, and whatever you upload is protected.

More Than Leisure

While YouTube started out as a website where you could share videos with your friends, it evolved into so much more. For many, YouTube remains an entertainment platform that hosts funny cat videos, ridiculous car crashes, conspiracy theories, and music. However, the platform must not be underestimated for its educational potential.

YouTube has a lot of value to offer in education. You can find anything from instructional videos on how to fix a leaky pipe to university-level machine learning lectures. Out of the hundreds of hours of video content that is being uploaded every day, we can find educational content on any topic we can think of. The thirst for easily accessible knowledge has also pushed a number of NGOs to offer entire collections of lessons and lectors for free.

Many programmers, artists, and writers start out by learning from those video tutorials and lessons on YouTube. As a result, schools are starting to integrate the video platform and specifically a number of educational YouTube channels into their own curriculum. Many professors started recording their own lectures so that they can share them for free with anyone who's curious and willing to learn but maybe lack the funds to get a formal degree.

YouTube is flexible enough to allow anyone with knowledge and skill on a certain topic to teach others. Content developers, teachers, tradesmen, and hobbyists alike post videos on a regular basis on every topic you can think of. Whether it's leatherworking, fitness, or astrophysics, the entire world has something to learn thanks to YouTube. This very same flexibility brought TED (technology education and design) conferences on the mainstream stage. With over 2,000 free lectures presented by leaders from every field, viewers can learn from the comfort of their own homes without spending a cent.

YouTube is leading the charge, changing the education system from a strict, rigid format, to an open easy-to-access model that works for everyone. As life starts getting in the way of many, it's of utmost importance to still have access to education. YouTube offers this access allowing even those with limited budgets or full-time jobs to learn a new skill through bite-sized video content instead of hours after hours of traditional schooling. Knowledge has never been easier to attain than it is now. All it takes is a bit of motivation and minimal digital know-how to access the right educational content.

Chapter 2 - What Makes YouTube Unique?

Social media is everywhere and it is true when they say that if you don't have social media, it is as if you don't exist. It's not just about people using it to communicate with each other, to make friends, and make themselves seen. Companies use social media to advertise themselves, to find new employees, to establish their audience, and to grow their business. Politicians use social media to easily give the people access to their agendas, but also to launch their election campaigns. Musicians, photographers, various crafters, game developers, and others use social media to establish their presence and to reach out to their audience. But social media is ever-changing, and no matter what your business is, you should make a call and decide which type of social media is right for your business, and which platform can meet all your expectations.

There is no type of social media yet that can beat direct communication, but some of them can make your business sound and appear more personal. Through various platforms, you can advertise yourself and also reach out to your audience on a more personal level. This interaction between you as a creative drive behind your product (be it video, music, or simply a commercial for a product) and your audience is important and should be maintained. All social media will allow you to do this, but it is up to you to decide which of the platforms will balance out your online presence the best. In the end, you cannot focus only on the audience, you also have to think about the quality of your material, the design of your brand, the monetization options, and what you have to offer.

This chapter will show you the differences between various social networks and how they compare with YouTube. You will also learn why you should choose YouTube and how to grow your business through it. But in the end, don't forget to have fun. Whether you strive to become a YouTube star, or if you just look to expand your business, using YouTube shouldn't feel like doing chores.

YouTube vs. Other Social Media Platforms

Before you can choose the social media platform that suits your needs the best, let's see what is out there, what choices you have, what can each of them offer, and why you should choose YouTube! Many people are surprised to learn that YouTube is considered a social network, but the truth is, it has all the elements of one. However, YouTube is a unique social network and a perfect choice for everyone who is trying to communicate their message through video. But let's not get ahead of ourselves, and let's see what other platforms have to offer, their pros and cons, and how they perform in comparison to YouTube. This way we will answer the question of why YouTube is such a unique place on the World Wide Web.

Facebook

Probably the best-known social network out there is Facebook. And it is a great platform because it offers so much to individuals as well as businesses. It incorporates almost all media formats, such as text, audio, and video. Facebook is used by a large segment of the global population, and such a big audience attracts many businesses to the platform. However, despite Facebook offering special sales and marketing tools to business owners, it is almost never the first choice for business owners. This is due to it not being the best option for the development of a brand. Businesses should always establish their brand, grow it, and use Facebook only to increase their reach. Facebook is a platform that can bring the awareness of your business to the next level because it allows you to be seen and for your content to be shared among millions of its users.

For videographers, Facebook is probably an ideal second choice. Just as any other platform, it will allow you access to a wide audience, but when it actually comes to videos themselves,

Facebook often falls short. This is precisely because this platform tries to incorporate so many media in itself. Just like a Jack of all trades, Facebook is a master of none. It cannot offer high-quality service to videographers. Facebook's many users like the simplicity of having it all in one place, and for their needs, Facebook came up with "Facebook Watch", a separate tab within the App, or website, for all the video content lovers out there.

Facebook Watch offers easy access to videos that were published on Facebook, however, there is a trick to it. A video needs to come from a very reputable page, such as the ones with more than 5,000 followers. If you are new to making videos and you are just beginning to spread your influence, you would have to dedicate a lot of time and money to become one of the reputable pages in order for your videos to be seen. This is something that is limiting you as a creator. Ask yourself if you even have enough time to dedicate to both creating quality content for your video and managing your social presence, all for only one platform?

Facebook Watch was created in 2017, with the intention to offer the viewers only the videos which were commissioned by Facebook. That means that in its early stages, the users of these platforms were not able to share their videos. The very next year Facebook Watch opened up to all of its users. But it was always intended to be a limited platform with a limited offer. Because of this, once everyone was able to upload their videos the platform itself had to change. The problem is, that Facebook Watch is still changing, and very often too. Constant updates and tweaks to the algorithm are what a creator has to deal with if he chooses to use Facebook Watch. This unpredictability of the platform is off-putting for many of its users.

In 2019, Facebook started offering its users a percentage of the money made from the ads that are played during their videos. This was a great change, however, the unpredictability of Facebook's algorithm makes it a very unreliable option for anyone who wants to earn money from videos. Some users have been complaining that one month they would earn a decent amount of money, but the next month they wouldn't see any revenues at all. And all of this just because Facebook suddenly decided to make some changes to how their algorithm works. These updates forced content developers to adapt continuously. While earning money using this platform is possible, it demands you to constantly keep track and update your marketing tactics to be able to keep up with Facebook. This means you would waste your time on managing your page more than creating quality video content for your audience.

Many people ask why not combine Facebook and YouTube, why not cross-post? This is always an option and something you should definitely consider doing. But even if you opt for cross-posting you would have to decide which social media would be your main video sharing platform. Facebook works completely differently than YouTube. Most of the time people don't search for videos intentionally when browsing Facebook. It comes as recommended on their newsfeed, and Facebook utilizes silent autoplay. This means that your video would have to be designed specifically to catch the attention of a person scrolling down his news-feed. A person is less likely to click on a video on Facebook if it doesn't have a flashy or colorful thumbnail or autoplay which would attract the eye quickly. Facebook users tend to prefer visual stimulation to auditory, and they tend to keep the sound off while watching a video. If you want to create videos that rely on sound, maybe you should consider Facebook as your secondary option.

Creating video content that caters to both Facebook and YouTube at the same time is nearly impossible.

Unlike Facebook Watch, YouTube is considered a consistent platform. That doesn't mean YouTube's algorithms never change, but some parts of it became codified. This means that YouTube is generally a more stable option that will strive to bring you equal revenues even if there are some changes implemented. YouTube is reliable when compared to Facebook Watch, but it does attract a different kind of audience. Its search engine is so advanced that newer generations are starting to use it as an alternative to Google.

YouTube is meant to be used as a separate app or website. As such, the platform is completely dedicated to videos, which means it will guarantee quality delivery to your audience. YouTube users are many and even though its algorithm is capable of suggesting videos based on the users' viewing history, it is mostly designed for a direct search. But this is not limiting at all. This means your videos will reach the audience that is interested in the type of videos you are making, and not just anyone. While it is true it's harder to reach new viewers, it does spare you from negative comments and ratings coming from people who were not interested in seeing your video in the first place. This is something that Facebook doesn't offer you. Another great aspect of YouTube, in comparison to Facebook, is that you can make the content as flashy as you want, or you could make it purely an auditory experience, it doesn't matter. In the end, it will always reach the right audience for you.

The major advantage of YouTube is that it can be shared on all other websites. It can be embedded in blog posts, news articles, newsletters, or it can be shared on other social media platforms, even on Facebook. The success of a video posted on Facebook purely depends on its news feed algorithm. But when it comes to YouTube, the content creator has full control of its success through SEO. This is because Google indexes YouTube videos. In other words, your video will pop-up as a Google search result, while a video posted on Facebook won't. That means that millions of people who use Google every day can become your potential viewers. YouTube is not as limiting as Facebook and ultimately it is a better choice. Your videos can be shared, can reach millions and millions of users, can bring you a stable income and you can fully control the quality of their display as well as their success.

Twitter

Twitter is a social network used for what is known as "Microblogging". It allows its user to post only up to 280 characters, but this number is occasionally increasing (it started from 140 characters). It is an easy-to-use platform with a newsfeed that will show you "tweets", or posts, from the people you follow. You can reply to their tweets, you can post your own, or you can re-tweet or share other people's tweets. Twitter is a great way to communicate your thoughts and messages in a very direct manner. It is used by various types of people from politicians, scientists, influencers, institutions, and businesses. It is a great way to reach your audience and express yourself. But if you are a video content creator, you may find Twitter extremely limiting. While it does allow linking your videos from other platforms, Twitter itself is not a good choice as the main platform from which to share your videos. This is because the platform allows very short formats, and the maximum length of a video is 10 minutes. However, this is available only to companies that want to share their video ads. Tweets in the form of a video are even shorter, as the maximal length is 2 minutes and 20 seconds.

That being said, Twitter is constantly evolving and changing its rules, and with the further development of technology, this platform pushes its limits. Video length might be increased in the future. Twitter is, primarily, designed for very short and direct content. This shouldn't discourage you from using Twitter at all. It is still a great place to share links to your YouTube videos, to spread your brand's presence, and attract an audience. Because of Twitter's time limits, videos designed for this platform are easy and quick to make. For example, you can create a preview of your main YouTube video and tweet it as a commercial. Twitter is perfect for commercializing your YouTube videos because the links can be embedded within a tweet and look as if it's part of it. Aesthetically pleasing and easily accessible links are a major plus!

TikTok

Similar to Twitter's microblogging narrative, TikTok is a micro-vlogging platform. It is a social network, completely dedicated to short videos with a maximum length of up to three minutes. TikTok is also available only to smartphone users as it is basically a smartphone app developed for IOS and Android operating systems. Nevertheless, the content shared on this platform reaches over 2 billion users worldwide. It is a powerful app and its popularity is skyrocketing. More and more companies, as well as small business owners, are using TikTok to promote their products and businesses in a creative way.

For a full-time video content developer, TikTok is a very limiting platform. The fact that it works only on IOS and Android smartphones will influence your ability to reach certain audiences. Furthermore, TikTok users form an unreliable audience as they are usually in the search of and quick entertainment. In addition, TikTok doesn't offer a share of the revenues to content creators and people who earn money through this social network do it mostly by advertising products and directing the traffic to online stores. However, this is a tactic a YouTuber could also use. Just like with Twitter you can create short and catchy commercials for your main YouTube channel, and use TikTok to direct the audience to it.

Instagram

Instagram is home to many businesses, influencers, bloggers, and vloggers because it uses stunning and expressive visuals to attract the audience in order to promote products or content.

This is why Instagram should be very carefully considered by video makers. Like Twitter and TikTok, Instagram is best suited for short and quick content that catches the eye of the audience. But the advantage of Instagram is that if your audience is younger than 40, they are most likely using this app.

Originally, the app was created for smartphones to share pictures, but nowadays Instagram strives to cater to everyone and the possibility of creating, uploading, and viewing videos was introduced too. These are usually selfie-style videos, perfect for vloggers and influencers who want to make a quick promotional material and direct the audience to their main platform.

That being said, Instagram should never be used purely for vlogging. As the networks described above, it is a limiting platform that allows short videos and limited content. If you are using it, remember that visual stimulation is the most important part of Instagram and you should focus your effort on making separate short videos only for Instagram. This app is to be used only for cross-posting and marketing. So why should you opt for Instagram above all others? Because of the size of the audience. If you have doubts about whether to use Instagram, Facebook, TikTok, or Twitter, simply go with Instagram because it's rarely a mistake. But remember, this app is not an alternative to YouTube, but only an additional marketing and outreach platform.

The Verdict

As you can see, there is no real alternative to YouTube. Facebook Watch came close to making a worthy competitor, but ultimately it failed because it was trying to cater to the demands of its whole user base. YouTube remains the only social media platform that is optimal for video content. Whether you want to be a vlogger, influencer, create intriguing gaming or science-related content, or if you want to talk about books, perform interviews, or promote your music, YouTube is the perfect place. It even offers you various ways to communicate with your audience. But just like any social network out there, YouTube is evolving and constantly changing. It follows the latest trends and who knows what the future will bring. Remember that YouTube is the second most used search engine out there after Google and many people use it on a regular basis for entertainment or to learn something new. The average time spent on YouTube is constantly increasing. This gives you, a video content creator, the freedom to choose the length of your videos, their content, and their visual and auditory appeal. This is why YouTube is so unique.

Why is YouTube the Best Choice for You Right Now?

YouTube is probably one of the most successful social media platforms out there because it benefits not only its developers but also its users. Whether you're a simple user or a content creator, or even a brand or a company, YouTube has something to offer you.

As a content creator, YouTube will reward you no matter if your channel is successful or if it fails. Instagram and Facebook, for example, do not have the option of direct payment to the content creator. However, YouTube does. To some degree, the platform offers you protection. But the compensation you might get from YouTube is not always money. Sometimes it comes in the form of networking. YouTube is famous for connecting you with professionals in the industry because YouTube strives to reward quality videos. Otherwise, everyone would make low-quality content just so they could make money from views. If the content is low quality, the users will leave, and so would the companies that pay for commercials, and the platform would fail. The better the quality of your content, the more compensation you would get.

Another reason why YouTube is the best choice for content creators is that it is the only social media platform that rewards creativity, but it is also completely driven by creativity. Just as Instagram is a home for photographers who try to put themselves on the scene, YouTube is a platform for video and audio content creators. This means that if you're a filmmaker, but you don't have the access to the big industry yet, YouTube is the perfect place where you could start. It will not only allow you to store your videos so you could show them off, but it would also compensate you for the hard work you put into making those videos. YouTube is doing this so it could mobilize talent that is usually underrepresented. It is your talent that attracts the users to the platform, and YouTube recognizes it.

Everyone on YouTube gets the same opportunity to present himself, and succeed. YouTube doesn't discriminate, and the platform allows a healthy amount of competition. The platform itself will not close itself to musicians because there are too many music creators out there. It is up to you, the content creator, to make your videos shine and attract the audience.

That being said, the most important reason why YouTube is the best social media platform for you is that it allows you to nurture your passion, to learn, grow, change, shape yourself and while doing this you can even start earning. You can either use YouTube as a side business, which will give you that extra income you could use. Or you can make YouTube your platform of choice on which you would launch your career. This is why a "YouTuber" became a profession, and you can even pay your taxes by signing yourself as a YouTuber. There are many stories out there of people who quit their 9 to 5 office jobs just so they could pursue their passions and become YouTubers. There is truth to that saying " if you do what you love, you won't work a single day". And many would say that YouTube is oversaturated, that everyone is becoming a YouTuber or an influencer. Some even doubt you could earn money by doing what everyone else is doing. But this is simply not true. You can still succeed on YouTube, even if your passion is largely represented already. You just need to find your own voice, do it in your own unique way and people will want to watch your videos.

To the young generations, YouTube stars are as famous as any rock star out there. They gather their fans into tight-knit communities and these fans are their primary audience. You don't even need to have millions of subscribers to experience this phenomenon. But remember that YouTube is about healthy competition, and anyone can become successful if they have something of value to offer. It's easy to say "be unique", or "just keep pursuing your passion and you will make it". However, YouTube reached a certain point of maturity, technologically and content-wise. It is not easy to become a hit overnight, but it's not quite impossible either. There are many ways to make yourself noticed. From offering high-quality content, which is probably the most important aspect of a YouTube channel, to creating collaborations with other YouTubers who could attract new audiences to your channel. In order to succeed on YouTube, you should develop a proper marketing strategy, or maybe even think about hiring a specialist who could help you push yourself out there. Having a plan and following it will eventually yield good results.

Using YouTube to Grow Business

You don't have to be a YouTuber to use this platform for your business purposes. Like any other social platform, YouTube is an excellent way to grow and expand your business. It will allow you to reach not only new customers but also the people with who you can work and collaborate. In other words, YouTube is an excellent networking platform for any kind of business out there. This is simply because, in the 21st century, social media marketing is the most important form of marketing we have. It completely replaces the traditional methods of advertising, and every business needs an online presence. We already discussed how YouTube, besides being a social media, is also the second most used search engine. Google is also indexing YouTube videos, and if done properly, your video ad can be among the first results Google displays.

Here are a few benefits of using YouTube to grow your business:

1. **Reach a bigger audience!** YouTube has billions of users and hundreds of hours of videos uploaded daily. This means that this platform puts at your disposal a huge audience that can potentially become your customers or fans. Of course, YouTube won't do the marketing for you, and you still have to think about how to drive that audience to come to visit your channel. There are many ways to attract people, but keep in mind that everyone wants to see quality videos. Once you focus on that, you can start generating a high number of views as videos with high numbers attract even more people and potential customers. The best way to do this is to share your YouTube videos through other social network platforms such as Facebook or Twitter.

2. **Generate Traffic!** Yes, you can use YouTube to generate traffic to your website. Simply place the link to your website in the description of your video ad and you will gain clicks. People are curious, and if your video attracts their attention, they'll want to find out more directly from your website. Another way to generate traffic through YouTube is to collaborate with vloggers and influencers. Find a suitable YouTuber who you think would present your product or your service the best. They will work hard to spark the interest in their own audience for your product, and that audience would happily click on the link which would lead them to your website.

3. **Increase your Google presence!** YouTube is part of Google. Google's search engine algorithm started considering videos a valuable and trustworthy source of information, and YouTube videos are highly ranked. But in order to make this feature work for you, you will have to follow a few rules. You will need to mind the use of keywords and create your titles, hashtags, and video descriptions accordingly. You need to organize and categorize your content properly, and if you have a blog on your website, make the videos a part of them. If your video content complements the text, Google would rank it even higher.

4. **The economic value of YouTube is unmatched!** Not only is creating a YouTube ad cheaper, but it is also much faster in generating traffic. The traditional marketing methods take time. They need to reach a wide audience but they are limited as they are not available to a large enough audience. YouTube will reach the targeted audience immediately and you will see the first results in no time. Time is money, and the faster you reach your audience, the faster you will start developing your business.

5. **Stay in touch with your audience!** YouTube, just as any other social network platform, will allow you to communicate with your audience through comments. But it will offer you even more than that. You can ask your viewers to be a part of your campaign by recording their reviews of your products and services. Make them feel that there is a human behind the videos and make them a part of what you are doing.

6. **Build brand awareness!** Through contact with your audience, you can raise brand awareness and loyalty. But for this, you would need to create a special connection with your viewers. You can do this easily through a series of initiatives you can start on YouTube. People love social initiatives and they will want to know your company's stance on many of the modern social issues. Research the modern trends and share your views on them. It can be about climate change, Pride month, animal welfare, and any other pressing matters. Organize charities, lotteries, and give away prizes related to your business. You can even opt to give special discounts to your YouTube followers.

Developing and expanding your business through social media is a fun task, and doing it through YouTube makes it engaging, interesting, modern, and very economic. Remember that YouTube is not only a place where you will display your ads. It is a fun, ever-growing community that appreciates communication between professionals and users. YouTube is an awesome place through which you can show the human side of your business. Show the face that stands behind the brand, act natural, joyful and share your happiness and emotions with your audience. This will increase their loyalty and YouTube will improve your ranking.

Using YouTube for Fun

YouTube is popular because once you create your account and your YouTube channel, you will have total freedom to decide what to do with it and how to promote it if you choose to do so. Some people want to become internet famous, but others want to keep their videos private, and maybe share them with certain friends and family members.

There is no right or wrong way of using YouTube. In the end, it all comes down to personal preferences. Some people will never make their own channel and won't post their videos. They use YouTube to enjoy the content other people have to offer. These people are called viewers and they are attracted to YouTube for various reasons. The platform offers them quality content for free, and easy access to their favorite videos. They can keep track of their favorite content creators, follow them and enjoy their new videos as soon as they're posted. There are even options that will enable you to receive a special notification whenever your favorite YouTuber uploads a new video. YouTube users are also given access to new music videos, movie trailers, and popular brand reviews. Although YouTube strives to cultivate the unrepresented talent, most of the famous names out there keep their presence on YouTube too. This is because they recognize the advantages of this social network and use it to promote themselves and their work. But most of all, the viewers love YouTube because of its various possibilities. Through the video content, they can have fun, amuse themselves by watching various gameplays, cartoons, or any content design to make them laugh. But they can also watch documentaries, interviews with famous people, and learn about the science or social problems of our world. There is everything for every person's taste on YouTube, and it's so easy to access its content.

That being said, YouTube is also fun for creative people who want to make their presence known - the YouTubers! Being a YouTuber and sharing your videos is a fun experience. It gives you the feeling that your opinions matter, that your talent is finally being seen and that your products are reaching their targeted audience. It is a satisfying feeling to know you are out there, and people appreciate what you are doing. To creators, YouTube gives freedom to express themselves and put themselves out there. But it also gives them the opportunity to earn money, to be discovered, to find business partners or potential new employees. The possibilities are endless and this is why the platform is popular and growing exponentially.

Section 2: Starting Your Channel

Chapter 3 - Choosing a Niche

Being a YouTuber means creating satisfying content for your audience. However, "audience" is a very vast term and you can have as much of it as there are users on YouTube. It is impossible to keep them all satisfied and you should never strive to do so. Instead, you should find a niche for your YouTube channel. All businesses work using this model. They find a niche market and they establish themselves as the dominant power within that selected niche. Although there are some success stories about people who managed to create the audience for their niche. This is very unlikely and you should not risk it. Instead, you should always strive to work within a niche that already has its own audience. In this chapter, you will learn how to pick a niche filled with potential and how to develop a successful YouTube channel around it.

Identifying Your Goals

Choosing a niche is no easy task. There are so many options out there. Some of them may be your passion and you might already have a vague idea of how you would develop your business from it. However, YouTube is a very unique social network and you will first have to ask yourself what it is that you want to achieve with your own channel. Setting goals for your YouTube channel is an extremely important part of planning your future business. With a clear vision of what you want to achieve, it will be easier to decide further steps you need to take in order to succeed. While some people have a vision and know exactly what their goals are, it might help them to re-evaluate their decisions and see if those goals are achievable in the first place. Other people don't really have a clear vision and they are going to need some brainstorming sessions in order to put it on paper.

To succeed you need to understand that your YouTube channel needs to offer value to others. Although it might be about you, or something that you do, all of your videos will be made for your audience. You need to ask yourself who do you want to help or entertain, who is your target audience? This question is probably the most important one you should ask yourself before choosing your niche. Your audience is what makes your presence on YouTube a success or a failure. After all, they are your subscribers, and the more of them you have, the more likely you would be to succeed. Determine not only the interests of your audience but also the whole demographics. This will later help you shape your videos into a narrative suitable for the type of people you want to cater to. Decide the age, sex, and even the location of the people you want to reach out to.

Now is the time to decide if you want to make your subscribers laugh, think, or learn a new skill. This will help you further determine the tone of your videos as well as their topics. Every video will make its viewers feel something, and you are in full control to decide what that feeling will be. Do you want to do comedy videos or general entertainment, or maybe you want to discuss burning social questions, educate your viewers on technical topics, or maybe show them your unique talents.

The next step is to determine the skills that you need to make your videos likable. Ask yourself what is it in you that you have to offer to the world? Do you like to talk and know how to keep an interesting conversation about various topics? Do you sing, dance, or play an instrument? Or maybe you are a gamer or a painter. Once you determine the special skill that will set you apart, it will be much easier to determine your niche. Remember that even if you have just one skill, let's say you play an instrument, you don't have to create a channel where you will simply show off that skill. You could also strive to give YouTube lessons to beginners, or teach them the history of your favorite instrument, talk about the theory behind music, and react to other YouTube videos of people who play your chosen instrument. The options are endless and you don't have to limit yourself. Combining different types of videos, but keeping them in the same niche will yield the best results.

If you set the goals for your YouTube channel from the start you will have a clearer image of what your niche should be. Even if you already know the niche in which you will work, it is always useful to have the goals in front of you as they will help you develop your channel properly. You will have a clear vision of what skills you have to offer, and what skills you need to improve to better yourself and your channel. Having a successful YouTube channel is all about keeping up with the trends, developing yourself, and constantly learning about new methods you could implement to start a successful YouTube channel. However, that doesn't mean the first goals you set have to be set in stone. You can change your goals as time passes and set new ones. Keep it as an interesting game and regard your goals as achievements. Once you achieve your first 1,000 subscribers set a new goal to reach 10,000. Set goals about the context of your video, your marketing approach, or even about attracting sponsors to your channel. Make a collaboration video your next goal. Keeping the goals alive will make maintaining a successful YouTube channel fun, challenging, and most importantly rewarding.

Why Choose a Niche?

Chances are you have many skills and have a lot to say to your audience. You might ask yourself why you need to limit yourself within the confines of a niche, and why is it important to choose just one among so many things you are good at? While there is no rule that would forbid you from making content on various topics, or about showing off your different skills, there are some setbacks to it. The main one would be your audience. You want to create a base of followers, your loyal viewers, who would come back to your channel because they know what content to expect. But not everyone will like everything that you do, and keeping them all happy is impossible. Therefore, sticking to one niche will make it much easier for you to please your subscribers. Remember that you can always have multiple channels and create content for different niches.

But you would have to work twice as hard to maintain multiple channels and create quality content that would engage your audience and keep them happy. Having multiple niches spread across different channels may wear you out quickly and soon you will find out you don't have enough energy.

The unwritten rule of making a successful YouTube channel is posting at least one video per week. If you have, lets say, three different channels, you would need to create three videos per week. Do you think you can make three high quality content videos in one week? While this is quite possible, if you are just starting your own channel, you need to collect some experience first. It is better to keep yourself focused on only one channel and on one niche, at least in the beginning. Later you might develop more channels, or implement other niches into your existing one. However, even then you would have to be careful not to put off your existing audience and lose subscribers. Research niches that work together the best and evaluate how your subscribers react to them. Research will give you a general idea about what audiences are looking for.

Introducing the Various Worlds in YouTube

There are many factors that determine the popularity of various YouTube niches and categories. One of them is geography - the location of your channel, as well as the geographic location of your subscribers. For example, one of the most popular YouTubers out there is PewDiePie. He is originally from Sweden but he is based in England. However, his YouTube channel is registered in the U.S. This is what allowed him to gain millions of subscribers and reach the top.

An audience's interests depend on their country. Some are more interested in channels which deliver their content in their native language, while others are open to international channels. The U.S. is by far the largest YouTube audience, and in general, English speaking YouTubers have higher chances of succeeding.

Aside from geography, the category you choose will play an enormous influence on your success. The type of content you create will determine how many possible subscribers you can have. Entertainment is by far the most successful category. It is followed by gaming, which we can say belongs in the same entertainment category. Next up is the "how to" category with various do it yourself and life hacks channels that regularly create quality content. These three categories alone are consumed by the vast majority of viewers.

You should keep this information in mind when trying to decide which niche to focus on in your own YouTube channel. But these categories are very general and broad. It doesn't help much to narrow down your ideal niche. So, if you still have trouble deciding on what to focus, here is a list of the most popular and highest earning niches you could consider:

1. **Vlogging**: A vlog refers to a video blog or video log. When a regular person picks up a camera and records the events of his every-day life, he is creating a vlog. Vlogging became popular because it caters to the social animal that dwells in all of us. Getting to know other people by observing their lives gives us satisfaction and the inspiration we need to better ourselves. But it could also simply entertain us by indulging our voyeuristic needs. Vloggers are many and in order to be successful in this niche, you could narrow it down to what makes you a unique individual. There are family vloggers, travel vloggers, musician vloggers, and so on.

2. **Tech**: Tech is something that is continuously developing and new products are launched every day. This means you have an opportunity to pick a niche that will never dry out. However, tech is also a very saturated niche and it is best to focus your efforts on a certain type of tech. You can choose anything between computer processors, cameras, smartphones, house appliances, TVs, drones, cloud services, and anything else that has some connection to technology. You can do product reviews, talk about their development, or make videos that will teach other people how to properly use a certain product. Tech is a general niche that can be broken down into hundreds of sub-niches. This is a good thing because you have the opportunity to start talking about something new that nobody else had covered before.

3. **Tutorials**: Are you a make-up specialist? Or maybe an excellent cook? Perhaps you're a skilled plumber or you're excellent with cars. Teach people how to unclog a pipe, change their oil, or replace a tire. YouTube is frequently used for educational purposes, so start teaching your audience how to do something you're good at. Tutorials are especially popular among the younger generation that is just getting their independence. Be that reliable guy or girl on the internet on which they can rely. That being said, you should focus on a specific skill. Talking about beauty and car engines on the same channel will quickly alienate parts of your audience.

4. **Healthy lifestyle**: You may be proud of how you turned around your life and transformed yourself from a couch potato to a healthy guru. Help other people lose weight and inspire them with your own transformation story. Show off your diet, teach your audience how to prepare a healthy meal. Set an example for others by showing them your workout routine. Health is another broad niche, but it is one of the most popular ones and it has a lot to offer. All you need to do is find something that hasn't been done to death or present your content in a unique, creative way.

5. **Storytelling videos**: If you have the amazing ability to tell stories about events from your past or present, you are a game changer. More and more people are searching for videos that would entertain them with storytelling. Keep in mind that you have to be entertaining, you have to be able to engage your audience and that your stories have to be very interesting. It is not as much about the topic of your stories as in how you present them. In this niche charisma is everything. However, "storytime" videos are rarely a niche on their own, but many YouTubers use this type of videos to present themselves to the audience and to make themselves approachable. You want your subscribers to know that

you are just as human as they are, and they will relate to you. Storytelling videos are often used as a tactic to gain fans loyalty and new subscriptions. Consider using them as part of your chosen niche.

How to Choose Your Niche?

Now that you know why it's important to focus your efforts and your YouTube channel on one niche, you might ask yourself how do you choose the right one? There are certain steps you could take to determine the right niche for you that will turn your YouTube channel into a success. You might have a specific skill you would want to exploit, or a passion which you can monetize through YouTube, but are these really niches that you can exploit? Let's say you play guitar. This is a very saturated area as many people play this particular instrument. What can you do to set yourself apart? This is the most important question you can ask yourself. Maybe beside playing guitar you are also a collector and could show off all the instruments you own and make reviews about them? This is only an example, but there is a way you could determine a niche that is right for you even if you are uncertain what skills you would like to present through your videos.

Start by thinking about broad categories. Maybe you like gaming, which is another very saturated niche. But maybe you particularly enjoy playing retro games. This is a more focused category. Start thinking about your favorite gaming platform, and soon you will come up with a niche that could sound something like "retro games on the sega mega drive". This is a very specific niche, and maybe it even feels limiting. But remember that you are just starting out and your goal is to build up a following. This kind of limit is good for new YouTubers who are looking to gain their first subscribers. Once you produce several videos on this topic and gain a core audience, you might want to expand your niche. Start playing retro games on other platforms, or create different kinds of videos. Make "Top 10 retro games" videos and keep your audience interested but also attract new viewers. Even the most obscure niche has a lot of potential simply because not enough people create that content. It's much easier to sell your content to a starving audience instead of fighting thousands of competitors for the same audience.

However, not everything can be solved with brainstorming. You should always do some research and see what is out there and how successful those niches are. You need to know what people want to see in order to create high quality content to attract them. The research should be done directly on YouTube as this is where you will see the best results. To keep your browser history from influencing your research, you might want to do it in an incognito window. For example, you can directly search for "retro gaming" on YouTube and filter your results by channels. This is still considered a broad category but it will show you what is out there, what other people are doing in this niche and how many views and subscribers they have. You will quickly determine if gameplays have more views than "Top 10" lists, or the other way around. You should do this type of research for all the relevant keywords of a certain category.

Once you choose the general category (retro gaming in our example), and you do your research and have an idea of what's out there, you should return to the goals you set for your channel and decide if you want to educate people, entertain them, or make them laugh. This will narrow down your choices. Maybe you find out that creating informative videos on retro games can pay out more than simply showing the gameplay itself.

After doing all your research and picking your niche, you have to think how to monetize it and if you can keep producing videos on the topic for a sustainable period of time. Make a plan for the future expansion of your niche and extend on what you can do to keep it relevant and interesting for your subscribers. Keep researching even when your channel reaches your set goals. You need to follow the trends and keep yourself in the game. Use tools such as Google Trends to determine the longevity of the topics you are covering in your videos. Also, keep yourself updated on all YouTube and Google marketing tools and algorithm changes and plan your business strategy accordingly.

Chapter 4 - Setting Up Your Account and Channel

You've brainstormed an idea, done some research, and you decided on the niche you want to work in; you are ready to start! You could immediately start making videos and upload them on YouTube, but there is so much more behind a successful channel than shooting videos.

First, you need to set up your account, but you will also have to think about branding your channel. A successful youtuber is more than just a name, or a personality. It is a one-man company, a business, and a brand. You want viewers to recognize your videos when they pop up in their suggestions feed and you want them to be able to search specifically for your channel.

There are many challenges and difficulties on the path to creating a successful channel and we will also discuss how to deal with all of them. Anyone can set up an account on YouTube and create his own channel, but if you want to achieve success, you will have to invest both time and money. You're investing in yourself and in a business, even though sometimes it doesn't feel like it.

Branding Your Channel

People love familiarity and having a routine. This applies to YouTube, and they are more likely to search for the channels they already watched, subscribed to, and enjoyed. Returning viewers are the key just like returning customers matter to every business, and if you want your channel to succeed, you will have to look at it as a business.

To have returning viewers, you have to make it easy for them to recognize you. This is where branding comes in. Branding is important because it's what makes you recognizable, and what makes you stand out from your competition, at least at a first glance. This first glance, the first impression your channel makes is extremely important, just like a book cover draws in a potential reader. People don't know you yet, and they can't decide whether they like your personality just by looking at a single video you created. But the way you present yourself, the way you look, or how your channel in general looks, will leave a very deep impact on viewers.

Your brand identity is the way people perceive you. In this case, you are trying to be likable to YouTube viewers, and make them want to return to your channel. This is why you need to make a good looking channel. Your brand identity needs to express the idea of your channel through your logo, color scheme, typography, thumbnails, your voice, and body language. If you're creating a YouTube channel to promote your already existing business, then you should match the branding of your website with your YouTube channel. After all, the channel is an extension of your business, if not its essence. If you look at some of the most popular YouTube channels, you will notice they are pretty recognizable even without reading the channel name. This is what you want for your channel too. You want people to be able to recognize it instantly and look forward to seeing your new videos.

The first thing you should consider is updating your channel art. Start with a banner because it is the first thing people will see. Decide what colors you will use, as well as the fonts and images. Make them fit the tone of your channel, and correspond to your chosen niche. Although bright colors attract the attention easily, you don't want to use them if your channel has a more serious tone to it. You also want to avoid mixing too many colors, because to a viewer that would be too distracting and confusing. But if you want to start an entertainment channel, you might want to consider the power of flashy and colorful banners. It all depends on your niche and a professional graphic designer might come in handy.

Once you have your banner set up, extend the same branding to your videos and thumbnails. Use the same or similar color scheme, fonts, and overall design. If you use text in your videos to present some data, make sure you use appropriate fonts that fit with the tone of your channel and niche. Thumbnails are extremely important. They are the first thing a viewer sees before even playing a video. If you brand them consistently, people will start recognizing your videos and would click on them just because they are sure of the quality of your channel.

That being said, branding is much more than just the looks of your channel and videos. Although the first impression your viewers are going to have of you is visual, you should strive to extend your brand onto the more technical side of your channel. It is important to understand that people like familiarity. They like consistency, they like their videos to have a beginning, middle, and an end. Because of this, you should consider following a script for your videos. They don't have to be detailed scripts like for TV or radio shows, but at least an outline. Have a good idea in which direction you want to take your audience. That doesn't mean your content will always be the same. You can make it as diverse as you want, but make certain you always follow the same recognizable format.

To discover the format you're going to follow, be creative and feel free to experiment in the beginning. See what works the best for you and your niche. For example, if you have a one on one conversation with your audience, if you're speaking directly to them, consider jump cuts. This way, your viewers won't be distracted, and their attention will be 100% on you and what you're talking about. But if your channel is more visual than auditory, (let's play channel) consider smooth and slow transitions. A good way to decide on your editing style is to research what your competition is doing. This doesn't mean you should copy their style, but get inspired and learn what works and what doesn't.

Finally, you should consider a personal brand even if you don't show your face on the camera often or at all. Sooner or later your viewers will want to learn who is behind this awesome channel they've been following. You need to present yourself in your best light. Keep in mind this is not at all about your looks, although it can play a major role. You need to think about how you express yourself, the way your voice sounds, the words you choose and even your accent. Everything that makes you a person will be judged by your viewers and you should present the best version of yourself. Remember that your viewers are your customers and you should strive to present yourself as you would to your business partners and clients. That doesn't mean you should be strictly professional and serious. Just be yourself or create an entertaining persona if it suits the niche you're focusing on.

What You'll Be Up Against

There are many challenges you will have to overcome as a new content creator. Even when you reach success and you consider yourself in the right place, you will have to deal with some old challenges as well as new ones. The best way to handle them is to anticipate them, be prepared, think two steps ahead, and plan for them. Do not let this discourage you. Remember that you are not the only one who has to deal with these challenges.

Aside from careful planning, there are support communities out there that will gladly help you, give you advice and nudge you in the right direction. Challenges can be very personal and sometimes feel like they're impossible to face. In those cases you might want to consider hiring outside help. But the majority of the obstacles you will meet as a new YouTuber are pretty common and easy to overcome. Let's examine the most common challenges together. This section will give you an excellent idea about facing future challenges, including unpredictable ones.

Expenses

Starting a YouTube channel that offers value can be a costly endeavour. YouTube is free to all of its users, and anyone can shoot an amateur video on their smartphone and upload it. However, if you want to succeed, you will have to turn to more professional equipment such as dedicated cameras, expensive video editing software, backdrops and lights, and even outside graphic design services. All of this can cost you thousands of dollars if you want a professional production. But remember that expensive gear won't guarantee YouTube success. You should rather concentrate on delivering quality content that offers value to the viewer. The keyword is "value".

Although you should start planning for potential expenses early, you can start small and upgrade as you go. Your viewers will notice the improved quality of your videos, sound, and the production overall and they will appreciate it. But they will stay mainly because your videos are fun to watch, and they deliver exactly what they need.

Don't let yourself be discouraged. Video content creation is a business like any other and you invest into it for your own future. Nowadays, you can buy almost everything you need for less than $1,000 and upgrade as your audience grows. That is a significantly smaller expense than what any other type of business would require.

Search Engine Optimization

YouTube is a search engine on its own, but it also works perfectly with Google because it is part of it. To have your videos rank high on search pages, you need to have an understanding of how SEO works. You need to learn how to optimize the titles of your videos, their descriptions, tags and even comments. SEO is crucial to success and you will often find yourself optimizing your content.

Learning the basics of search engine optimization is a challenge and a requirement if you can't afford to outsource this task. However, there are many tools out there that can help you analyze keywords, trends and help you optimize your channel so it shows up as one of the top search engine results. You can even search for YouTube channels that will teach you how to become a competent SEO specialist.

Competition

YouTube is open to everyone. As a result, sometimes it feels as if your videos are just whispers in a very crowded room. In order to be seen on YouTube you need to stand out. This is one of the biggest challenges you want to address early on in your YouTube career. But the solution to this problem boils down to the goals you set in front of yourself. These goals are a measure of what success is to you. After all, success is a very individual thing. You might consider yourself very successful if you gather more than 10,000 subscribers, or you might strive to gather a million. To beat your competition you will need to offer quality content, value, and choose your niche wisely. If there are many people already doing what you're doing, try to come up with different types of videos and new ways to say what others are already saying. Consider beating your competition with your shining personality or a unique way to present information (such as using cartoons).

In either case, competition can feel overwhelming, but you can learn from it. Study those to succeed and eventually you'll succeed as well.

Time

Being a successful content creator means investing time in your YouTube presence. Ask yourself how often can you post videos, and keep them interesting and of high quality? Do you have a 9 to 5 job that you need to dedicate your time to, or maybe a family that requires your attention. Your subscribers want you to upload your videos regularly. They want to be able to anticipate new content from you. But how frequent you upload content doesn't depend only on your personal time.

The type of content will dictate how often you need to post. For example, tutorials and let's play videos are usually posted three times per week, while educational videos or trivia heavy content would require you to upload a video once a week. Vlogs can be posted daily, weekly, or even monthly, depending on the type of vlog you are doing. There are many factors that will determine how often you need to upload new, engaging content, but most important of all is to set a schedule and stick to it. Be regular and keep your viewers happy.

Earnings

Many people think that successful YouTubers are rich. But success doesn't necessarily equal money as many youtubers are doing it just for fun. There are many ways to monetize your YouTube channel and it can be a real challenge to do it.

The first method that comes to people's minds is advertisement. But the truth is ads don't pay well for the effort you put in your videos. Furthermore, YouTube as a platform will take its cut of the cake from advertisement, leaving you with a smaller share. Ads also pay only if the viewer interacts with them, and doesn't skip them. Nowadays many users skip ads altogether by using free ad blockers. This makes ads a very unpredictable source of income.

Although you shouldn't completely disregard advertisements, there are other ways you can monetize your videos. You can affiliate sales and product promotions, offer various services, engage yourself in larger projects and become a public speaker, or let the fans donate money for your work using platforms like Patreon. Many YouTubers have found success by providing free content without ads and allowing the viewers to support the channel via donations.

Finally, since your youTube channel is a brand and a business, you can always opt to sell your own merchandise to subscribers. If you plan ahead, earnings will come if given enough time.

The Process of Creating Your Channel

Setting up a YouTube account takes only a minute and anyone can do it for free. Even starting a channel is one click away. However, optimizing your YouTube profile to achieve maximum reach is another thing.

In this section you will find a step-by-step guide on how to get your account set up, how to create your own channel, as well as how to optimize it. Don't forget that you need to research before starting your channel and decide on some key points such as: who will be your audience, what is your niche, how successful is your possible competition, and what is the ultimate purpose of your channel.

Step 1: Set up your account.

Because YouTube became part of Google, it doesn't take much more than having a Gmail account to sign up for your YouTube account. You can sign in to YouTube using your smartphone, computer, or tablet. All you have to do is fill in your information. Once your account is created, YouTube will require you to verify it. You will find a code has been sent to your inbox. Use it by following the instructions and your account will be fully set up. It's time to get down to business and launch your channel.

Step 2: Create a channel.

In the top right corner of your screen you will find your profile icon. Click on it, and then choose the "Create a channel" option. This is also where you will have to make your first decision. Do you want a personal account or a business account? The difference between these two options is that with a business account you can set up a different name to your channel and share its management with other people. Once you decide on the type of the channel, give it a unique name.

Step 3: Personalize your channel.

Once you create a new channel, you will notice a new Google account was created with the name of your channel. This is so you can use your brand name to interact with people on YouTube, leave comments on other videos and like/dislike them.

The new Google account comes with its own settings and YouTube history. Through it, you can further customize your channel by adding the description of your channel and inserting links to your main website or other social network platforms. All of this information increases your chances of being found and it increases trust among your viewers.

Step 4: Art

You'll need some digital art to personalize your channel. You can create some by using Photoshop, if you are skilled enough, or you can pay a professional to do it for you. But you could also opt to use free image creators such as Canva or Adobe Spark. They come with YouTube art templates you can use to customize your art to your liking. But keep in mind you should follow the optimal size for the art that YouTube recommends. A single image should not be larger than 2560x1440 pixels. To play it safe, any text you want to include in your art should be within the minimum of 2048x1152 px area to guarantee it won't be cut off when displayed on different devices. Recommended file size is 6MB or smaller.

Step 5: Add a profile picture.

Each channel you create will have a dedicated spot for a profile picture. This is the icon that will show up next to each of your videos, and therefore it's part of your branding strategy. Take note that the profile picture is limited to 800x800 pixels, so think of something that would look good at small resolution. You can use your logo or the initials of your channel's name. To upload the profile picture, simply hover your mouse over its placement and you should get the option "edit". Click on edit and simply upload your new profile picture.

Step 6: Optimize your channel description

The description space of your channel is limited to 1000 words and you have to be creative and make each one of them count. Remember that description is also indexed by search engines and that is why you should include a relevant selection of keywords and a call to action. The first 100 to 150 words are the most important ones for good SEO because of how search engine algorithms rank them, so make sure to use keywords that accurately describe what your channel is about. However, don't overwhelm the text with them. It should read natural, otherwise Google will lower your ranking due to keyword stuffing.

Step 7: Add relevant links to your channel.

If you click on the "Customize Channel" button on your homepage, and then on the gear icon in the upper-right corner, you will see a Channel Settings lightbox. In order to add links you will have to turn on the "Customize the layout of your channel" option. Now you can go back to your channel's homepage and you will see the "Edit Links" option in the settings menu. Clicking on it, you will get the option to set up links that will be displayed over your cover art. Use this option to make yourself more visible to the search engine and potential viewers.

Step 8: Add a trailer to your channel.

A channel trailer is the best way to introduce yourself and your channel to the viewers. You should create a short, to the point video in which you explain who you are, what your channel is about, and what type of content you have to offer. This trailer should be designed in such a way to attract new subscribers. Make the trailer grab the viewer's attention as soon as it starts, but keep it in the general tone of your channel. These trailers will appear only to the viewers who didn't subscribe yet to your channel, and their purpose is to persuade them you have quality content to offer.

Exploring Your Channel

Congratulations! You just created your first YouTube channel. Now is the time to explore your possibilities. There is a significant difference between the YouTube users who never opt to create their accounts, and the users who have their channels set up. Millions of people use YouTube casually and they never create their own account. But they are at a loss. YouTube allows you to view videos and even share them without ever logging in. But in order to become an active member of the community, you need your own account and channel. This will allow you to upload your own videos, comment on videos, whether they are yours or someone else's, and cut your own corner on the YouTube real estate market. You will also be able to save links for easy retrieval and create your own personalized playlists.

Take some time to explore your account settings, and especially the channel settings to become familiar with the environment. Perform all the steps mentioned above to fully optimize your channel and prepare yourself to create your first YouTube video.

Section 3: Creating, Editing, and Posting Videos on YouTube

Chapter 5 - Creating Content

You have an idea for your YouTube channel, you did your research and you know your target audience. You chose your niche, thought about the types of videos you want to make, and set up your own YouTube account. Now the time has finally come to create the content and say "Hello" to the YouTube community.

But how do you do it? You sit in front of your camera and you shoot your first video? Is it really that simple? Well, yes and no. Yes, YouTube is about video content and everyone can upload something and be seen, but not everyone will become successful. Behind a successful youtube channel lies the recognition that the content is so much more than just a video.

First, you will need to establish your own content plan and develop the strategy behind it.

It Depends on Your Niche and How You Strategize

All the great videos out there on YouTube are carefully planned by their creators. Of course, you can make an awesome video without following a strict plan, but could you really keep doing that regularly? You would either have to be very lucky or extremely talented. All the successful YouTube channels strategize their content, and they even go into such details that they write scripts. This planning phase is called pre-production, and if you do it correctly, you will save both time and money.

The first thing you should do is think about who will be watching your video. Who is your audience? But don't fall into a trap thinking you know your video will be viral and everyone would see it sooner or later. You need to understand that your audience is a group of people with different experiences and interests. That group of people will have overlapping interests and you should always strive to create your video content having these overlaps in mind. You need to narrow down your video viewers to a single persona with a set of interests. That way you will be able to create a much more relatable video. Don't strive to please everyone. Think about the age, gender, location, economic status, education level, hobbies, and career of your audience persona.

Once you define your audience, you will have to define the message you are trying to convey to them. There are numerous ways to work within your niche, and you have to make a decision for each video you are making, namely what is going to be its main purpose. Are you going to entertain, educate, or maybe you want to show off your own product? It is incredibly important to tailor a video to carry out a specific message. Planning the message of your content will make it easier to create more fun and engaging videos in the future.

Another thing you should take into consideration when planning your content is the budget. Budget in this sense doesn't necessarily have to mean money you would spend making a video. You can opt for videos that don't require any investment at all. But you should consider the recording equipment you have, and if you need to buy or rent a new camera, light, backdrop, and any other tools. If you have a tight budget, remember that the most important thing in a successful video is the message it's trying to convey. You can be creative and record an interesting video with your smartphone. However, if your niche demands professional visual appeal, you might need to work on getting more adequate equipment.

The script is incredibly important whether you are making a prank video, an educational one, or a simple commercial for your product. If needed, you can write down what you want to say, word for word. But if you are a talented speaker and think you have enough charisma to win over your audience, you could opt to work with a basic outline. This means that planning the script for your videos isn't just writing down the sentences you will be saying. It also involves writing down the visuals you want to use in the video, or when to play music, and when to stop it. Review your script often, and if you're working with more people, listen to their advice and work together on the script.

While writing your script, consider putting your best in the first eight seconds of the video. That is normally how much an average person allows a video to peak his interest. A viewer that clicks on your video in the first place, will click away from it if his attention isn't engaged early on. That doesn't necessarily have to be a bad thing. You don't have to start your video with the most interesting information you have to offer. You can use these first eight seconds to intrigue your viewer, make him want to stay on your video without revealing too much. Think of it as the first paragraph in a new book. It has to grab the audience into a new world. Avoid long and boring introductions in which you would explain the video your viewers are about to see. You should never underestimate your audience's ability to understand your videos.

Determine the length of your videos. The message you want to present to your viewers should determine how long your video presentation should be. There is no need to make it longer than it needs to be. But there is also no need to rush and create short, fast-paced videos so you could save up on time. However, keep in mind that generally, people are not as interested in seeing long videos. Shorter videos have better engagement. This is again connected to the attention span of your audience. Generally the short videos are watched until the end by a large number of viewers. However, if your video is engaging, interesting, and speaks to the right audience, then its length is less important.

Next, you need to plan the location, lighting, outfits you will wear during the recording session, make-up, guests that you will interview, and everything else your video will involve. All these small details are what make the content of your video engaging and interesting, and they should not be taken lightly. But remember, everything needs to be synchronized with your niche and target audience. Don't wear a sports outfit if you're giving a presentation about job interviews. Your audience wouldn't take you seriously. You should also avoid shooting your job interview video guide at a zoo, for instance. The location needs to give a viewer a visual representation of your video's message. Create a simple office setting, or use a neutral backdrop. Planing all these details is part of the creative process. The message you want to spread across YouTube and the internet starts with an idea, not in the camera. Careful planning will help you choose the best possible way of representing yourself, your business, or simply your niche and YouTube channel.

See What the Other YouTubers are Doing

Because YouTube is the second most visited website, right after Google, it holds great potential for many businesses and people who want to succeed. This platform has a space for everyone, from big brands and famous individuals to self-proclaimed YouTubers and influencers. But they didn't succeed by accident, they all used a strategy that helped them be unique. They used data and analysis methods to determine the most effective way to gather subscribers and views. Let's discuss some of the tools you could also use to deduce how well your videos are performing.

YouTube has its own analytics system and it is a great tool for anyone who is just starting their own channel. Known as YouTube Analytics, this tool offers you a very in-depth analysis that will help you understand the performance of your videos. You can also use it to understand your audience and determine its demographics.

You can find this tool in the Studio section of your channel, and you will see that it has many sections and options for you to explore. But it will take you only a short time to find some of the data that will give you an insight into how well your channel is performing. You can see the overall traffic over time and determine when was the point your channel had the most visitors. This is an excellent way of determining at what period your channel is peaking, and you can concentrate on posting in the given time frame. You can also see the view duration of your top-performing videos, and the location of the people who are watching your videos. Swipe to the audience tab and discover the age, gender, and location of your viewers. Sometimes we are simply not reaching the audience we want, and you can make adjustments to your content accordingly.

There are many such tools out there that enable you to see the data behind your channel and analyze it. Some are free, others come with a subscription, but they're equipped with so much more than what YouTube's analytics system has to offer. It is up to you to determine which tools you want, but the general advice is to use at least two and to compare the data you are getting from them. These tools are content marketing tools, and they come with their own integrated YouTube Analytics. Here are a few of them for you to explore: BuzzSumo, Brandwatch, and Social Blade.

Besides analyzing your own channel and videos, you should make an effort to also analyze your competition. By doing so, you will learn a tremendous amount of information that will help you succeed. This is called "competitive benchmarking" and through it, you will see what makes your competition succeed or fail, and you will be able to develop your own strategy around it.

If you notice that your views are dropping, and your main competitor's views are rising, it's time to investigate. See what it is they're doing to attract people and analyze what you're doing wrong. You can even do competitive benchmarking ahead and plan for the future. You don't have to wait for something extraordinary to happen in order to benchmark your competition. Do it before you even start your own YouTube channel just to get a general idea about their success and how you should organize your channel.

There are two ways you can do competitive benchmarking. You can opt to do it manually and look at your competition's views, go through their comments, and learn how they interact with the audience. You can also search for both positive and negative feedback your competition receives to draw your own conclusion on what works and what doesn't. However, if you want more in-depth analytics, you could use some of the aforementioned tools. Unfortunately, YouTube's own analytics tool won't allow you to see your competition's data, but tools such as InfluNex, Rival IQ, and SocialBlade will.

The Win-Win Solution

If you think competition benchmarking is like spying on your fellow YouTubers, be assured that is what everyone is doing and no one will take it as something bad. Learning about other YouTubers, their methods, and successes, as well as failures, will allow you to take your channel to a new level. Content creators are aware of the amount of success they can achieve and that they can prosper if they work together. In the YouTube content-making sphere, this is known as collaboration; collab for short. You should plan in the near future to search for a collab opportunity, because of the many advantages it can bring you.

YouTubers connect with each other through personal outreach, or through apps like Grin. They do this so they could work together and present themselves to each other's audience. There are many YouTubers who create similar content, but while some are famous, others are unknown even though they offer quality content. But YouTube is massive and finding a content creator who caters to all your needs is a difficult task. But if two YouTubers, or more, work together, they can cross-post their collab video and intrigue, engage, and gain a new audience. Sometimes, famous YouTubers will endorse smaller YouTubers by mentioning them in their videos. By introducing this less known channel to their own audience, they can funnel traffic to that channel. Doing collabs is always good for business, but it might not always have the same results.

Collabs need to be planned carefully, and the best thing you could do is to collab with other people who create content in your own niche. This is because if you share the niche, you most certainly attract the same type of audience. If you are doing make-up tutorials, doing a collab with a person who does wildlife content won't bring you many views. But if you collab with a hairstylist, you will reach an audience interested in beauty tips. But sometimes, doing a cross-niche collab can yield success. Let's say you are doing those make-up tutorials because you're a make-up artist. You could collab with a history channel and discuss and demonstrate make-up fashion through various historical periods. This type of cross-niche collab will bring together two audiences and increase traffic to both of your channels.

Sometimes a few smaller YouTube channels can band together and create a strong bond. They can grow into a different, separate channel and attract a huge audience. However, when it comes to collaboration, the trick is in finding the right people to work with. There are millions of YouTubers out there and you should not send the invitation just to anyone. You need to do some research, learn about the top content creators in your niche, and reach out only when you are sure something good can grow out of collaboration. There are forums such as YTTalk, the SocialBlade forum, or TheYouTubeCommunity where you can get to know other content creators and find collab partners.

Once you reached out to other YouTubers and received a positive response, brainstorm together to find the perfect way in which you could collaborate. There are many things you could do together but stick to your own niche. You can interview each other, or simply talk about the interests you share. You can also do a fun video where you challenge each other, or even do a collab intended to raise donations for a noble cause. The options are numerous and they all yield results. Be creative, but also listen to your new collab partner and appreciate their ideas too.

There are other types of collaboration worth mentioning. They wouldn't be with YouTube content creators, but with already established brands that are searching for new ways to advertise themselves. While they are prone to search for famous YouTubers who would do a simple commercial for them, your audience wouldn't appreciate such a collaboration, especially in the beginning. You need to find a way to implement this brand into what you're already doing. Reviews are always a good start, particularly if you already established a level of trust with your audience. Just make sure to stick to your niche and only arrange collaborations with brands that you know will appeal to your audience.

Read This Whenever You're Lost on What to Create Next

There comes a moment in every YouTuber's life when he or she is simply out of ideas what to do next. All artists and crafters have this creative block and everyone deals with it in his own way. However, if you plan ahead, and think of a system that will ensure you never run out of ideas, you won't be in trouble when your channel picks up. This will also help you be consistent in publishing your new videos as you won't waste your precious time brainstorming new ideas.

There are different systems you could use, and the general advice is not to rely on only one. Here are a few things you could do to keep your videos fresh and interesting for your audience:

Read comments and listen to feedback: Your own audience will leave comments on your videos. Sometimes praising and admiring your work, but once in a while, they will leave you suggestions on what you could do next and what they would love to see you do. Take their ideas into serious consideration. Answer your viewers' demands and questions to establish trust and loyalty. You will show that you acknowledge them, you listen, and you cherish their input. Your own viewers will surprise you with some awesome ideas for your next videos!

Do your own research: There are many ways to research new topics. You can read articles, books, or watch other people's videos but you have to confine yourself to your own niche. There is no point in doing research on topics your niche doesn't correspond to. You can even share the story of how you found the information on the topic with your audience. They would love to hear where else they can read or hear about the topics you discuss in your videos.

Get inspired: Inspiration comes in many forms and from many sources. Watch documentaries or movies, even tv shows, read books, and listen to music. All these sources can inspire your next video. Even just simple talk with your friends and family can lead to a new great idea for the next video. Inspiration is all around us, you just have to harvest it. Getting inspired from everyday life is a skill you need to learn. All you have to do is observe everything around you consciously and ask yourself how you can implement what you experience in your videos.

Recycle other YouTubers: Other YouTubers are great sources of inspiration. You should never strive to copy them, but there is no harm if you give your own opinion on the topic already covered by someone else. You can even mention how you were inspired to talk about this topic or to create a video on the given topic by watching another YouTuber. You can even create react videos and argue your point of view. Just make sure to credit them by mentioning their channel, as that could lead to a potential collaboration and spread the news about your channel. Don't be afraid to go to their videos and see the topics they covered even years ago. Some topics are always trendy and you might be able to bring a new perspective.

Here is a list of ideas that can serve you throughout your YouTube career:

- Accept another YouTuber's challenge
- Have an in-depth discussion on the topic belonging to your niche
- Do a reaction video, but keep it closely connected to your niche
- Create a tutorial and show your audience how to do or make something
- Tell a story from your life, people love to connect with YouTubers on a more personal level.
- Include breaking news from your niche
- Go live, and show your audience what you are doing at the moment

- Host a trivia quiz and invite guests and experts from your own niche
- Make first impression videos
- Create unboxing videos if you review a product
- Do a Q&A and answer the questions your audience is asking you
- Include bloopers, and make funny videos of your own recording failures
- Create a "Best of" compilation once in a while involving only the topics of your niche
- Create a comparison video where you compare two similar products
- If you have children, think about including them in some of your videos
- Go outside and interview strangers on the street
- Create a "history of" video where you explore the origins of your chosen topic
- Discuss your favorite movie, music, or book. Again, whatever your niche is, your audience would get a chance to get to know you personally if you include such videos occasionally. Just don't overdo it.
- Include myth-busting videos. Learn about the myths in your niche and show your audience the truth behind them

Constructing Scripts Your Way

The importance of the script can't be underestimated. There are two different ways to make a script: you can opt to write the lines of what you plan to say, or you can simply do an outline of the video which you would follow. The script can be detailed or not. It is there to guide you and make your video production process an easier task. But there are instances where you don't need a script, or where it would even pull you back. For example, you can do an interview with an expert, and prepare all the questions in advance. You can think you are very well prepared for the interview, and your guest will smoothly answer all your questions. But those kinds of interviews can sound posed and feel fake. Prepared questions are always good, but that doesn't mean you need to follow the script in a rigid fashion. Feel free to ask new questions that pop in your mind during the interview, or to construct more questions based on your guests answers, and simply push the conversation in an exciting direction.

Having a script will raise the quality of your videos, make them more cohesive, and let your audience follow your videos naturally. However, you need to be aware that there are certain rules to writing a script, and in order to have successful videos you should try to follow them. All videos must have an introduction, a middle that will contain most of the actual content and a conclusion. However, it is up to you to balance these three sections.

Introductions can often be unnecessarily long, boring and your audience will lose the attention and move away from your video. Instead, start a video with the most interesting detail of the topic so you grab the viewer's attention, and then move on. Keep it short, to the point and make your message crystal clear. In the discussion section you should go back to the most interesting fact about the given topic and continue building your message there. The point of the message is there, in the main body of your content. As for the conclusion, it serves as the end of your video. Here you can end your video with your own thoughts on the topic, or you can let your guests have a final word (if you choose to host them). Just as the introduction, the conclusion should be kept short and to the point. Try to end your videos with fun facts, a quick summary, or tease your audience with "whats next". Keep them interested and they will want to come back to your channel.

Here are some tips on how to write good scripts:

- Write down the basic elements of the scripts such as the character, ideas, main message, setting of the entire project, and props you would be using.

- Consider your audience, their demographics, maturity level and interests and only then decide on what kind of narrative you want to introduce in your video. Work the idea of your main message around that. Should it contain a dose of humor, be completely serious or maybe you want to present your message through animation?

- See if your viewers had some questions in your previous video that you could answer in your next one. By including your audience and addressing their questions and concerns, you will gain their trust.

- Include emotions, the audience loves to get emotional. You can either express your own passion towards the topic you are discussing, or show emotional footage. Don't forget that happiness is also an emotion and you can use this to make your audience laugh or simply feel satisfied and relaxed.

- Keep the pace of the video steady. Don't rush through certain segments just because you think they are less interesting. Your audience might not agree with you, but that doesn't mean you should drag the video to impossible levels. Keep them flowing naturally and don't limit yourself by strict time limits. Follow the structure and keep your audience engaged.

- Once you are done writing the script, ask someone for their opinion. Use their creativity and work together to improve your script. You can seek a writer's opinion and you can even work with a small test audience to see you your script from the viewer's perspective.

- Review your script several times, and don't be afraid to delete parts of it. Even the best script writers rewrite up to several times. Make sure you are completely satisfied with the script before starting the recording sessions.

Chapter 6 - How to Create or Record Your Videos

Back when YouTube was still a young platform, there were only two kinds of videos: bad and worse. In those days, most people had access to low-quality camcorders and that's about it. Nobody even imagined making professional YouTube videos as a career, so nobody invested in studio equipment and video editing software. The few who did, still struggled making bad videos. Keep in mind that today's cheapest smartphones record better quality videos than most consumer-grade equipment people had access to.

Since those dark times, both hardware and software evolved significantly. Smartphones are more than capable at shooting good-quality videos, professional cameras are quite affordable, studio lights are cheap, and editing software has never been easier to work with. Consumer level video production can be surprisingly good with minimal investment.

That being said, there are no more excuses for creating bad content that includes audio distortions, terrible exposure, and a shaky cam. All you need to know is the basics of recording and creating a video. So, let's discuss what it takes to create high-quality entertaining YouTube content.

Creating vs. Recording

Video content is valuable and many people prefer it over text. However, not everyone is made to be in front of the camera. Fortunately, to be successful on YouTube you have two choices: you can create your own content or record it. A lot of people who want to get into YouTube content creation falsely assume that they need to show their face and be charismatic to draw in the crowd and be successful. That isn't true. Both video content creation methods are equally viable.

Creating content doesn't necessarily involve any type of recording. You can produce high-quality videos without recording any footage, sounds, or even voice. Everything is generated and put together using software. On the other hand, the recording method implies recording your own video and audio content.

Recording your own content is probably the biggest challenge for most people. You're probably worried about it as well, wondering about your looks, the quality of your voice, your accent if you're not a native English speaker, your demeanor, as well as other human factors. These are things that have to do with you and they're difficult to change. If you aren't made for the camera, you're going to either struggle or have to invest a lot of time and effort teaching yourself how to act. Additionally, there's the hardware factor to consider as well. You would need a camera, or at least a capable smartphone, a tripod, background, studio lights, and all of this costs. It doesn't have to be expensive, but everything piles up. But this doesn't mean you should avoid recording content. It can be extremely rewarding. However, you might want to start off easy by creating content until you learn the ropes and then make the big step towards recording.

There are many ways to create content and make it visually pleasing without ever recording yourself. You can create PowerPoint presentations and source them up with animations, background music, and narration.

Alternatively, if you love writing, you can use intelligent software, like Lumen5, that creates slides automatically after analyzing your text. Afterwards you can add the music, audio, and render the whole project as a video. This method also leads to the creation of the so-called "explainer" videos. This type of content relies on short slide-based presentations to explain a certain topic. It is highly popular nowadays for people that want a quick solution or explanation to a question they have, and there's a lot of programs that provide just that. Adobe Spark is such a program that is available for free and provides you with predefined story structures you can use to create the slide show.

Equipment for Recording Videos

YouTube is highly competitive nowadays with many content creators offering commercial-quality video content. Viewers grew accustomed to quality video and audio production, so you can't get by with a noisy microphone and a cheap camera. However, that doesn't mean you need to go so far as to rent film-making equipment and professional editors. All you really need is the following list of items:

1. **Camera**: This is the most important piece of equipment. While nowadays there are plenty of options, all you need to focus on is having a camera capable of shooting in HD (1080p). Whether it's a webcam, DSLR, mirrorless camera, or a GoPro, it doesn't really matter. Each type of camera comes with its own set of advantages, but first you need to figure out what you actually need. There's no point in getting the most feature-rich mirrorless camera if you're going to film your face to appear in a tiny window on the side of a gameplay video. That being said, DSLR cameras are the best choice overall because they can shoot HD videos, they're affordable, and they offer you a great deal of control over exposure, depth of field, shutter speed, and ISO.
2. **Microphone**: Audio quality is just as important as video quality. If the audio is bad, the viewer will lose interest and throw you a dislike instead of subscribing to your channel. Your laptop's built-in microphone is not enough, and you should invest in an external one that can eliminate any background noises. But not just any external microphone will meet all your needs. Before you buy one you should learn which type and brand will suit you the best. While the USB microphones are very easy to use, many opt for the Shotgun microphone as the best option. They pair well with small cameras and will record high

quality audio. They can reduce mechanical noise that comes from around the microphone itself and they are capable of capturing clear sounds without picking up ambient noise.

3. **Stabilizer**: In order to make your videos look professional you will have to get rid of the unsteady and shaky footage. It will make your viewers dizzy and less likely to return to your channel. You can opt to use a tripod or a gimbal stabilizer. They are both amazing in stabilizing your videos and photos, but which one you choose depends on the type of videos you're creating. The tripod is a more affordable option but you should invest in a good one as it will provide better stabilization as well as the opportunity to record from different angles. It can even collapse for low angle footage, and it may come with a ball-head which you can turn and shoot from different angles. Gimbal stabilizers are usually used for light cameras such as smartphones or GoPros. They have built-in motors or weights that will balance the camera for recording much smoother videos. Choose based on your setup and budget.

4. **Lights**: If you plan to record your videos indoors or in low-light light conditions, you should consider purchassing lighting equipment. However, even if you're shooting with plenty of bright light, additional lighting can set the mood of your video, or break the sharp shadows often created by hard natural light. There are various types of lighting equipment and you should choose according to your needs. A softbox is good to start with because it softens the natural light coming through the window. Umbrella lights will also create soft light, but you will have more control over them as they're easy to move around as needed. As for ring lights, they're ideal if you record yourself indoors. It emits light around the subject isolating it and making it the centre of viewers attention. Finally, if the lighting conditions are bad where you're filming, you should purchase one or two studio lights to act as the primary source of light.

5. **Video Editing Software**: Now that you have all the equipment you need to record your first video, you will also need a little extra to push the quality of the video through post-production and shape it into the final, presentable product. Video editing software will help you make amazing videos by allowing you to control their length, effects, filters, insert text, animations, edit sound, add music, and so much more. You will discover most of your creativity in post-production. There are many programs to choose from, such as Adobe Premiere and Corel VideoStudio, but most of them come with a subscription fee atached. If you need a basic editor, you can get away with YouTube's YouTube Studio but it comes with limited options. Try finding one which will suit all your needs and you will have no trouble learning how to use it. Most of them have the same features and the only major difference lies in the interface.

Guide for Recording Videos

Bad videos stick out like a sore thumb and viewers won't return to your channel if you fail to deliver quality. When it comes to good videos, it is hard to pinpoint a single element that makes them good. Good videos are attractive, informative and they make us feel a certain emotion. YouTube experts and seasoned content creators always speak about the importance of story and that a video without one is considered bad even if it is technically executed to perfection. However, that doesn't mean you should ignore the technical aspect. Your story won't be interesting enough if your video makes the viewers feel dizzy due to shaky camera work. Aside from story, the video shot with a steady camera, under good lighting conditions and with top-quality audio, will attract more viewers. People are attracted to good visuals. A good video is just that, a story, but you want to offer the best. The best video is the combination of the two factors: story and technical execution.

In order to get the best out of your storytelling abilities, as well as out of your recording equipment, here are some tips for shooting professional YouTube videos:

1. When you shoot your own video you have full control over the process. To execute it properly, you should make a storyboard and include the illustrations of the scenes you are planning to shoot. The storyboard will be your guide during the shooting but it will also help you finalize your video in post-production. A storyboard should also contain information such as the schedule of shooting, venue, the equipment needed, and the perfect time of the day for a certain scene. It's similar to a script, but it allows you to visualize your plan of action so that you can implement it step by step.

2. No matter if you use your smartphone, GoPro, mirrorless or DSLR camera, remember to shoot horizontally. Vertical or portrait footage is a clear sign of amature content. Horizontal, or landscape footage will play without problems on all devices, while vertical looks ok only on phones.

3. Mind the location of your videos and what you can use for the background. Make an effort to choose a simple background which will not distract the viewers' attention. There should be no action in the background, and if possible, use neutral colors. Many people use a simple wall, some kind of backdrop, or a green screen and these are all good solutions. Your subject should always be several feet away from the background. This separates the subject better and draws the viewer's eye to focus on it.

4. Improve the composition of your scenes. Even if you have an awesome story to tell, and the high-end equipment to record it, your video won't turn out professionally if your composition and framing are bad. You should always strive to arrange all the visual elements in the scene in a way to tell a story. This will also make the scene aesthetically pleasing and enjoyable to watch. One of the basic composition rules for videographers is the **Rule of Thirds**. You should place your main subject's head slightly above the centre of the frame, and leave plenty of room on the side which the subject is facing. If you're doing close-ups, and if you have to cut off your subject, do it from the top.

5. Use manual focus on your stand-alone cameras or exposure-focus lock on your smartphone. This will allow you to set focus using your own eyes instead of relying on the camera. Autofocus is very handy, but it will often bring the subject in and out of focus if

there is movement in the scene or the light isn't constant. Manual focus will also help you to have control over the depth of field and if used properly, manual focus will help you tell a story.

6. Expose all your scenes evenly and adjust the white balance on all your devices, if you're using multiple cameras to record. This way you will avoid having different exposure, light color and temperature.

7. Shoot with editing and post-processing in mind. This means that while shooting you should keep editing in mind and maybe take a scene from different angles, make safety shots, and plan for the cuts and transitions. This will save you a lot of time in the editing software, and you will have different material to choose from and not settle for the bad scenes just because you have no other. It will also save you from re-shooting if something goes wrong.

8. If you're shooting with your smartphone, avoid the front camera. Use only the back one. Front cameras are usually of lower quality and will produce worse video and audio.

9. Clean your lens. No matter if you record with a camera or smartphone, lenses will often gather dust and dirt which can be seen in the final product or cause focusing issues. You want your videos to be clean and focused on your subject. A speck of dust can distract the viewer or, if large enough, ruin the whole video by covering up a part of your main subject.

10. If you don't have a stabilizer, hold your camera or smartphone with both of your hands, close to your body and if possible, lean against a wall or a tree. This will stabilize you, and in return stabilize the camera. This method is not as effective as having a tripod, but it will reduce the shaking. Besides, modern smartphones and cameras come with the lenses equipped with image stabilizers (not nearly as good as actual stabilizers). However, you should always strive to give it as much stability as possible.

11. Avoid using zoom, especially on your smartphone. Zoom tends to create unstable scenes because the movement it captures is difficult to control. Smartphones use digital zoom instead of optic zoom and the result is digital noise which will make your videos look unprofessional.

Creating Videos without Recording

There is a reason why YouTube named its users "content creators" rather than "video makers". Not everything posted on YouTube is recorded, and there is no rule that says video must be included. If you ever used YouTube to listen to music, you are certainly familiar with the fact that musicians often use their album cover to display as a steady image instead of a video, while the song is playing. This is not only cutting the costs of video production, but it also allows listeners to focus on the audio rather than video. There are many reasons why some YouTubers prefer to not use cameras and create their content in different ways. Maybe they're shy and don't like being in front of the camera, or their talents lie in storytelling rather than visual presentation. If you are among the people who want to explore alternative ways of creating content for YouTube, without using the camera, here are a few popular methods:

1. **Use artificial intelligence.** Yes, AI can make videos for you from scratch using tools like Vedia AI and Softcube. Technology has come a long way. All you have to do is type what you want your video to be about. Enter the text and the AI will choose the appropriate royalty free images and videos, as well as speech, music and sounds. AI will also use automated editing tools and create a finished product. However, keep in mind that there is no AI platform which is fully automated. You will still have plenty of control over the video being created.

2. **Opt for Screencast.** If you have no time to record and edit videos, but you need content for your YouTube channel, live streaming is always a good option. You can stream directly what you're doing on your computer. It can be gameplay, or you could show off your photography editing skills. You're a digital artist? Show how you draw and what tools you're using. Teach people how to create short and funny animations. Screencasts can even be live streamed, and YouTube will record it for you so you can share it at later times. That being said, this option can be applied only in certain niches, so keep that in mind.

3. **Create a PowerPoint video.** Yes, PowerPoint allows you to export videos. But making a video using this program can be time-consuming and the results might not be as you would expect. However, it is still a good way to create content without using a camera. You can record only a voiceover or you can use AI to read the prepared text that would accompany the video. Many tutorials are created this way.

4. **Create an animated video.** Animation will allow you to be creative and you'll have full control over your video. You don't have to be an artist or professional animator to create this type of videos nowadays. There are online services that will allow you to create animation videos using only your own sketches. The sketch will guide the program how to create a polished animation as an end result. However, for the high-quality animations you should still invest in a skilled artist.

5. **Use stock images to create a video.** You can use video editing techniques to create an interesting video out of still images. This type of content solution is best suited for informative videos such as news, history facts, short commercials, and various tutorials. To keep the video interesting you can try zooming in and out, panning, transitioning and different effects and filters which will make your end product aesthetically pleasing.

6. **Use stock videos.** Just as you have stock images at your disposal, you have stock videos and clips too. By carefully choosing stock videos you can create an awesome video which will successfully convey the message, tell a story and evoke an emotion in your viewers.

7. **Repurpose existing videos.** If you have a rich YouTube channel with plenty of content but no time to record a new video, you can recycle your old content. Simply repurpose segments of different videos and be creative with the material you already have. Maybe you saved some unused material from previous shootings and now you can use them to create new content for your channel.

In the end, you can combine all of these methods for non-recorded content. You can combine animation with still images, or screencast. The possibilities go as far as your imagination can carry you. Be creative and come up with your own ways to create YouTube content without using a camera.

Chapter 7 - Editing Videos Like a Pro

Editing videos is a time-consuming process, but a necessary one. Be prepared to learn various tools and even when you think you know everything, you might surprise yourself by discovering new features and ideas.

To edit your own videos you will have to learn how to use editing software, but you will also have to learn some fundamental techniques experienced film makers have been using for decades. This chapter will teach you how to finish your videos and turn them into presentable final products. Start editing like a pro!

The Makings of a Great Video

The editing stage of video creating is usually referred to as post-production. No matter how tedious this step feels like, nobody should skip it. Otherwise, your product would be a pile of mess and unpresentable to the audience. Video editing and post-production in general, are there to put all of the aspects of the video together. It will give your video a perfect flow. With cuts, pacing, and sound effects, your video will become a perfect piece, enjoyable to watch because the narration and pacing are consistent.

Video editing involves blending images and sounds together in perfect harmony. It is the editing that will emotionally connect the viewers to your video. But be aware, bad editing can harm your videos even more than an unedited one. That's precisely why it is important to master the video editing skills on your own. Even if you intend to use a professional editor, you should know the fundamentals of editing otherwise you may end up conveying the wrong message.

Before you dive into editing, you should learn the file formats, resolutions, and conversions you will work with. Knowing these will help you make editing decisions and produce amazing final videos. Modern editing programs are able to handle these on their own, but you still need to know your options.

Videos are large files, and in order to handle them more easily you will have to compress them. Video editing software is able to use certain calculations to squeeze high-quality video and sound into the smallest possible file size. Without compression, your videos can be up to 50 times larger than the final product.

The part of software which handles the compression is called a codec. There are different types of codecs and if your video editing software uses, for example, codec A, you won't be able to watch that video on a device which supports only codec B. However, YouTube supports the most common ones.

Some of the popular codecs out there are: Apple ProRes. Windows Media (WMV), Digital Video (DV) and MPEG-4. Codecs will compress your videos and together with the additional information (video title, synchronization, subtitles) will save them as a certain file format. The file format can be Flash Video (.flv), QuickTime (.mov), Windows Media (.avi), MP4 (.mp4) or MPEG (.mpg). When a video is saved in one of these file formats, it can be played with different kinds of codecs. Modern editing programs can work with any of these file formats. However, there are some exotic file formats and if you encounter them there is a possibility you will have to convert them to a format your editing software can recognize. There are video conversion programs out there, but your main editing program might already have one integrated.

Beside file formats and codecs there are other video editing terms you will have to familiarize yourself with. Here you can learn the meaning of the most commonly used ones:

- **Aspect Ratio**: is the relation between the height and width of your videos. The dimensions are expressed through aspect ratio, and the most common ones out there are: 4:3, 16:9, 1.85:1. YouTube is capable of changing the aspect ratio of your videos based on the device a person is using to play it. However, avoid adding borders or vignettes to your videos as they can confuse YouTube's algorithm into displaying a wrong aspect ratio.
- **B-roll**: is a supplemental footage that is used to make the transition between the scenes smoother. For example, an additional scene can make the viewers' eyes transition smoothly to different points of view. B-rolls are commonly used in movies, news, and interviews.
- **Bit Rate (Data Rate)**: is the amount of data used in each second of your video. It is measured in kilobits per second (kbps), and they can be constant throughout the video or they can change.
- **Color Temperature**: refers only to the visible light in the video and it can range from cool to warm. This is because cooler colors have a bluish tint, while the warm ones are closer to orange and red. The color temperature is measured in Kelvins.
- **Compositing**: is a process of combining the images using the video editing software. Graphical elements can also be added to the video and this type of compositing will produce a different kind of a single screen image.
- **Crop Factor**: is a number that represents the ratio of your cameras sensor's imaging area to that of a full frame sensor. It is typically presented in numbers between 1.3 and 2.0.
- **Frame Rate**: is the video information captured by the camera's sensor in 1 second. The frame rate is represented through frames per second and the common ones are: 24, 25, 29.97, 30, 50, 60. Shooting at 60 FPS offers the smoothest experience, but 30 FPS is still commonly used.
- **J-cut**: refers to the point where the audio of the next scene precedes the video. They are used creatively to stir emotion in viewers before they are even able to see the next scene. Don't confuse J-cuts with Jump-cuts, those are two different things.
- **Jump-cuts**: are abrupt changes between the scenes. They can make your videos look unprofessional if used wrong and you should avoid using too many of them.

- **L-cut**: is the opposite of the J-cut. The audio of the first scene continues into the next scene.
- **Resolution**: is the number of horizontal and vertical pixels in your video. But sometimes, the resolution is determined only by displaying the number of the vertical pixels (480p, 720p, and 1080p).

These are just some of the video editing terms you should remember. There are more and in time you will learn them. The best way to learn video editing is to simply dive into it and experiment. You can make a short test video and practice on it. You'll learn a lot more that way and a lot quicker. Once you feel confident enough, you can start creating videos for your YouTube channel.

Using Video Editing Tools

Video editing involves using your raw footage to create a final video product out of it. However, you can't turn bad footage into a high-quality production. There's no magic way around it. You should strive to obtain good footage from the start and improve it through editing. Fortunately, for most of the viewers, the quality of the video comes from its ability to tell a story. It's not about the pixel count, but about the message you are trying to send, and about the way you're doing it. Video editing will help you create the best possible way of conveying your message. There are various video editing programs, some are free, others are expensive, and they all come with their own unique features. It is quite possible you will end up using more than one editing software to create amazing videos. But nobody can tell you what to choose and what to stick to. It depends on your budget, technical requirements, and willingness to learn. Here are some ideas of what is out there so that you can find what suits your needs.

VSDC is a free program for editing and it is a good choice for beginners. The program comes with options such as blend overlays, as well as mask and key options. It will allow you to control the speed of your videos as well as transition filters. Some users claim this program is not user-friendly, but the fact it's free still makes it a solid choice for a beginner to practice the basics.

iMovie is another free editing tool for beginners, but only for Mac users. This program offers you various templates that enable you to create quick finished footage. It also has a variety of animated titles and transitions that will give an extra spark to your video without any effort. However, iMovies lacks elaborate options and while it is good for quick clip cutting and putting together different scenes, it will not make an elaborate, high-quality video. That being said, it's still a great option for a beginner.

EaseUS Video Editor is a powerful and easy to use platform which will allow you to create beautiful end-product videos without much technical knowledge. It is beginner friendly, and it comes with over 50 special effects and transitions you can use. It will also teach you how to use more elaborate editing components such as hue and saturation, speed, multiple audio tracks, and much more. It also allows voice-over recording without ever leaving the program.

Adobe Premiere Pro is an advanced editing program and lots of people choose it as their only editing program. You will need some time to learn how to best use this program because of a myriad of options, but once you get the hang of it, your video editing process will become very simple. Furthermore, Adobe Premiere Pro has some automatic features as well that speed up the process. Use this software once you familiarize yourself with the basics, otherwise you may feel overwhelmed.

PowerDirector comes for a price, but it's worth it. This program is extremely user friendly and it has advanced video editing options such as 360-degree footage, motion tracking, and keyframing. PowerDirector will allow you to create complex videos for any niche.

Adobe After Effects is probably one of the most powerful editing programs out there. It is a complex software that will allow you to integrate animations with your videos and will allow you the usage of third party plugins. It is meant for experts but anyone can learn how to use it. The possibilities with Adobe After Effects are limitless. If you can imagine it, this program can do it. However, the learning curve for this program can be steap. There are various tutorials out there, and a supportive community of users that can make the learning process more enjoyable.

The Actual Process of Video Editing

Each video editor has his own workflow and will do the job in his own, unique way. In time, you will find your own way of editing and you will be able to add your own signature to the videos you're making. However, there are six basic steps you could follow and make the job much easier.

Video editing is done in stages, and aside from knowledge, you need to know how to organize your workflow for maximum efficiency. Each step of the video editing process needs to build upon what was accomplished in the previous stage. This way your video editing process will not only be efficient, but the end result will be a coherent video.

The Preview

This stage is part of pre-production and post-production as well. Start by visualizing what you want your end result to be. Write down the ideas and shoot accordingly. Then you can start reviewing the material you got and discard unusable clips. This way you will save time by not importing unusable scenes into the video editing program in the first place. If you're missing some material, now is the best time to re-shoot.

Planing

With your end goal in mind, plan the construction of your video. Which footage needs to be in each segment of the video. Plan the beginning, the middle, and the end of your video and choose the clips you want to include in these parts of the video. Write down all the ideas you have and elaborate them on paper before you import your clips to the editing program. Planning ahead of time will save you from a lot of frustration and wasted effort.

The Rough Cut

At this stage you should prepare your images and clips in the right order. You should also choose the sound effects and music, and include them in the video. The rough cut will give you an idea how various clips and images work together to make the final video. If something works differently than what you imagine, it's not too late to change the concept, or even reshoot.

Scene Editing

Once you're satisfied with your rough cut, it's time to start working on the details. You can cut your clips to the exact point where you want them to start and end. You will now decide on the type of the transition between the scenes and clips, but don't forget to be consistent. If you use multiple transition types your viewers can get confused and have trouble following the flow of your videos.

Effects

Once your overall cut is ready, it's time for the most fun part of post-production: adding the special effects. Keep in mind that simple is almost always better. You are not a Hollywood movie editor playing with CGI (unless that is your niche and specialty). This is the time to add the titles, music, sound effects, and other fine details to your video. Maybe you opt to use slow-motion, color filters or time lapse footage. Keep in mind that the effects need to help you tell the story. Avoid unnecessary flashy effects that will distract the viewer.

Rendering

The final stage of the video editing process is choosing the file format and saving your video to upload it on YouTube. There are different rendering requirements for each file format. The best option is to choose the format which matches the frame size and frame rate of your video. Many editing programs can make this process easy for you as they offer different templates for different streaming platforms. YouTube is always among them. Depending on the length of your video, its complexity as well as the power of your computer's processor, rendering time can vary.

How to Add Music

Music is a really important element that enhances your videos. It speaks to the viewers on a different level. Together, the auditory and visual stimulants complete the message you're trying to communicate to your audience. Music is often used to add the emotional depth to your videos. We all know watching videos without any music feels really strange.

The first thing you need to do when choosing music is making sure it's not under copyright. Now, you might think that means you will need to create your own music. But this is not true. You have options. There are various stock sites which can sell you or offer you for free, music samples and audio tracks. Once you download it, you receive the rights to use it for your videos. They work just like stock images and videos.

The video editing software of your choice probably has an awesome tool which will help you implement the audio. But there are also separate tools that can do this job for you. They all work similarly so you will have to take into consideration the following aspects: your budget, the interface, input formats, and audio control. The tools can also be online or offline. Some of the most popular online tools are Pixico, Kapwing, MP3 Care, Animoto, and of course YouTube Studio. Among these, YouTube Studio is probably the simplest to use. All you have to do is choose the music which is already uploaded to YouTube. Once you start uploading your video, YouTube Studio will start automatically adding your chosen music to it, and it will synchronize the two components. Other online tools are more complex and they will give you more control of the audio settings. However, they usually come with a price.

If you want to use offline tools to add the music to your video instead, you can opt for any of the video editing programs we explored earlier. They come with this option, but be aware they support only certain music file types. Furthermore, offline video editing programs are usually more sophisticated and will give you many options. However, they can be too confusing and not as user-friendly as tools like YouTube Studio. If you're a beginner, you might stick to one of the online tools and focus on building up your video editing skills first.

Tricks to the Trade

Post-processing is mostly about creativity and less about technical knowledge. However, that doesn't mean you can go creating awesome edits without any technical knowledge. This is why it's important to choose the right software, the one you find easier to use, and that can perform all the actions you need. Consider the interface, the available features and its usability and find the one you will enjoy using the most. The latest and the most advanced video editing program is not always the best choice because it can be less suitable to your own editing style. If you're just starting out, using tools that are industry-standard will most likely push you away from the content-creation process.

Furthermore, you need to pair video editing software with a good computer. It doesn't really matter what you choose, but it has to be fast enough to be able to render your videos in due time. Video files are huge and your computer also needs to be able to offer you a smooth workflow in video editing software. Choose a good processor with a high core count, invest in a fast storage device (SSD), and increase your computer's memory (RAM).

Once you have a powerful computer that can render quickly and a good video editing software, it's time to be creative. Instead of impressing your audience with flashy animation and special effects, always strive to edit your videos for the story you're trying to tell. Your video has to be aesthetically pleasing but also to evoke the right emotion from your audience. Select appropriate music that matches your video and make sure it sets the right mood. You don't want a love ballad in your compilation of funny animal videos. It simply doesn't make sense. You can also choose to add texts and graphics to your videos which would explain the details and facts about your topic. However, this greatly depends on the type of the videos you're creating.

Here are some video editing tips and tricks you can use to make your videos look more professional:

- **Montage**: This technique places the accent on the passage of time. Quick cuts are put together to give a context to the story. It is mostly used to show how a character changed over a certain period of time. Think about the Rocky Balboa exercising scenes in the movie "Rocky".

- **Cross Dissolve**: This is another technique that can be used to signal the passage of time, but it can also be used in many different ways. For example, you can use it to show parallel storylines which are happening at the same time.

- **Fade in/out**: Again, we have a technique used to present the passage of time. One scene is fading out while the new one is fading in. This technique is often used to fast forward in time without too much explanation or to change locations. It is also used to show the transition from day to night and vice versa.

- **Cross Cuts**: Also known as parallel editing, this technique is about switching between two scenes happening at the same time but in different places. Cross-cuts are often used to add tension to the video, expectation and uncertainty. But they are used in other ways too, for example to amplify emotion.
- **Pull focus**: This trick will help the audience focus on the text or a title, while the scene is running in the background out of focus. This way the background is blurred, but the letters are sharp and easy to read.

Chapter 8: You Don't Just Upload a Video

You might think your video is ready for upload once you're done editing it, and although there is no rule which would prevent you from doing so, you should think about several factors. Remember that careful planning is the key to YouTube success, so you will have to include the video details, thumbnails, and your upload schedule in the initial planning. In this chapter, you will learn the importance of having a video schedule and everything you need to know about the details that accompany your video. At the end of this section, you will find a detailed guide on how to upload your first video to YouTube.

The Video Details

Many people think once they finish editing the video and they upload it to YouTube, it's out there, ready to be seen, and that's that.. However, that's not quite how it works. Any piece of content on the internet needs to be properly described in order to be discovered. This description comes in three parts: the title, description, and tags. Together they are referred to as the metadata of the video and they help your viewers find your video. They also notify YouTube about the content of your video and how to categorize it.

Titles are a big part of the YouTube ranking algorithm, but they are also what your viewers will most likely search for. This is why you need to think about the audience's possible choice of words before creating the title for your video. These keywords need to accurately describe your video and they have to make sense when put together. You can't simply throw in all the words that are related to the content of your video. For example, If you made a video of your dog barking at a postman, you can't just title it "barking, postman, dog, at". Put it in order to make sense for the viewer as well as the algorithm, and type something like "a dog barks at a postman". Or for even better searchability, add more details: "funny German Shepherd dog barking at postman". This way your title will capture the attention of those who search for funny videos, dog lovers, and those who exclusively search for German Shepherd videos.

Avoid using personal names in video titles unless the video is about a well-known person. As time passes, some titles get less and less traffic. You should occasionally review them and update them with new, high-traffic words. Avoid clickbait and misleading titles, this will greatly influence your ranking. Keep the titles under 70 characters if possible, and put non-essential details such as the number of the episode or brand name at the end of the title.

Next, we have the description. The description is a longer section of metadata and it will allow you to use as many keywords as you want. You can use up to 5,000 characters to accurately describe what your video is all about. It is highly desirable to use all of them. If you put well-researched keywords in the video's description, it would be a huge boost to visibility. YouTube will accurately index and rank your video, making it available to a wider audience. The YouTube description should be well planned because the search page will display only the first 120 characters. This doesn't influence the indexing itself, but rather how the audience perceives your video. Dedicate those first 120 characters to carefully selected words to grab the viewer's attention and make them want to watch the video.

There are many practices when it comes to writing a good description. Aside from using carefully chosen keywords, you might want to add time codes (timestamps). This will help your viewers jump to the parts of your video that are of interest to them. But do this only if your video is very long. You can also add links to your description section. They can lead to your website, your profiles on other social networks, or your other YouTube channels. Credit the people who worked with you on the video, and also credit the music and images that are not yours, but you used them to create your video. At the very end of the description, you may want to call the viewers to subscribe to your channel or direct them to other videos you created on a related topic.

Finally, you have to pay attention to tags. The tags are what will help your video get discovered by people who search a certain keyword in the search bar or even search engines such as Google. The better tags you chose, the higher your video will be ranked on the search results page. However, you must understand that search engines don't tolerate using irrelevant tags. In fact, if you use tags that you know are generating high traffic, but are not related to your video, you will eventually be penalized by the algorithm. Research the relevant keywords, place the most important ones first, and the least important ones last. Youtube has three different types of tags: specific, compound, and generic. Each one of them has a different purpose and you should always treat them separately. Only that way you will get the best results and attract the audience to your channel.

The specific tags are keyword-oriented and they notify YouTube about the content of your video. Without them, YouTube won't know how to categorize your video or how to rank it. Once you start typing these keywords, YouTube will immediately recognize the content of your video and it will try to suggest some of the keywords that are related, which should be helpful.

The compound tags are tags that use more than one word. Some users even tag the whole title of their video. But YouTube allows only 500 characters to be used as compound tags and if you want to use your title as a tag, you will have to keep it short. When writing compound tags avoid using prepositions such as: or, as, and, if, etc. Not only will you save room for more important words, but YouTube also ignores prepositions completely when it comes to ranking videos.

Last but not least, we have the generic tags, which are one or two-word descriptions of your entire video. They should be used in all of your videos, across your entire channel. Because they are repeating and constant, these tags are very important, so don't forget to include them when you upload each new video.

Creating YouTube Thumbnails

Thumbnails are like billboards for your videos. They instantly tell the viewer that the video is interesting. This is why they are extremely important, and a well-designed Thumbnail can attract the attention of a new audience for your channel. You can always opt to simply use a freeze-frame to tell your viewers what your video is about, but this usually doesn't attract much traffic. You need to make it engaging!

The thumbnail is a small, clickable snapshot and it is as important as your video's title. Because YouTube's ranking system also considers how many clicks your video generates in the first hour since the upload, you want your thumbnail to attract the audience to actually click.

However, Keep in mind it isn't enough to have just a flashy thumbnail. YouTube actually registers for how long a viewer watched your videos. If he just clicked and immediately left because your video wasn't interesting, YouTube will take note of it, and rank your video lower. This is why it is important to use a thumbnail to attract the right kind of audience. Your thumbnails should always portray what your videos are about. This way they will attract only the audience that will stay and watch your content until the end.

More than 90% of content creators have custom-made thumbnails. This is because thumbnails are the first thing a viewer will see when he searches for a certain video. The thumbnail should always contain key information about your video and go well with the title. The two go hand in hand to inform the audience that the video is worth watching. Choose an image that looks great in large and small format and is eye-caching and appropriate for the audience you want to attract. You can opt to use text in the thumbnail, but make it short and easy to read. Use a large font that is clear and concise. Thumbnails show up in different sizes on YouTube and on external websites that contain links to your videos. Therefore, it's important to create a thumbnail that will look good in different sizes and on different devices.

Using misleading or clickbait thumbnails and titles is a sign of sensationalism and is off-putting to the audience. Your viewers might get offended or annoyed by your misleading thumbnails and will most likely not recommend your video to others. Your goal is to grow a loyal audience and once you become recognizable, include your brand in the thumbnail. This way the audience will look forward to seeing the new videos you created. Avoid deceiving your viewers and misrepresenting your video. Keep it simple and to the point. Refrain from using offensive language or images. Never promote violence or sex through images, text, or the video itself. It will not only discourage the viewers from clicking on your video, but you will also lose a chance to monetize your content. Many advertisers choose carefully with whom they want to be associated, and they exclude the YouTubers who promote sex and violence. Finally, you should also avoid using ALL CAPS letters in thumbnails and in your video titles. Most people find it off-putting.

Once you have your thumbnail set, you can use YouTube Analytics to see how they perform. Observe what a viewer does once he clicks on the video. You will easily come to the conclusion whether your thumbnails and title work well enough to attract the desired audience. If you find they don't, you can make the necessary changes easily. There are plenty of free online YouTube thumbnail creators, and they will even give you a variety of templates to choose from. But you can always upload your own photo, add the text you want, or the desired clip art. You can even change the background and the color of the thumbnail. Once you are done with the creative process, all you have to do is download the finished product to your device, so you can use it on YouTube. It is that easy to make a thumbnail. Here is a shortlist of thumbnail makers you can try for free:

1. **Canva**: It has more than 2 million images in its database, hundreds of fonts, and it will allow you to customize the background, colors, and text however you want.

2. **Adobe Spark**: It comes with built-in themes you can use. All of them come with their own color choices, fonts, and layouts, and they are already designed to catch the eye of potential viewers.

3. **Crello**: This service will allow you to quickly blend images, text, designs, and objects. It's an easy-to-use program that will allow you to explore your own creativity.

4. **Picmaker**: Picmaker comes with a huge database of stickers, photos, backgrounds, text, icons, and much more. But it will also allow you to erase the existing background on some of the images, so you can use them as creatively as you want.

5. **Snapp**a: This program has a big assortment of templates, as well as customizable text, images, and objects that you can use to create thumbnails for your videos. The simple drag and drop functionality will allow you to do it fast even if you are not an expert.

Setting an Upload Schedule

In previous sections, we mentioned that scheduling the publishing of your videos is very important. It is one of the best ways of growing your audience and subscriber base. But being regular will also keep your existing subscribers interested as they will know when to look forward to your content. A schedule will also keep you disciplined and you will look forward to creating the content for your YouTube channel. It is often difficult for some creative people to stick to a schedule because they are inspired in the moment and inspiration might not visit them for months. However, with YouTube, it is unlikely to grow a substantial follower base and become successful if you're posting your content on the spur of the moment. It is essential that you make great content that you are passionate about, but remember that it isn't the only thing that will bring you success.

Even if you are not used to making schedules and organizing your creativity, you can still do it. It is a matter of discipline. Here is what you can do to get into the routine:

1. Be specific! Don't simply say to yourself "I'm gonna post two times a week". That is not enough. You have to decide on a specific day and set even the specific time frame when you will post your new content. Let's say you set your posting time to be each Wednesday at 2 PM. Your viewers will know exactly when to log in and see your new content. Remember how we said the first hour is very important for your video to get ranked? Well, this is how you do it. Your fans will watch your video immediately, allowing your video to rank higher and attract new audiences.

2. Make your posting schedule public. You can post it in the description of your channel, intro video, or on your banner. The audience will want to see your schedule and anticipate your new content. It will also allow your new subscribers to get to know your routine.

3. Remember that uploading a video takes time. You also have to dedicate time to writing the description, title, and creating the thumbnails. It might be easier if you prepare yourself in advance. Write down everything you need to have it ready on the day of upload.

4. Resist posting ahead of your schedule. It might happen that you feel extra creative, and you make two videos instead of one. Resist posting them both at the same time, or one immediately after the other. Bank your extra video and have it ready for the next scheduled publishing period. This way you will always have a video ready to post, even when you don't feel creative enough to create new content.

If you have a verified YouTube channel, and by this point, you should, YouTube will allow you access to a neat feature called "scheduling". This feature will allow you to upload a video ahead of time, but publish it only on the specific date and time you set. Uploading and publishing used to be synonyms in the world of YouTube, but not anymore. However, to use this feature you will have to go through a bit of effort on setting it up. Make sure your video status settings are not set to Public, Unlisted or Private. They should be set to Scheduled. Once you do this, you will have to choose your date and time of publishing the video. YouTube will need you to confirm your settings through email. Once everything is set up, you can relax and YouTube will automatically publish your content on the date and time you chose. You might as well be on a vacation and not worry about your schedule or channel!

Yet another trick to successfully scheduled YouTube videos is determining the perfect day and time of publishing. You can do this by checking YouTube Analytics and determining on what day and at what time your videos are most viewed. This will highly depend on your audience demographic. If you want to succeed worldwide, YouTube suggests posting on Thursdays and Fridays between 12 and 3 PM. This is because, on those days, YouTube itself has the most visitors. Following the same data, you can determine the worst days for publishing your content and avoid those days.

How to Upload Your Videos

Now that you know how to fill in your video's details, add metadata, tags, a proper title, and a thumbnail that will attract your audience, it is time to learn how to upload the video. You can either opt to use YouTube's application or do it via your web browser. There is not much difference between these two options and most of the steps are the same. But this chapter will teach you how to do it properly no matter what device you are using.

Uploading a video through the web browser:

1. Using your favorite web browser navigate to YouTube.
2. Log in if needed.
3. On the top of the screen, you will find the "create a video" button, click it. In the drop-down menu find the option "upload video" and select it.
4. YouTube will take you to the upload page where you will find "select files to upload". Choose the status of your video: "Public, Private, Unlisted or Scheduled". Public videos can be seen by anyone. Private means only you have access to it. An unlisted video is still up on youTube but available only to people who have a direct link. Scheduled videos are stored for later publishing.
5. To upload the video you can click the large arrow to select the file, or you can simply click and drag the file directly from your computer.
6. While waiting for the video to upload fill in the information such as the title, description, and tags.
7. To complete the process click "Publish". For this, you don't even have to wait for the video to finish uploading. However, your video will not appear online unless you click Publish.
8. Depending on how long your video is, YouTube will need some time to process it. It can take up to a few minutes for your video to become available to your audience.

Uploading a video using the mobile app:

1. Launch the YouTube app on your device
2. At the top of the screen, you will find the upload button, tap it. Your device will ask you for permission to access your camera and photo library, allow it.
3. The next screen will take you to where your videos are stored. Choose the one you want to upload. At this point, you can also access your camera and start recording a new video, or opt to go live.

4. Select "Next".

5. Enter the information of your videos such as the title, description, and tags. At this point, you need to choose a privacy setting of your video- Public, Private, Unlisted, or Scheduled. Then tap "Upload" at the top of the screen and you are done.

Your videos are uploaded and ready to be seen by millions of people all around the globe!

Section 4: Growing Your YouTube Channel

Chapter 9: Your YouTube Audience

People chose to become successful YouTubers because they want to put themselves out there, and they want to be seen and to interact with the viewers. But who are exactly these viewers and how do you get them to see your videos? YouTube attracts 1.9 billion users each month. That is almost ⅔ of overall internet users. They all watch videos and enjoy the content YouTube has to offer, but they are not all the same. Every person will search for what interests them. It can be news, entertainment, tutorials and how-to's, or product reviews. Among younger generations, YouTube became a substitute for television. They don't get their information or entertainment from TV. They turn to online media and YouTube. But if they all have different interests, and search for different videos on YouTube, how do you get them to see yours? After all, viewers have billions of videos to watch, and how can you get all those people to choose your video among myriads of others? It is not a simple task, and you should avoid creating content for everyone. You should strive to create a loyal fanbase, made out of people who share an interest (or more) and attract them to subscribe to your channel.

The YouTube Community

Simply put, your audience, the viewers of your videos, are the people interested in watching the content of your channel. Not every viewer will become your audience. Your videos can be seen by people who will never again return to your channel as they are simply not interested in the type of videos you are making. Remember that they are not your audience, they are only passing by. You should never strive to please them. Concentrate on people who genuinely want to see the type of videos you are making. They are the reason behind your success, they are loyal to you, and they are here to stay. Your audience is your community, and once you determine what type of videos you want to make, it is time to determine what type of people you should strive to attract and subscribe to your channel.

Youtube is used by both men and women, by the elderly, and by children. The demographics of the viewers are vast. But still, the analytical data shows that YouTube is no place for bursting the stereotype bubbles. The majority of the audience is male, between 18 and 25 years old, and they mostly search for entertainment. This doesn't mean you should create content just for this type of audience. YouTube users are actually divided fairly equally between males and females. The only difference here is that males tend to spend more time on YouTube. The same goes for the age difference. Younger people tend to stay on youTube longer than the older ones. And it is true that women mostly search for beauty and fashion channels, while men prefer sport, gaming, and news channels. However, if you take gaming as a large category the divide between male and female viewers is 50-50. The same goes for lifestyle channels, if observed as a large category it attracts an equal part of male and female viewership. This demographic divide is most obvious when it comes to small niches. The narrower your niche is, it will attract specific kinds of demographics. You will notice that older men prefer sport, while younger ones prefer console gaming. Older women prefer storytelling channels while younger girls like make-up tutorials. There is only one niche that unites all of the youtube viewers. No matter the age, gender, or where on the planet earth they are located, everyone loves pets!

Knowing your audience will greatly help you determine who is watching your videos, and what type of videos you should strive to make. But never address your audience presuming you know them. Never address their age, their gender, or their location. Don't presume only men watch your videos because you are making only "let's play" type of content. Not only will you offend some of your viewers, but you will also lose the majority of them. People don't like to be generalized and put into categories.

Where Do Viewers Come From

Attracting the audience to your YouTube channel is not as simple as creating quality videos that will interest them. People still need to find your videos, and you need to learn how to reach them. To do this, you need to find out how the people learn about your video and where they are coming from. Did they search for your channel's name on YouTube or Google search bar, or did they follow an external link to your channel? If you know where the majority of your traffic is coming from, you will be able to create a promotion strategy and attract even more subscribers.

There are ways to see how people found your channel. For example, YouTube Analytics has an option to show you the traffic source types report. Through it, you can discover from which external websites and apps viewers came to your videos. Or see what videos they were watching when you came up as suggested. Youtube also allows its users to create playlists, and perhaps through some of them, your audience found you. Analytics will allow you to see the playlists that led viewers to your videos. In the end, you can always see what phrases did the viewers search for in YouTube's search bar when they found your video.

Understand that more than half of your viewers will come from search and suggestions simply because that is how YouTube's algorithm works. There is nothing much you can do about it, the algorithm is out of your hands. However, this only underlines the importance of optimization and metadata on your channel. Search and suggestions love good titles that are clearly describing what your video is about. The more accurately you do your SEO it is more likely for your video to show up in brows results and suggestions.

External and Embedded player traffic will tell you more about where your videos are being shared, which external websites are leading to your videos. YouTube Analytics will include other social media in its report and you will easily find out if your audience prefers Facebook, Twitter, or some other platform. Once you find that out, you can start sharing your videos on those platforms and generate even more traffic.

Getting People to Subscribe and Hit that Notification Icon

On YouTube, success is measured in numbers: of views, likes, and subscribers. You might ask yourself why are subscribers important? Isn't it enough to have as many views as possible? The answer is that subscribers are your viewers, but they are also the force behind your video that will get you even more views. Once again, it all boils down to the YouTube algorithm. The subscribers bump up the number of how many times your video was played, they also increase the watch time and the engagement. The YouTube algorithm will notice this and rank your videos higher making it able to reach new viewers easier. The more time your subscribers spend on your video, YouTube will consider its content relevant and will put it as a suggestion to the new viewers.

Having a large number of subscribers is also important if you want to monetize your videos. After all, you can't even start benefiting from the ad revenues if you have less than 1,000 subscribers. The more subscribers you have, the more money you can make from YouTube as the platform will offer you benefit levels. But if you don't want to become famous, viral, and successful, if you want to use YouTube as a digital marketing strategy for your already existing brand, you still need subscribers and you still want to up their numbers. The reason is simple, more subscribers mean more views. More views lead to new audiences and your videos will reach more people who will learn about your brand, and what you have to offer. Sure, you can always opt to buy YouTube subscribers, but that is not a good option. Bought subscribers are bots, and they are there only to pump the subscriber numbers. But they don't engage, they won't pump your play numbers or watch time. YouTube even has a fake engagement policy that will penalize you for using the bot subscribers. And finally, your real audience wants engagement, not only with you but also with other subscribers. And if all you have to offer them are bots, the real subscribers will leave because of the lack of engagement.

Buying YouTube subscribers is simply not worth it. But how do you get real ones? Here is a short series of advice on how to attract people to subscribe and how to get them for free.

1. Ask! Sometimes the best strategy is the simplest one. Ask your viewers to subscribe to your channel. Do it after you make your audience laugh, or learn something new, or do it at the end of the video. You don't need to ask them to subscribe every minute of your video, you will risk putting your audience off. Once is enough. You can personally ask by recording yourself, or you can write a text. The viewers sometimes need a reminder, and if they liked your content, they will want to return to it. Also, remind them to turn on notifications to receive reminders about your new videos.

2. Create anticipation. End your videos with a teaser of what you are working on next. This will intrigue your viewers and they will want to come back and see what's next. They will subscribe in order to have a reminder to watch your next video.

3. Form a relationship with your audience. Engage your viewers and be friendly towards them. Respond to comments and follow them back. People genuinely appreciate the engagement and will want to come back to your channel.

4. You can run a contest. Offer your viewers a prize that will intrigue them, and mention that they need to be subscribed and that they need to turn on notifications in order to participate in the contest. Be fair, and reward your viewers for their loyalty.

5. Partner up with other channels. We already talked about collaboration with other YouTubers. It really works and it will bump your views and you will gain new subscribers.

6. Don't miss an opportunity to partner up with celebrities. Whether they are Youtube or other celebrities, it doesn't matter. This is a hard one, you need to attract the celebrity to your channel, make them want to work with you. But if you make it work, the number of your subscribers will skyrocket.

Engaging with Your Audience

To build your YouTube community, increase the number of your subscribers, and attract new viewers, you need to devote some time to audience engagement. By doing so, you will turn them into loyal fans and they will anticipate your videos not only for their high quality but also because they feel valued and cherished by you. Keep in mind that there is a wrong way of engaging your audience, and it will leave them frustrated, disappointed and they will unsubscribe. But you might still wonder what the audience engagement actually is. It is the actions that your audience takes on your YouTube page, or on the page of one of your videos. These actions can be comments, likes, and dislikes, shares, new subscriptions, or unsubscriptions.

Don't expect the audience to engage just because you have an awesome video. There are many awesome videos out there, and you need to show that yours is worth their time. You will do this by reaching out first. Initiate the interaction with the audience by answering their comments under your video, or on other social media. Listen to their advice and concerns, put an effort into your reply. This will show that you value their opinion and will make them want to come back to you. You can also use your video to call the audience to action. Simply say that you would love to hear their opinion and that you can't wait to read their comments. This is a call to a conversation and the audience will be eager to start one. Another way to initiate action is to ask your audience for the ideas for your next video. Ask them what they would like to see, or if they have some questions for you.

Rewarding your loyal fans is always a good way to make the audience engage. You can organize competitions or giveaways. You can include in-video shoutouts, where you would personally thank your audience by mentioning some of their names. Feel free to go even further and ask them to participate in your next video. You can even organize meetups, and personally get to know some of your fans. Organize it online, through skype, hangouts or any other platform. Finally, join a cause and promote it through your videos. You will find that many of your viewers will appreciate the gesture. Raise money for a charity, invite guests to your channel to talk about climate change, or bring in the animal shelter workers to promote adoption. By promoting the cause you are passionate about, you will connect with your audience and they will want to engage on your page.

Tinkering with the Community Settings

Once you reach 1,000 subscribers, you will open access to Community Tab (it will replace the Discussion tab), which allows you to interact with your viewers using rich media. This means you will be able to create polls, to send text, images, and videos to your community. The community posts will allow you to interact with your subscribers separately from the videos on your channels. The Community Tab will appear in Home or in the Subscription feed allowing you easy access. The community tab is a Facebook-like experience where you can post status updates, or simply chat with your viewers or share gifs and images with them. But you should know that the visitors to your page can answer your posts only by text. Your subscribers will be notified of new community posts if they turn on notifications for your channel. In fact, try introducing your Community Tab in your next video, link it and invite your viewers to subscribe and turn on notifications. Here is how you can use Community Tab in different ways and for different purposes:

1. Your first community post should state its purpose. Welcome your audience and let them know what your intentions are. This will help you build a strong and loyal community.

2. You can always use community posts to market your product. You can post an image of your product, and include a link to your online store. Offer special discounts for your subscribers and advertise upcoming sales.

3. Promote your latest or next video. Post a teaser image or a short trailer that will announce your next video. If you have already published one, you can use community posts to link it.

4. Promote your old videos to the new audience. Even the old subscribers might enjoy remembering your previous content.

5. Use polls to find out what your audience thinks. This is an interesting feature that will allow you an insight into the mind of your audience, and maybe even help you prepare for your next video.

6. Host a Q&A on your Community Tab, or use it to promote your upcoming live Q&A video session.

7. Ask your audience some questions and let them be the creative drive behind your videos. Ask them for ideas and suggestions.

8. Share gifs and memes. This will allow you to connect with your audience on a more personal level. Nothing connects people quicker than a good laugh.

9. Promote a cause through your Community Tab, and rally your followers to the cause. You can even gather donations for a charity through community posts.

10. Use the community tab to post other people's channels. It is an excellent way of promoting your collaborations and channel partners. Drive the traffic their way through your Community Tab and they will do the same for you.

Consider Doing a Livestream

YouTube has an option for live streaming and it is a great way to reach your audience in real-time. Going live means your video will be housed in the Live section and it will attract the viewers who are interested in seeing their favorite YouTubers in real-time. Of course, not only those who are interested in live content will see it. Anyone who subscribed to your channel, or anyone who watched one of your videos, or videos of other people but similar to yours, will have your live content suggested to them by YouTube. Going live is a special way of engaging the audience because there will be many viewers, all watching it at the same time. It will give them the experience and excitement of live events, but this time, made especially for their eyes. Live is a very unique way of presenting your content. Even if you are selling a product or promoting a brand, going live will get you a new audience, or make you stand out because you are doing it in such a unique way.

YouTube Live is a very popular option and the numbers are there to support this claim. More than 80% of adults prefer live videos instead of reading a blog post or the news. Around 82% of adults prefer to watch live videos than to browse through social media posts. 70% of the adults claim YouTube is their favorite platform for live content. These numbers make it obvious why you should consider going live. This doesn't mean you should do it all the time, but keep it occasionally, when you feel inspired or have a need for it.

Keep in mind that you can't just simply go live and expect people to watch you. You will need to do some promotion of your live event, just like a concert needs one. There are several ways of promoting your live event. The most obvious one is getting the word out there through social media. Everyone is on Facebook, Twitter, or Instagram. You can even use your Community Tab on YouTube to announce and promote your live streaming. You can even opt for Facebook advertising campaigns to give your promotional campaign a little extra push. The good thing is that you can limit your expenditure on ads and keep them as small as you want, but still secure viewership through them. Just make sure you post advertisements and promotions on time. Do it at least several days in advance.

Now that you planned and promoted your live streaming session, it is time to consider what you can do to ensure its success. First of all, brainstorm the content of your live video. Just as if you would do it with a recorded one. You can't go in front of the camera unprepared and rely only on your good looks and skills. If you are doing a live Q&A, be certain to prepare some rules and explain to your audience how it is going to work. Encourage your viewers to participate in the live stream. To do this, enable the real-time chat function and ask your audience for an opinion, or their suggestion. Encourage them to ask you questions. Make your live stream fun! Maybe your priority is to inform your audience, but that doesn't mean you should be completely professional. The audience will expect live streams to be fun and enjoyable and you should give your best to give them that experience. Be creative, play a little game with your audience, or tell a funny story from your life.

Chapter 10: Managing Your Channel

In this section, you will learn how to get the most out of your channel. Making and publishing high-quality videos is just one-half of the job and being a Youtuber also means running many channel-related tasks that are not at all creative, but necessary to keep you going and reach success. In his chapter, you will learn how the YouTube Algorithm works, how to make the best out of it, and what other options are out there when it comes to owning your own YouTube channel.

Welcoming Your Audience to the Channel

Once a potential viewer comes to your channel for the first time, he will want to see all that you have to offer in one place. The best place to do that little presentation is a channel trailer video. It is exactly like a movie trailer, it will quickly present all that your channel stands for, and tease the viewer making him want to see more. The trailer for your YouTube channel will directly influence the viewers' decision whether to subscribe or not. This is why the trailer needs to make an impact on the audience, and hook them up! If you wonder what should go into your trailer video here is a quick guideline:

1. Welcome the audience to your channel. Treat your channel as your home, you want the guests to feel comfortable. The best way to do it is to address them personally and welcome them.

2. Assume they are visiting your channels page for the first time. Many of them will be there for the first time, and your trailer video should be targeting them. Introduce yourself, or your brand and make them see what you have to offer.

3. Tell your viewers why they should subscribe and ask them to do so. When the video finishes, your video will have an end card that will enable the viewers to subscribe immediately.

4. Plan your trailer video and write a script. Decide what the tone of your trailer video should be and what emotions do you want the audience to feel upon watching it.

5. Add graphics and music to make your video more attractive and engaging. This will help draw in your audience and make them want to see what content you can offer them.

6. Although there is no perfect length for the trailer video, you will want to keep it short. Think of movie trailers, they are ace paced and short. The length should be just enough

to intrigue the viewer, spark and interest, but not reveal too much because the real content is waiting for them in your other videos.

7. Use storytelling powers. This doesn't mean that you should bore them to death with talk. Instead, use imagery to tell the story. After all, most viewers prefer visual stimulus. Keep away from using written text in your trailer video.

8. The first few seconds of the trailer video are crucial. That is when the viewer's attention gets hooked or not. The intro of your trailer should be interesting and engaging. Start with a fun fact, or a question that will make your audience wonder.

Make Use of Playlists

If you can think of it, YouTube has a playlist for it. Your favorite music band, or the funniest scenes from the Simpsons, there is a playlist for that. YouTube playlists are an awesome way of engaging your audience and you should use them to grow your brand and to maximize your marketing strategy. But first, you need to learn what is a YouTube playlist, and how to use it. A YouTube playlist is a set of videos that play in order. When one video finishes, the next one will start automatically. Users don't have to take any action to play the next video. All they have to decide is which playlist will suit their momentary needs. Do they need to cheer up? Maybe they will search for a funny video playlist. Do they need relaxing music for work? There is a playlist with all the mellow, chill, and relaxing tunes that will help a person concentrate.

But for YouTube content creators, the playlists are the ultimate content curation tool. This means that you can use a playlist to engage your audience, instead of doing it with just one video. The playlist does need to tell a story and you should avoid putting together a playlist of random videos. The viewer's experience will be enhanced because he doesn't have to do any content search. The possibilities for playlists are endless, and the way you will use them is all up to you. You can put together all the Q&As you did in the past. Or pair videos that address the same topic. Make two separate playlists of funny dog's videos and funny cat's videos for the audience that is interested only in their favorite animal.

To create a playlist on YouTube, simply go to "My Channel". Select the "Customize Channel" option to access the video manager. This screen allows you to edit your entire YouTube channel including the description, banners, and videos. Now select the "Playlist" tab in the middle of the screen and click on the button "New playlist" to create a new one. Enter the title for the playlist you are making and click "Create" (the title can always be edited later, in case you change your mind). Now that you created a playlist, it's time to add videos to it. Click the "edit" button then "Add videos" and simply select the ones you want to use. Now that your playlist contains some videos in it, it's time to share it with the rest of the world. Do this by simply clicking the "Share" button. You can share it through email, social media platforms, or embed it in your website or blog post. Creating a playlist is simple and YouTube's interface will allow you to do it in no time. Why not use this awesome feature and make it easier for your viewers to find the videos of their interest?

Are You Properly Utilizing YouTube Stories?

If you manage to get 10,000 subscribers, YouTube will enable you to share stories with your fans. They are short, mobile-only videos that will offer you the opportunity to connect with your audience in a unique, casual, and "in the spur of the moment" way. Use the stories to engage your audience and make them into your loyal subscribers. Stories will be visible for only 7 days, and then YouTube will remove them. The concept is similar to Facebook and Instagram stories, but it will offer you a dynamic way to connect directly to your YouTube audience, without using other social media platforms. Keep in mind that if your channel is labeled to be for children, this feature will not be available to you. You will be able to add stickers to your stories and to interact with your audience through comments and replies, and you will have direct influence over the short video and delete it even before the 7 days time period expires.

YouTube stories can be created only through the YouTube Play app, and not through YouTube Creator Studio. This is what makes them a perfect marketing solution for smartphone users. You can add images or videos to your story from your phone's library, or you can create them on the go. Remember that story videos can be only 15 seconds long, so whatever content you choose to put, make it short and to the point. You can add music, use filters, insert links and add text and stickers to your story. Once you are happy with the end result, tap Save and only then tap Post and your story will be delivered to your audience.

As a content creator on YouTube, you have to strategize the use of the stories. Use them to engage the audience, ask them questions, and get inspired by their answers. Build a relationship with your audience by addressing their comments personally. Hit a reply button and answer their questions, or compliment their insight. Use the YouTube story to announce your newest video, or to advertise your products. Stories are a great way to market your brand, especially because you can add links to them. They will ensure your main websites get organic traffic too.

How YouTube Videos are Ranked

More than 300 hours of video per minute are being uploaded on YouTube at any given time. It is hard to get noticed and to succeed as a content creator. While offering quality content will guarantee that your audience will return, it is the SEO that will attract the audience to your video in the first place. In order to do a proper SEO, you need to understand how YouTube ranks the videos. In this section, you will learn the most important ranking factors that you will continuously use to optimize your presence on YouTube. Optimized YouTube channel will help search engines understand the content of your video, and increase its ranking both on YouTube search pages and within search engines such as Google.

Keywords

YouTube's algorithm pays much attention to the metadata of your video. The keywords you choose to use are a significant part of the metadata. Keywords are simple, one or two-word descriptions of your channel or your video, and just by glancing at them, the users will know what your content is about. Keywords can be added through the advanced setting in the Creator Studio within YouTube itself. You have to understand the importance of the proper use of keywords. They are effective only if they are carefully chosen and relate closely to your brand, the niche, and the content of your videos. This is why you should always do some keyword research before choosing them. There are many useful tools that can help you with keyword research, such as Google AdWords Keyword Planner or Rank Tracker.

Pay special attention to how many keywords you are using. If used in great numbers, they will start diluting the importance of each one of them. Keep it in between 5 to 10. To get some ideas for your channel keywords visit your competitor's channels and see what works for them. Another method of finding the right keywords to use is YouTube search suggestion. Start typing a phrase relevant to your channel and see what YouTube will suggest to you. These keywords are great for the simple reason that you don't have to wonder if they are popular. If YouTube is suggesting them, it means people actually search for them. If you are recording the speech for your content, say your keywords during the video. Make them fit in the content naturally. This is important because YouTube automatically transcribes your videos and uses this transcription to understand its content.

Video Title and Description

As you already know, metadata is extremely important for YouTube to rank your videos properly, and the titles are part of the metadata. This is why you should pay close attention to how you title your content. Titles give a first impression about your video, not only to the viewers but also to search engines and YouTube itself. A video with a good title will attract more traffic to your channel and will increase the number of views your videos will have. Shorter titles work better because the long ones often get cut off in the search bar. Try to limit your titles to five words or less. Your main keyword should be at the start of the title, and it should be the most relevant one for the content of your video.

The video description is very similar to the title of the video, but the good thing is you have more room for keywords. The description will help Google and YouTube understand the content of your video. Start the description with the most relevant keywords and keep it at least 250 words long. Include links to your other social media, blog, or website in the description and you will helpYouTube rank you higher. Don't be afraid to repeat the keywords in the description, but this doesn't mean you should make a list. The descriptionn should be relevant to the readers too. Try to limit your repetitive keywords to 2 to 4 times. Avoid being spammy, and be as informative as you can.

Video Tags

Tags are short, one or two words, descriptions that will help YouTube understand the topic and the content of your video. Tags generally don't have the impact on the ranking as keywords do, but they still play an important role. They will not only help the search engine rank your video, but they will also help users find it. Tags are keywords and it is important to use the words and phrases you think users might search for. Keep them relevant to your video, otherwise, they won't do their job. If you are doing beauty tutorials, make sure to use tags such as "make-up tutorial", "evening make-up", or "home beauty treatment". Keep the number of the tags in mind. You don't have to type a whole bunch of them. Ten well thought tags will do a better job than 20 irrelevant ones.

Tags may not be the most important thing when it comes to YouTube rankings, but they do play a role in making your video a suggested one or a related video in the sidebar area. If a viewer is watching a video about gaming from another channel, if your tags are relevant, YouTube will suggest to that viewer to watch your gaming video next.

Video Quality

YouTube loves HD videos and promotes them. Any video, on any given topic, will rank higher if it's in HD. But the quality of your video will have the most important impact on the user's experience. High-Quality videos attract more traffic, and the more traffic you have, the higher your video will rank. YouTube focuses on users' interaction with the videos because it can't use backlinks like Google does to determine the relevance of your content. If the user's engagement is negative, your video will rank lower. But High-Quality videos don't necessarily mean HD. You can have the viewers spend more time watching, commenting, and liking your videos if you offer them quality content. This means that no matter how well you do your SEO, if your video has no quality to offer (resolution, content, or both), it will not rank well.

User Experience Metrics

In the Video Quality section, we mentioned the importance of users interacting with your channel and your videos. YouTube simply places a lot of focus on this interaction when determining how to rank a video. It uses several metrics to do so: comments, number of new subscribers after watching the video, likes and dislikes, and shares. YouTube uses these numbers as a basis on which to determine the quality of your video and its relevance. Videos that are capable of engaging the users, making them like, share and comment, will definitely rank higher. The time a viewer spends watching your video is also important and falls into this category. If your video is 10 minutes long, but the user stops watching it after only one minute, YouTube will receive a signal that your video content is not interesting, of no relevance, and will rank it lower.

Closed Captions

If you use spoken words in your videos, you should consider using closed captions. There are two major reasons why you should do this:

1. Your videos will become available to a much larger community, as the people who do not speak your language or are deaf, will now be able to follow it.
2. Search Engines analyze closed captions and include their value in the ranking system.

YouTube will offer you the option to upload your own subtitles, or to use automatic captioning. The automatic one is not perfect and in order to ensure the overall quality of your video, it is recommended to upload your own.

Mastering YouTube Analytics

A tool that content creators use to measure the success of their YouTube marketing efforts is called YouTube Analytics. You can access this tool from the YouTube Studio dashboard, it is integrated with the YouTube website, and you don't need to do any installation on your part. This tool is capable of tracking everything that is going on on YouTube, but that doesn't mean you need to have an insight into everything that exists. YouTube Analytics works with raw data, and if you don't know how to translate it, what's the point? You should concentrate on observing the data that helps you turn a viewer into a subscriber. Understand what your audience values, and how to keep them engaged, and you will hit a jackpot.

To use YouTube Analytics, you need to log in to your YouTube account, click your profile icon, select YouTube Studio and then select Analytics. In the upper right corner select Advanced Mode for a detailed breakdown of the channel and video data. Now you can opt to download this information, directly from the Advanced Mode. You can also click the Compare To option in the upper right corner and this will take you to a new screen where you will be given insight into various parameters, past and present, and you will be able to compare them.

Youtube metrics

To be able to read all the data YouTube Analytics presents to you, you will need to learn each metric measured, why is it important, and how to use this data to improve your performance.

Subscribers: This represents the number of people that subscribed to your channel. YouTube Analytics will allow you to see how many new subscribers you gained over a certain period. To see how this figure compares to your typical subscriber growths, simply however over its icon.

Realtime views: This is the number of views your last published video received in the period of the last 48 hours. This metric is an excellent way of tracking how well your YouTube Live or recently published video performed.

Top Videos: will display a snapshot of the videos that performed the best over a given period of time. YouTube Analytics will allow you to adjust the time frame, and you can easily conclude which of your videos is the all-time best performer.

Channel Views: This will allow you to track how many times your channel was viewed over a given period of time. You can compare different periods and determine if your channel performed better in the past or in the present. If you notice your view counts are lower now, you may see what you did well in the past and repeat it to attract the audience back to your channel.

Channel Watch Time: will give you tidal hours people have spent on your channel. You can compare this number to the average watch time simply by hovering over the icon.

Audience Metrics

To better understand your viewers, use audience metrics. It will help you adjust your content and community management and digital marketing strategies/

Unique viewers: This represents the number of people who watched your video at a selected period of time. This metric doesn't include multiple views that come from the same person.

Average views per viewer: This is a metric that tells you the number of times one viewer watched a video on your channel. It will include multiple views of one video, and the views of multiple videos.

When your viewers are on YouTube: This is a chart that displays days and hours that have the most viewers on your channel. This info is important because you can base your publishing schedule according to it.

Audience demographics: This will let you know the age, gender, and location of your audience. Use this information to plan the content or your viewers, or maybe even content that will attract the demographics missing from your channel.

Youtube Discovery Metrics

This metric will allow you to learn how people find your videos and how they discover your channel. Whether they visited your channel through external links or found it by using the YouTube search bar. Learning these metrics will help you to adjust your SEO.

Impressions and CTR: Each time someone sees the thumbnail of your video, the impression is recorded. But impression click-through rates will display the number of people who clicked on the thumbnail to access the video. If you have a high click-through rate, that means your keywords and your thumbnails are effective. But in order to see how the video itself is performing, you will need to see the watch time and average view duration.

Traffic sources: will tell you where and how people find your videos. Traffic sources include YouTube search, suggestions, and playlists. Other sources are measured too, and you can find out if people used Direct URLs or External links.

Top YouTube search terms: you can see these if you go to Traffic Source and then YouTube Search. This is how you will find out the top searched terms that people used to find your videos. This will give you a clue if your SEO strategy is performing well, or if it needs adjusting.

YouTube Video Metrics

This section will help you track the metrics for a certain video and determine how well it performs. Based on the data collected, you can conclude what you need to do differently in your future videos to perform better.

Views: This metric shows you the number of times a video has been watched overall. This includes repeated views from the same person.

Video Subscribers: This represents the number of people who subscribed to your channel after watching a particular video.

Watch Time: This will tell you how much time people spend watching your video overall. This number is accumulated after a certain period of time.

Audience retention: This metric will tell you how far people made it through your video. It is an average view duration, and you will learn at what point of the video people lose interest.

YouTube Engagement Metrics

This section will tell you how and when your audience is engaging with your channel. Use it to plan interaction with the audience, such as replies to comments, or asking them to subscribe, like, and share.

Likes and dislikes: Sometimes they are considered vanity metrics, but they are important. They will tell you what people think of your content and if you need to change something to perform better.

Card and end screen reports: These reports will display the metrics for the interactive content you added to your video. The report from this secretion will tell you if they worked, and which cards worked best.

YouTube Revenue Metrics

This section is very important to the content creators who monetize their videos, as it will help them track their earnings.

Estimated revenue: This will tell you how much your channel earned during a specific period of time. The figure you get includes all sources of revenue.

Revenue sources: This metric will display a breakdown of all the sources your videos use to make money through YouTube.

Let's Talk About Copyright

YouTube takes copyright very seriously, and you should mind how you use the intellectual property of other people. But before you understand why this is important, you need to know what copyright is and how you can avoid copyright infringement. When a person creates an original work, be it music, sound, image, or written word, he automatically owns the copyright to this work. That means he is the only one who can make copies of his own work. But he can also give the right to others to use his work. The copyright law is different in different countries, but YouTube takes it very seriously. The laws are set in place to protect the creators and their work, and give them certain rights. If a musician allows his work to be used without any copyright protection, he wouldn't be able to make a living out of his own music. Here are the types of works that are subjected to copyright:

1. Musical compositions and any sound recording
2. Audiovisual works such as TV shows, online videos, music videos, movies, etc
3. Visual work such as photographs, posters, paintings, etc
4. Video games and computer software
5. Written works such as articles, books, poems, musical compositions, etc
6. Dramatic works such as musicals, scripts, and plays

It is important to understand that facts, processes, and ideas are not subjected to copyright. It may be immoral to steal an idea, but the deed itself is not protected by copyright laws. Only creative works fixed in a physical medium are eligible for copyright. But be cautious, as anything else can be protected by patent and trademark laws.

YouTube punishes the users who infringe on copyright. The video that is violating other people's copyright will be taken down, and the user will be punished by a strike. If a user gets three strikes YouTube will take away your channel. There are precautionary measures you can take in order to ensure this doesn't happen to you.

Have permission. The rules are simple, everything you created belongs to you and you own the copyright. But if you choose to upload the content created by another person, you better have their permission to use it. Remember that copyright is not only created as soon as the work is done. It is also in place for as long as the creator lives, and even some time after his death. That means that there are some intellectual works out there that are open for public use and you are free to use them.

If you decide to use someone else's work you need to get their permission. Simply stating that something was created by someone else, or adding the name of the copyright owner is not enough. This is still a breach that will lead to video being blocked, and you get a strike from YouTube. What you need to do to be able to use someone else's work is to get a license for it. However, the licenses often come with some kind of restrictions. It might be that the license states that no monetization is to be made through the use of the copyrighted material, or that you can use it only for a limited time. Be sure to read the rights and limitations of such licenses in detail.

There is always an option of Fair Use. This is when you copy the copyrighted material for a limited, and transformative purpose. In other words, you are allowed to comment, criticize or make a parody out of copyrighted material. This can be done without the permission of the author of the copyrighted material. However, Fair Use is somewhat tricky, because it can be implemented only in videos that are out there to inform or educate. You cannot monetize from Fair Use.

Chapter 11: YouTube and SEO in a Nutshell

Not so long ago, the internet became a perfect place for all types of marketing. At first, it was enough to publish a high volume of marketing material in order to secure the views and traffic. However, with the increase of internet use, it became impossible to find relevant information in a sea of content out there. Search engines had to be modified and made able to filter relevant material from the spam content. Various algorithms were made to do this filtering and the marketers had to change their tactics. Suddenly, the volume wasn't enough and they had to produce high-quality content which would also be optimized in such a way that search engines would discover it and rank it high on the result pages. Only several years ago the algorithms were able to work only with the written word. But now they are able to work with videos, images, and even sounds. Through smart optimization of text, sound, images, and video, you can make your content rank high. This is what SEO is all about and why you should do it properly.

SEO, in General

SEO stands for Search Engine Optimization and in simple terms, it means improving your internet presence (through website, blog, YouTube channel, etc), to increase its visibility. The truth is, you need to rank high in order to be noticed by the users who search for the content you are creating. When using search engines such as Google, people pay close attention only to the first page. This is not because they are lazy, but because search engines rank the relevance of the content. This means that the first result displayed is probably there because of high-quality content that will satisfy the consumers. The further down you go, the displayed results lose in relevance. Your goal as a content creator must be to show up on the first page of the search engine, and if possible, to show up as the first result.

But how do search engines know what is high-quality content? Simply put, they were designed to crawl pages on the web and collect information. They index the information and analyze it. There are hundreds of ranking factors the algorithm would use in order to determine the order in which the pages should be displayed. Some of them are the usage of keywords, the construction of the content (if it was written for humans or for machines), and even the architecture of the website (if it was constructed for browser use or if they are also mobile-friendly). you can take into account all of these factors and create a website, or a YouTube channel that would help you rank higher on the search results page. The search engine algorithms are constantly evolving, learning, and changing in order to give the users the best experience. This is why SEO is a marketing branch that requires constant updates and adjustments to the work routine.

How SEO Works on YouTube

SEO for YouTube is a little bit different than for search engines like Google or Bing. This is because instead of using backlinks, YouTube prefers to analyze the user experience and determine the quality of the content based on that. That means that if your YouTube video engages the audience, if its content makes them stay, subscribe or interact with your channel and video in any other way, it will rank it better. In chapter 10 we discussed the importance of user experience metrics and how to comment count, the length of the video, the number of views, likes, shares, etc will influence how you rank on YouTube. You should dedicate your time to improve your user engagement methods and attract your audience to subscribe and stay on your channel. But there are other things you could also be doing in order to improve your rankings and here is what theta re:

1. Keyword research. By now you understand the importance of having a good set of keywords that will be related to your content and describe it in the best possible way so that search engines will understand what your videos are about. However, you should pay special attention to researching your keywords often and with the right tools. The popularity of keywords changes over time and a keyword that worked perfectly yesterday might not work for you tomorrow. This is why it is important to periodically check your keywords and how they rank. Google provides you with a free tool you can use to check the popularity of the keywords and discover new ones. It's called "Google Trends" and it already comes with a YouTube search option implemented.

2. Track the rankings of your videos on YouTube. You don't need to do this manually, there are tools out there, both free and paid, that will help you keep track of your positioning on both Google and on YouTube. One such tool is Ubersuggest.

3. Be consistent. While becoming viral is a great thing, it will bring you a short burst of fame. The key is consistency. You need to build your subscribers base and turn your viewers into fans. This can be done only over a long period of time. Keep producing high-quality videos that are published on schedule. Having two viral videos in a row is impossible, and forget about making all of your videos viral. Only by building a strong community of viewers and through their engagement with your channel, you will have a consistently high ranking.

4. While it is true most people will give a video maybe a minute or two to intrigue them, that doesn't mean you should keep your videos short. Put the most intriguing information at the beginning, but keep the video at least five minutes long. Google ranks better longer videos because it means they can charge for more advertisement. High-quality, long-form content allows running more ads, therefore more profit for YouTube.

5. The first 48 hours are critical. Prepare your SEO before you publish a video. Better yet, before you upload it. Never publish a video without properly done SEO, thinking you can

do it anytime you want. As soon as you give YouTube's algorithm the information about what your video is about, it will rank high enough to attract viewers. These viewers will interact with your video through likes, comments, and subscriptions, and will push its rankings even higher. The sooner this happened the better. It is possible to go back and repair the SEO of your older videos to keep them relevant. But once the algorithm judges your video, it is very hard to change that judgment.

Applying & Improving SEO on Your Channel

To get the YouTube SEO right, you will need to dedicate a lot of time to optimize your channel, playlist, metadata for each video, their description, titles, thumbnails, and even the video content itself. It is important to think about your videos as text and even transform them into text. This will help you rank higher not only on YouTube but also on Google and other search engines. The power of transcripts, closed captions, and subtitles are not to be ignored. This is how search engines learn about the content of your videos and it is the text they use to process the information and decide how to rank the video. Here are some tricks you can apply in order to take your YouTube SEO skills to the next level:

1. Add Closed Captions. YouTube will automatically transcribe your videos, but its auto-caption is only 70% accurate. The mistakes it makes can influence the ranking of your videos as the search engine will not understand fully what your content is about. This is why it is important to provide YouTube with 100% accurate captions. But there is one more draw-back from automated-captions. Google will penalize you for using the random words as captions, as it will treat them as spam. If they sound like gibberish, and most likely they will, Google will decide the captions are unworthy and will rank your video lower.

2. Add the transcript of your video to its description. Since the description field allows you to type 4,850 characters (including spaces), this should be enough to fit a transcript of a dialog-heavy video that lasts up to 10 minutes. If your video is longer than that, you can make a short version of a transcript, but include a link to the full version on a separate web page. This is done because the description section of your videos is where the search engine's algorithms will crawl first in order to index your video.

3. Translate the video transcripts and captions in different languages. This is more important if your content is not in English, or if you are targeting a population from a certain location in order to expand your audience. Search engine algorithms will include the translated transcriptions and captions and rank your videos higher in the countries where those languages are native.

4. Use the video SEO embed in order to inject the video's metadata into the head of your webpage. This will allow search engines to crawl and index the video properly. Try out 3Play Plugin to make the videos SEO-friendly. Optimizing your videos not only for YouTube but for search engines too will bring you more views. And even though Google prioritizes the videos on its search page, it won't be able to do so if the SEO is not done properly.

5. Use playlists and subcategorize your videos. Make playlists by grouping 4 to 6 relevant videos. This will not only increase the users' engagement, but it will also make it easier for your audience to share multiple videos at a time. This way, more of your videos will reach a new audience.

Chapter 12: YouTube Marketing

Social media marketing became a huge opportunity back in the early days of Facebook, Twitter, and Instagram. But recently, marketers are turning to YouTube as they see the great potential video marketing on social media has. After all, YouTube is a social media platform too, as well as the second largest search engine. With over 6 billion people using YouTube each day, marketers would lose so much if they chose to ignore it. Maintaining the presence on different social media is how businesses and brands reach out to their audience and how they engage with them. YouTube is nothing different. People from around the world use YouTube and this platform became a unique way for marketers to reach new audiences. Video marketing is increasing because video accounts for over 70% of internet traffic in general. In this section, you will learn how to use YouTube and advertise your brand or service and how it will help you grow your business by reaching new audiences.

The Basics of Marketing

Marketing is a set of activities one makes in order to sell or promote a product or a service. It is what you say in order to convince the people your product or service is worth their time and money. Marketing is not only advertising, it also includes the sale and the delivery of the product and service to the people. After all, you want your customers and clients to keep coming back to you. Because marketing is a complex idea that drives a business, there are third-party affiliates that do marketing professionally and offer their services to companies and businesses. Big companies usually have their own marketing departments that take care of the advertising and searching for new potential markets on which to sell their company's product. Promotion is not a synonym for marketing. It is just one of its branches. Promotion is marketing done on specifically targeted audiences in order to expand the business.

Marketing is not only about drawing in customers and clients. It is also about maintaining the relationship with the already existing ones. Keeping in touch with past clients, as well as reaching out to potential ones is an important part of marketing. It may even involve writing "thank you" notes, emails, sending gifts to prospective clients, and socializing with them. But people often think that marketing is about pushing the product just to everyone. However, it is more nuanced than that. Marketing is about matching the product with the people who need access to it. This is one of the reasons for the existence of the Four Ps of marketing: product, price, place, and promotion. When put together, these elements make up the essential mix a company needs in order to successfully market its product or service.

Product: This is the item or service a company wants to offer to the customers. Before trying to market the product, marketers need to understand it, and to learn how it compares to the same or similar products that the competing company is offering.

Price: The price is the amount of monetary value the company wants for its product. There are many factors that enter the process of establishing the price for a product or service: unit cost price, marketing costs, packaging, and distribution expenses.

Place: This is the location where the product will be distributed. This includes making a decision if the sale will be in a physical store or through online platforms.

Promotion: In other words, this is a marketing communication campaign. It includes advertising, selling, various sales, direct marketing, public sales, guerilla marketing (unconventional interactions with customers in order to promote a product), and sponsorship.

Online sales are increasing each year. Only in 2017, they reached an unbelievable 65% of total sales. Considering the lightning-fast increase in popularity of online sales, online marketing is a critical part of the overall marketing strategy. Digital advertising and the use of social media platforms have become a norm. Youtube has joined the world of digital marketing as both a place to host the advertisement and a place to reach a new audience, as well as to keep in touch with the already existing customers.

Social Media Marketing (SMM)

Social Media Marketing became one of the largest aspects of marketing. Because the general population is using social media platforms on a daily basis, it became incredibly important for businesses to reach their audience through Facebook, Twitter, Instagram, Youtube, etc. Social media platforms give the opportunity to brands and businesses to directly speak to their audience. If you are not doing it, you are missing out! It is not news that social media usage surpassed that of the TV or radio. Marketing on social media will bring great success to your business, but that doesn't mean it is an easy job. There are nuances to be used in order to maximize your social media outreach. Another difficulty is staying in trend. Social media platforms are ever-changing, and as social media marketer, you need to constantly be up to date and follow the rules of the game.

Social media marketing is a branch of Internet marketing and it involves creating content for social media which will ensure that the marketing and branding goals online are achieved. Activities that make up social media marketing include posting text, images, and video updates, in order to get the audience to engage. Another aspect of social media marketing is paid to advertise.

How SMM Works

Strategy: Social media marketing campaigns need to be planned in detail. But before you even start, you need to think about what are the goals of your business and what exactly do you want to achieve with the campaign. Only after you are certain you have these figured out, you can start planning your marketing strategy. If you start the marketing complaint without any plan, you will soon become lost and overwhelmed. Instead of aimlessly wandering the social media field, try asking yourself some of these questions, in order to determine how to define your social media marketing goals:

1. What is driving you to start a social media marketing campaign?
2. What do you think you will achieve with it?
3. Who is your targeted audience?
4. How would your targeted audience use social media?
5. Which platforms, groups, pages would they visit the most?
6. What is the message you want to send to your audience, through social media?

The type of your business will greatly influence your social media strategy. This means that if you are in the travel business section, you can opt to use highly visual stimuli to reach your audience. This means that the best social media platforms for your business would be Pinterest, or Instagram, as well as YouTube. Twitter or Linkedin would be a better option for a marketing company or business to business outreach.

When determining the goals of your social marketing strategy you should think about whether you want to raise awareness about your brand or to drive traffic and sales. Social media is an amazing place to create a community that would be encouraged to engage with your brand. This is why you should think about starting customer support through social media. And that will lead you to the next step in the thought process. Which social platform is perfect for your business. There are a lot of social media platforms, and although you should establish a presence on more than just one, that doesn't mean you should do it on all of them. Think about your targeted audience and where do you think they hang out the most? Pick a few platforms which you know with certainty have the highest possibility of reaching your targeted audience, as well as satisfying your business goals. Facebook and Instagram are great for driving traffic and sales, but Twitter might be a better option for raising awareness.

Planning and Publishing: Once you have your strategy up, it is time to plan the content for your social media marketing. You need to think upfront about what you want this content to look like, will you use videos, images, GIFs, etc. You should also write a script and text for everything you plan to publish. Also, make a schedule for publishing and determine when exactly to publish each post. The timing and frequency of your publishing are incredibly important. You want to maximize the reach and you should determine at what days and at what times most of your audience is active on social media.

Listening and Engagement: Once you published your first social media posts, you should monitor how users and customers are interacting with it. Read comments, count the likes and shares, see if anyone tagged someone else to attract the attention of their family and friends to your business. Remember that people might talk about your brand or business without tagging you. You won't know when this happens, so you will need to do some manual search. However, this shouldn't be a difficult job. There are many tools out there that can help you monitor the engagement of your audience.

Analytics: If you want to know how your social media marketing is performing, you will have to analyze some raw data. This will tell you if you got any new followers, and what their number is compared to the previous month; or how many positive mentions you got. You will also know if people are using your brand's hashtag and if they are sharing your posts. The social platforms will provide you with some of the information you need, but to get the best results, you should consider using some of the tools specially designed to keep track of the analytics.

Advertising: Social media platforms allow you to post ads too. These are paid ads that will ensure you reach the widest possible audience. These social media advertising tools are so powerful that you can specify your targeted audience based on their location, gender, age, interests, and even based on their interaction with your competitors.

Marketing on YouTube

YouTube is a platform that reaches around 95% of the world's population, and it can be accessed in 76 different languages. It is no wonder the businesses are hurrying up to establish their presence on YouTube, and marketers are rushing to offer YouTube their services. You might think that YouTube is too narrowly specialized and that your audience is not there. But think again! Over ⅓ of the overall time people spend on the internet, they spend watching videos. YouTube has more than two billion active users, and the chances that your audience is there are great. Everyone uses youtube, even the elderly. And it's not only about reaching the audience. Correct use of SEO and YouTube can help you and your brand rank higher on different search engines. Most importantly, YouTube allows you to share unique content with your audience and ensure their engagement.

If you ever watched a video on YouTube, and the chances are that you did, you probably encountered YouTube ads. It is important that Marketing on YouTube isn't equal to running those ads. We will talk more about them in the next chapter. Now it is important you understand that marketing on YouTube means creating your own channel with the name of your brand, producing high-quality videos which will engage the audience and at the same time advertise your product. For example, you can host a Q&A session with your audience, or make an unboxing video, create tutorials on how to properly use the product you're selling, or simply make an intro class that will explain the service your business has to offer. The possibilities are enormous. Look at how other businesses did it. Some of the most famous make-up producers already have their presence established on YouTube and they are creating content for their viewers by hosting famous make-up artists.

If you are still not convinced that YouTube is perfect for your business, let's see three main reasons why you should seriously give it a chance:

1. Make your brand an authority in the field. Video marketing will help your audience build their trust in you. You will become a figure of authority to whom the viewers can always come back for the necessary information. Your presence on YouTube will say "Hey! I'm always here for you", and the customers will find it easy to connect to your brand. People appreciate the help and value they are getting through these business-driven videos on YouTube and find it easy to connect with the ideas and strategies behind those businesses.

2. Build Credibility! When it comes to customer acquisition, trust is everything. If your audience doesn't trust you, they won't buy your product or your services. Because of this, you have to take steps to build a relationship with your audience, grow your customer base and keep them informed. Offering information is the best way to gain someone's trust. Through videos on YouTube, you can put a face behind the information, someone your audience can connect to on a more personal level, and the credibility will rise.

3. YouTube is more engaging than other social media platforms. People enjoy watching videos and they do it more now than ever before. Videos are entertaining and the viewer doesn't need to put much effort into finding what they like. Since through videos you would be able to connect with your audience, you would step beyond the boundaries of traditional marketing. You can keep the communication between and your viewers going and add a personal touch to your brand's name. Make sure to reply to your viewers' comments and take their concerns and suggestions into consideration. Show them you care and they will become loyal followers and customers.

Branding on YouTube

If you are opening a YouTube channel especially for your business, you should consider several key points that make a difference between brand channel and personal channel. Your brand's channel is the extension of your business, and it should be treated professionally. Channel identity plays a major role in social media marketing. If you follow these few steps you will easily attract new subscribers and create a fanbase for your brand:

1. Channel name: The name of your brand's YouTube channel must reflect your business's name, and be consistent on all social media platforms.

2. Channel icon: The YouTube channel icon is similar to the Facebook profile picture, but since YouTube is part of Google, it will be used across all of your Google properties. The best option for brands is to use a company logo or a professional headshot in case you are the face of your own brand.

3. Channel art: Make sure that you chose the size and image for your channel art that scales well on all devices. You never know what device your audience is using to access your channel, mobile phone, tablet, PC, or TV.

4. Channel description. This is the perfect place for you to provide the audience with a detailed description of your brand or your company. Explain what it is that you do, and what types of videos you plan to share with your viewers. Use relevant keywords at the beginning of your channel's description to ensure search engines rank you higher.

5. Channel trailer: Keep it short and sweet (between 30 and 60 seconds). Keep it focused around your channel's idea, your business, and explain what your audience can expect to see. Don't forget to invite the viewers to subscribe to your channel.

6. Channel URL: If you have more than 100 subscribers, as a brand you might be eligible for a customized URL address. You also need to have a customized channel icon, channel art and for your account to be older than 30 days.

7. Channel links: In the About section of your channel, you should put the links to your business's website or other social media profiles. This makes it very easy for your audience to connect with you elsewhere.

Promoting on Other Social Media Platforms

YouTube is part of Google and if you do your SEO right, you will have no trouble ranking high in search engines. People will easily find your channel and videos whenever they are in need of your services or the product you have to offer. However, proper SEO will get you only so far. To maximize your audience outreach you will have to do more, you will have to promote your channel and your videos on other social media platforms. This is yet another reason why you should opt for multiple platforms and establish your presence everywhere you think your targeted audience spends their time. Facebook, Twitter, Instagram, Pinterest, Linkedin, TikTok, are all relevant platforms marketers regularly use in order to reach the people and display their brands. You should not miss out. But this is why YouTube is so special! Other platforms will allow you to embed and post your YouTube videos. This way, they will reach not only the audience that uses YouTube's platform only, but also the people who are not using it and prefer to spend their time on Facebook, or on Twitter.

But you will have to introduce your YouTube videos to your audience on other social media platforms, in the right way. Even if you have already established a presence somewhere else, there is no such thing as a bad time to introduce YouTube videos to your audience. But you should refrain from bombarding your fanbase with YouTube commercials. Instead, introduce them gently, in a teasing way. Announce something new is brewing within your company. Make the introduction of a YouTube channel something special, something to anticipate. Once your channel gets published, create a special series that your audience will want to watch, and eagerly expect the next episode. Be sure your YouTube videos are of high-quality both technically and with their content. Don't forget to create a special hashtag that will come with your videos and organize a YouTube playlist to maximize the enjoyment of your followers.

Sharing is one of the best ways of cross-platform promotion. It is quite simple, but many businesses don't put enough effort into it. But this doesn't mean you should simply share your YouTube videos on other social media platforms. Of course, you would do that. But even more important and valued promotion is if other people and other companies share your content. You can always invite them to click share, but this is something professional, brand YouTube videos should avoid doing. Instead, opt for engaging your audience by replying to their comments. Don't simply say "Thank You" and move on. Try to start the conversation. Ask them to suggest something, or if they want to see something specific. The more attention you pay to your fans, the more likely they are to feel appreciated and they will engage in your videos. It is similar to other companies. Return the favor and share their videos on your social media platforms.

Another option for promoting your YouTube content on other social media platforms is to promote your channel as a whole, not just individual videos. You can embed your channel URL in the posts you dedicate to other social media such as Twitter, or Facebook. Intrigue your audience by saying they can discover more on the topic in your YouTube channel and they will click to check what you have to offer. In the same manner, you can cross-promote older videos. If you are touching on one topic on Facebook, but you made a YouTube video on the same topic some time ago, it is a great opportunity to post a link to that video on Facebook.

Chapter 13: YouTube Advertising

Advertising on YouTube is not the same as marketing on YouTube. However, it can be a part of the overall YouTube marketing strategy. Brands advertise on YouTube because they know this platform will ensure they reach a wide audience. But advertising on YouTube is a complex subject and if you take some extra time to learn about it, it will bring you great benefits. This chapter will teach you how to optimize your time and money and how to properly invest in YouTube advertising. You will also learn different types of ad formats, what options as a marketer you have, and what are video ad campaigns and how to set them up.

What You Should Know About Advertising

Advertising is using a very persuasive message to influence the clients and customers into buying a specific product or service. The goal of advertising is not only to increase sales but also to attract new customers. Therefore, the targeted market must be specifically defined. Only then a business can approach it with an effectively designed ad campaign. The first step in the advertising campaign is to establish the targeted market. This is the same as establishing your audience. You need to know who they are, and where do they come from, in order to effectively reach them. Once you establish the targeted market, you need to check the level of competition for the product or service you are offering. There is a chance you will have to compete for the audience with other companies who are offering the same or similar product/service.

Advertising takes as many forms as there are mediums. It can take the shape of online marketing, newspaper advertising, Yellow pages, TV or radio commercials, cold calling, or banner advertising. The type of advertising you chose will much depend on your targeted market. However, online advertising is steadily taking over as more and more people have access to the internet, and use it daily. This is why marketers simply cannot ignore online advertising. But no matter the type of advertising, your ads need to convey a certain message. To do the best job, ads need to be specifically designed to persuade an individual your business is their best choice. There are five main components of all ads that make up this design:

1. The headline: is the key attention-grabbing component of an ad. A simple, but effective headline needs to stir interest in the audience and make them want to learn more.

2. Subhead: is used only if a Headline needs clarification. It has the same role as the subtitles of the book.

3. Body copy: This is the main section in which the features and benefits of the product or service you are offering are highlighted.

4. Image: This is a visual aid that follows the ad. Its role is to help the audience visualize a product or a service.

5. Call-to-action: is the very end of the ad, in which you will invite your audience to do business with you.

When it comes to online advertising, there are several ways to do it. There is paid search advertising or pay-per-click (PPC). Advertisers will display their ads above organic search results, giving the paid ads the top spot on the search page. There is also social media advertising and you can use it to sponsor or boost your posts. Social media advertising will put your ad in front of the eyes of your targeted audience, and encourage them to engage. Sponsor content is another way of advertising online. Brands can subsidize blog posts or articles and through them, they can reference or recommend a product or a service. And finally, there are banners and display ads that are using the top of web pages as promotional space. They work similar to PPC, but instead of using mainly text, they focus on visual advertisement.

Paid Advertising on YouTube

YouTube allows marketers, companies, and businesses to post ads on its platform. This is a paid service, but there are various sets of rules YouTube implemented to make sure that by opting for this service, you get the most out of it. This is why businesses and marketers pay for an ad, only if a viewer watches it for at least 30 seconds. This way advertisers don't lose money and YouTube obliges itself to promote your ads to the targeted audience. In this deal, everyone's a winner. YouTube targets the audience to which it would play your ad based on their search history, both on the platform and on Google. But it also followers the viewing behaviors of the audience which helps YouTube decide who is the right target. But that doesn't mean you can't control your ads once they are out there. YouTube will allow you full control over your budget and paying method. You can set a limit and tell YouTube to stop displaying your ad once it hits a certain number of views, or once the budget you set in advance is all used up.

There are three main types of the paid advertisement on YouTube: TrueView Ads, Preroll, and Bumpers. Here is what each one of them entitles and how they work:

1. TrueView Ads: These ads are the standard of YouTube advertising. You will pay for this type of ad only if the viewer watches it or interacts with it (clicking on call-on-action). YouTube requires that TrueView ads must be between 12 seconds and 6 minutes long if they are skippable. There are two types of TrueView Ads: Video Discovery Ads (display in search results, or as video suggestions and related videos), and In-stream Ads (play before, during, or at the end of a video someone is watching)

2. Preroll Ads: These are non-skippable In-stream ads, and they can play before, during or after the main video. Preroll ads must be between 15 and 20 seconds long. Since these are

shorter than the required 30 seconds of watch time, the unskippable ads use a different billing option known as CPM bidding (cost-per-thousand impressions).

3. Bumpers: These ads are the shortest type of YouTube ads. They last for six seconds and they always play before the chosen video. Since they are so short, advertisers need to be very creative about how to use this time and promote their business. Bumper ads also use the CPM bidding model of payment.

Launching a YouTube Ad Campaign

Once you have the video you want to use as an ad on YouTube, it's time to set up your ad campaign. Here is a step-by-step guide on how to do it. Keep in mind that the advertisement process on YouTube can be extensive and will require your time and dedication. It can also require some testing before you find the perfect strategy that will suit the needs of your business you are trying to promote.

Link YouTube channel with Google Adwords account. If you have multiple channels, repeat this process for each one of them. You will set up your advertising campaign using Google AdWords, but make sure the video is first uploaded to your YouTube channel. Once on the AdWords homepage, simply click on the "+Campaign" button. This will lead you to a new page where you will be able to choose the type of the campaign and set up its name. You should choose the "video" type from the drop-down menu. To ensure your video will be in TrueView format of the ad, select "In-stream or video discovery ads". Now you can set your budget, the amount of money spent per day.

Budget and Prices

There are various ways you can set up your budget and in order to do it properly, you need to understand some basic bidding strategies available to you. Most of the AdWords users use CPC (cost-per-click) bidding strategy. This is because people think the CPC strategy is less risky and easier to set up. But there is also an option to create CPV (cost-per-view) strategy.

1. Cost-per-click means that you will pay when users click on your ad campaign

2. Cost-per-view means you will pay for video views. This is the default setting in AdWords.

But YouTube will allow you to use only CPV bidding strategy. Although it would be nice to have options, CPV has a huge benefit. You will pay for the ad only if the viewer watched the first 30 seconds of it or the whole thing; or if he interacted with your ad. This means you are certain you are getting value for the money you are paying to YouTube. Once you set the bidding system, and you decide how much money you want to spend on the advertising, you are ready to go. But remember that you won't actually pay the price you set, at least not all the time. Here is how bidding works: if you set your price limit to be 0.20$ per view, but the next highest bid is only 15$, YouTube will charge you only 17$. The rule is one penny higher than the next highest bid.

Increasing your bid can help you get more traffic, but you need to keep in mind the money you are spending. You want to be comfortable with the price. Since the other advertisers are going to change their bid limits, the CPV system often fluctuates, and you need to keep track of it. AdWords will also allow you to set different bids for different target audiences. These are called customs bids and to set them up just click on the "Targets" tab under "All Video Campaigns", then click on "Bid". Now you should see a small icon that is labeled "Customize bids per format", click it and set bits for different targets.

Networks

AdWords will also let you decide where you want your ads to appear. You have two main options: YouTube Search or YouTube Videos. YouTube Search will display your ad on the search page, YouTube home page, channel pages, or as next to watch. YouTube videos will run your TrueView ad, and you can choose whether it will play at the beginning of the video, during it, or at the end. Most marketers opt for setting up different campaigns for YouTube Search and for YouTube Video ads. If you do it too, you will have better tracks of your ads' performance metrics.

Location, Language, and the Advanced Settings

If you want to show your ad only in a particular location, the next step of setting your campaign will allow you to just that. You have given options to include all countries or to choose for yourself. The location tab will also let you see how many people you can reach at a particular location.

For more advanced targeting, AdWords will let you specify the operating system and the type of device your targets are using. This means you can set up your ad to ruin only for people who are using their mobile phones. You can even increase or decrease your bid if the ad is played on a certain device. You can also set up the language your audience is speaking.

Under the Advanced Settings section, you can set times and dates for the beginning and the end of your ad campaign. You can create a custom schedule, and limit the daily views for users. These settings are in place to help you get the most value for the money you are paying to run the ads.

Targeting and Advanced Targeting

Adwords will let you set up your targeted audience by age, gender, parental status, and by their interests such as cooking, music, lifestyle, movies, etc. You can always run different campaigns with different target audiences and see which will perform better. Advanced targeting will give you an option to target the individuals by keywords, topics, or websites. Keyword targeting is a powerful tool, especially when you are targeting individuals who answer to visual stimuli. Be sure to do your research, test some keywords and groups of keywords to see which will give you the best results, most clicks, and conversions.

Don't Forget to Check the Results

Once you run your ads, it is crucial to follow their performance. You can do this only by looking at the metrics and analyzing them. Impressions, engagement, views, and clicks, will tell you if your ad reached your targeted audience, and if they responded to it. Following the metrics is easy. Start with the Reporting Tab which you will find within Google AdWord. You will get tables, charts, and reports that are easy to read and understand. Reporting Tab will allow you to see the following:

Impressions: This represents the number of times your ad was shown to the viewers.

Views: This is the number of times someone watched your ad for at least 30 seconds. But this also counts the number of times someone interacted with your ad.

View rate: The rate is the percentage of the people who watched your ad when it was shown to them. To get the view rate, Google Ads uses a simple formula: total views divided by total impressions.

CPV: will tell you how much money you spent every time someone engages with your ad.

Earned actions: This section counts the subscriptions, likes, and additional views you earn after someone watches your ad.

Video viewership: This metric will show you how many people watched 25%, 50%, 75%, or 100% of your ad video.

Call-to-action overlays: The overlays are interactive elements on the video and are used to provide the viewers with more information. They will drive the visits to your website, channel, or even other videos.

Remarketing lists: This will allow you to target the audience based on their previous interactions with your YouTube channel

Optimize Before You Launch a New One

After analyzing the metrics of your ads, you might come to a conclusion that your ads are not driving enough traffic to your website, or that there is simply not enough engagement of the viewers, you are not getting enough views. It is a perfect time to adjust some of the parameters and optimize your video campaign to perform better. Here are some tips on what you can do to give your ads a little bit of extra kick and drive the viewers to respond to them. By optimizing your ad campaigns, you will be able to reach new audiences, generate new clicks and conversions, and boost your search results.

Evaluate CPV

If you did everything you could to deliver a creative ad, able to capture the viewer's attention in the first five seconds, and if you did everything you could to find your targeted audience, but you are still seeing low views, it could be that you are being outbid, and it's time to adjust your CPV. If you find out you have to raise your CPV in order to reach a broader audience, it might mean two things: either your video is playing for several weeks and it reached creative exhaustion, or the competition is outbidding you. In both cases, raising your CPV bid would ensure that your video is played more often, to even more viewers and it could generate new conversions easily. However, if you find out that you can lower your CPV, it might mean that the competition is not strong at the given moment, and it is the right time to grasp the chance to gain more viewers and conversions.

Evaluate View Rate

View rate is the primary metric you should follow. It will tell you if your video ad is reaching enough people, and if they are interacting with it. In general, a video with a higher view rate will win more auctions, and it will pay lower bidding rates than a video that has low view rates. This is why you have to pay special attention to the targeting. It will ensure your video ad has more views than your competition, and that you would pay your ads at lower rates. You can do this by improving the creativity behind your ads. Shorter videos tend to have more views, minor tweaks such as adding captions, or improving the introduction can take you a long way. You might find out that you just adjusted your ad to reach a completely new audience of which you weren't even aware.

Evaluate CTR

This is an important measure if your goal is to use YouTube advertising to drive more traffic to your website. To achieve this, you should look into narrowing your targeted audience. Understanding what your viewers want and what they need is the first step in successfully picking the right demographic. If needed, adjust your audience's age, gender, parental status, interests, and affinities. But don't forget to evaluate the topics and keywords of your ads, as they play an important role in giving your audience just what they were searching for. If you want to exclude certain viewers, you can add topics and certain demographics to the exclusion list and your ad won't be played to them. This should be done only if the metrics show you that your ad has no response with a certain type of audience. By excluding them, you will ensure your video ads are played only to the people who find them relevant.

Section 5: Aiming and Achieving Your Long-Term Goals

Chapter 14: Becoming an Influencer

Influencer, someone who wields influence, is an aspiration of many modern young people. But the term itself bears dual value. It is used for people who are business owners, and experts in their field, and celebrities, but it can also be used as an insult to render meaningless someone's social impact. While some elected officials are considered influencers, so are some well-dressed pets. The influencer culture so popular today is tightly close to consumerism and the rise of technology. An influencer is anyone who has the power to affect the buying habits of people. They would resort to uploading original content, often sponsored, that drives their followers to desire and to buy certain products or services. Influencers use various social media platforms and upload photos, videos, blog posts, reviews, or stories in order to change people's online behavior and influence their spending habits. Influencers have to be creative and authentic, and they have to wield a certain dose of authority in order to be able to affect their followers.

What it Means to Become an Influencer

Influencers are people who already established themselves as creators on YouTube, they grew a base of followers and are now able to monetize their videos by influencing their followers' buying behavior. Influencers get paid by the sponsors, for their promotion of a certain product or service. But because of what they do, influencers are often seen as something negative and often unwanted. Nevertheless, they manage to drive the market for their sponsors, for various brands and companies. Marketers need influencers and they need their approach to the audience. But How are influencers different from YouTube content creators? They also create their original videos and upload them for everyone to see, just like creators do. The difference is in self-expression. While influencers are used by marketers and companies to promote the business, creators are doing it for self-expression.

But whether the term "influencer" will have a negative or positive connotation largely depends on the age of the audience or YouTubers. Old people tend to sneer at the term, but young generations see it as a career title to which they should aspire. While millennials tend to call themselves "creators" even if they indulge in the job of influencers, zoomers intentionally call themselves influencers. They enjoy the title because it proves they are able to turn their social connections into an income. Younger generations are also aware that if they wear the title of an influencer as a badge of honor, they would attract brands willing to sponsor them. Brands themselves quickly adopted the term and even the marketing agencies started allocating money for "influencer marketing". But the truth is also those creators tend to work on YouTube only, while today's influencers have to be present on multiple social network platforms. Building their presence solely on YouTube means limiting themselves to one type of audience. Instagram and

Facebook are becoming very popular options, especially since they also introduced the option of monetization through sponsorship deals.

YouTube Influencers in Every Field

Because YouTube is used by millions of people every hour, brands search for YouTube influencers with lots of subscribers, through which they would push their product. But not every channel with lots of subscribers is eligible to become influencers. The type of content one produces plays a key role. Here is a list of some of the biggest names out there who are recognized as the influencers to go to, in their respective niches.

1. Fashion, Lifestyle, and Beauty: This is a very broad category but this is because the lines between them are not very well defined. Make-up artists will often suggest interesting fashion combinations to wear and the fashion influencers often talk about their lifestyle and diet. Names worth mentioning in this category are Zoe Sugg and her fashion channel Zoella. She reaches 11.5 million subscribers all over the world and she offers beauty hacks, shopping sprees, make-up tutorials, etc. But the biggest name out there is Kids Diana Show, a lifestyle channel based in Ukraine that reaches astonishing 75.7 million subscribers. This channel is owned by a young girl Diana. She posts lifestyle-related videos targeting families and parents of young children.

2. Sports and Fitness: This is one of the most popular categories on YouTube and its popularity is still growing, mainly due to COVID19, lockdown, and people searching for new ways to stay fit during the hard times when they have to stay put. But the most popular channel in this category is actually integrating sports with comedy. Dude Perfect gathers 55.6 million subscribers.

3. Gaming: Another very big category is gaming. Since gaming became a mainstream culture, this category is not a small niche anymore. Its biggest star is definitely PewDiePie, with over 109 million subscribers. He is a Swedish YouTube star and aside from rocking the world of gaming, he is also the most subscribed individual creator on YouTube. The size of his subscribers and his charming personality make him one of the most wanted influencers.

4. Tech: Shoppers looking for tech products are the audience most likely to search for videos in order to decide on their choices. They also love to use YouTube to educate themselves about what is new out there! The name that stands out in this category is certainly Marques Brownlee, and his channel is named after his initials MKBHD (HD stands for High Definition). He has 13.7 million subscribers and offers amazing tech review videos that are highly engaging.

5. Entertainment: Watchtime for entertainment videos is incredibly high. Since younger generations use YouTube instead of TV, it is no wonder they prefer to search for quick entertainment on this platform. One of the biggest influencers out there in this category is Toronto-based Lilly Singh with over 14.9 million subscribers. She is diverse and creates comedy sketches as well as music videos, and much more.

6. Travel: The videos in this category are popular because they discover new worlds for their viewers. They are inspirational, informative, educational and they make us dream of unseen places. Among the biggest names out there is Jack Harries who gathers 3.78 million subscribers on his channel. But if you like to combine food enjoyment with travel, check out Mark Wiens with 7.41 million subscribers, or the Best Ever Food Review Show channel that has 6.6 million subscribers.

Your Checklist to Becoming an Influencer

Becoming a YouTube influencer is not an easy task. The area is highly competitive and challenging. Young people all over the world want to become influencers because it is a valid career option out there, it's relatively new and exciting, and it is highly engaging. But becoming an influencer is much more than just posting high-quality YouTube content and hoping that a brand would notice you and want to work with you. First, you must gather your followers base and that alone is a difficult task. But it is from your viewership base that you can monetize your YouTube channel. Although it is a hard task, it's not impossible. There are millions of examples of rising YouTube stars out there, and you can be one of them. All you have to do is dedicate to it, and invest time in your career as an influencer. Here is a short checklist you can follow to make sure your new career takes off in the right direction.

1. Think about your goals, and what you want to achieve. This is a step you can start doing even before you launch your YouTube channel. By asking yourself what you are hoping to get out of becoming an influencer, you will decide what types of content you need to create, and you will be able to define the targeted audience for your channel.

2. Develop your channel's goals and content. Although as an influencer you will work with brands and sponsors, you need to become a brand yourself. Once you establish what image of yourself you want to present, you will come up with the content that will support and follow that branded image.

3. Be consistent. Post frequently, at least once a week, and stick to your schedule. You are a brand, and your audience will want to know ahead when to expect new content from you. By being consistent and frequent you will increase your chances to attract new viewers.

4. Be original. this is a hard one, there are so many YouTube channels, and you have the impression all the topics are covered. However, originality is not only in the content itself

but also in the way you present that content. Come up with something new, original, and fresh that will capture your audience and make them want to stay on your channel.

5. Build a wide social presence for your channel. Create social media pages on different platforms and gather followers there. Cross-post your content and direct your audience from one platform to another.

6. Invest in your own website. Custom web design needs to reflect your brand and what you are representing. The website will be used to drive traffic to your YouTube channel, and you can even include a little store within it and sell your own merchandise.

7. Invest in the right tools. Invest in high-quality recording gear, and in a computer that will help you create high-quality content.

becoming an influencer doesn't happen overnight. Patience, hard work, and genuine interest in what you are doing will bring you a long way. keep an open mind and accept suggestions from potential sponsors, even if you never did them before. You might surprise yourself and discover many new things you are good at.

The Things You Can Do as an Influencer

Influencers are very powerful people. They are able to change the behavior of their followers, even more than Hollywood celebrities. The younger generations admire and follow more influencers than regular celebrities. Some of the influencers also have much more subscribers than celebrities. But why is that? The answer is pretty simple. New generations are more easily awed by someone who is relatable, who is just like them. The influencer is a guy next door. He is not an unapproachable musician or a movie star. He is the same as us, same as the most of the population, and he is a friend. However, there is a line that an influencer can cross, become a YouTube star, and stop being an influencer. Too many subscribers, too much fame, and an influencer will become unapproachable, he will lose his power to convince people into changing their behavior. When this happens, he stops being an influencer. As long as people can identify with you, and you present yourself as a dude from the neighborhood, you hold the power.

Brands are aware of this phenomenon that more popular influencers are less able to turn their viewers into customers. This is why recently, companies and businesses started turning to those influencers that have a smaller following base, but more loyal and more tightly targeted. These influencers are known as micro-influencers. They create a smaller base of subscribers, of carefully chosen demographic that will, for sure, easily turn into customers. Brands want to reach out to these smaller audiences rather than trying to mold a brand face out of one macro influencer (the one with a large base of followers). Speaking to the niche audience on more specialized subjects ultimately brings better results. But this is also how influencers are becoming more like brand's PR agents, and not their advertising weapon, a face behind the logo.

Companies and brands are missing a lot if they are not investing in YouTube influencers. The influencers are capable of not only bringing sales but also raising the awareness of the brand. Through their work, the influencers will drive conversions, generate leads, and a high ROI because their audience trusts them. This is why influencers may be an even better option than paid ads. However, the combination of the two gives the best results. Influencers are here to stay, and their popularity is not waning at all. The newer generations are identifying so much with them, that their dream job is not to be an astronaut, or a ballerina anymore. They want to become YouTubers, Influencers, and YouTube stars.

But before starting a collaboration with an influencer, do your research on them, and see if they are a good fit for your brand. You as a company won't have much influence over the content of influencer's videos. You can't control what they will say, how they will behave or what they will decide to show. Take for example Disney who had to break off their collaboration with PewDiePie, due to accusations that he is an antisemite. You don't want an influencer to ruin your brand's good image with his or her's unacceptable behavior.

Chapter 15: Making Money on YouTube

Content creators are not paid by YouTube for the videos they produce. The videos are not monetized by default. To make money from YouTube you have to go to settings and turn the monetization on. Still, this doesn't mean YouTube will simply pay for your content. Instead, it will offer you two different options: become a YouTube Partner, or have your video played on YouTube Premium. People think that only content creators with millions of subscribers can earn money on YouTube, but this is not true. The earning potential of your channel is determined by the engagement of your audience, not by the number of views or subscribers. Unfortunately, engagement isn't the only thing that will secure your earnings. You also have to carefully choose the niche you will cater to and explore the channel's revenues. Subscriber count does matter, but not in the scope it is believed.

There are YouTubers out there who earn millions from what they do. However, if you look closer, all that money is not earned solely through their content creation. They all have their own merchandise they sell outside of YouTube. They use their channel to drive traffic to the stores where they sell their merch. They all started small, by defining their targeted audience clearly, and delivering high-quality content. As their subscriber base grew, they started expanding their business from YouTube and creating a brand from themselves.

Earning a Living Through YouTube

Let's put aside the merchandise business of many YouTubers and concentrate first on how much money is possible to earn from YouTube alone. The amount of money YouTube will pay per view depends on many factors. Some of them are: the number of views, clicks, the quality of ads played during the video, the video's length, etc. The sum can be anywhere between 0.01$ to 0.03$ per ad view. On average, a YouTuber earns 0.18$ per ad view. That means that per 1,000 views, a YouTuber can earn on average around 18$. However, getting to the point where you can monetize your videos is hard work, and the people who get into the business usually do it out of their own passion to be in front of the camera, and to communicate with the audience. YouTube doesn't pay for the number of subscribers. But subscribers are still a valuable source of revenue because they generate ad views. They are also the ones who engage with your videos, they comment, share, and like, making your video visible to others. The more views your video gets, the more likely you would get paid.

A video can get you around 5$ per 1,000 views. But this is not an amount set in stone. The number will depend on the accumulated views as well as how many ads are integrated in your video. But this also means that 1,000,000 views will bring you around 5,000$. If you are a moderate influencer, this is already a significant amount of money you can earn. Keep in mind these numbers are estimates, and how much money you will actually earn depends on many factors. However, earning money from YouTube is a fast-developing economy and more and more companies are willing to spend their money on YouTube marketing. This also raises the chances of a good earning for content creators.

The ad placements are not the only way you can earn money through YouTube. Here are some other options out there for a YouTuber to earn his salary:

1. Affiliate links: Essentially, when a YouTuber is reviewing or mentioning a product of his "favorite brand" we're talking about affiliate links. When a viewer clicks on the link to the product (usually found in the description of the video) and makes a purchase, the YouTuber will earn a commission.

2. Merchandise: We already mentioned that YouTube stars usually sell their own merchandise through their own shops, hosted outside of YouTube. The most common things YouTubers who made a brand out of their channel sell are accessories such as shirts, bags, hats, etc. But some also make toys or fashion products of their own.

3. Sponsorship: If your channel has a large number of subscribers, brands will approach you for a partnership. They will want to sponsor you in turn for product reviews that will increase their sales.

There are millions and millions of content creators on YouTube, and most of them don't earn anything. But the majority of people who manage to monetize their YouTube channels, earn a decent living. It is not much, but it can do well as a side hustle or even an average monthly salary. And in the end, there is a small and elite club of YouTubers who is able to make an extraordinary income, counted in millions of dollars per year. They are YouTube stars, and there are just over 2,000 of them. Many of these stars are already established musicians such as Rihanna, but many more are just ordinary people who managed to succeed. The hardest part of earning a living from YouTube is the very start, earning your first dollar. But if you offer quality content and grow your audience, it will become easier. Once you establish your name and brand, things will just start to develop on their own as the brands will seek to sponsor you and to work with you.

The YouTube Partner Program (YPP)

The YouTube Partner Program is one of the easiest ways to start earning money through YouTube. This program will allow the creators to monetize their content by allowing the ads to play during their videos. If you join YPP you will become a part of the revenue-sharing model which helps both creators and YouTube to stay in the business. This means that when you allow ads to be added to your videos, and your viewers watch them, you will share the revenue with YouTube taking 45% and giving you 55%. But to become a partner, your channel needs to become eligible. The minimum requirements to apply for the YPP are:

1. Have a minimum of 1,000 subscribers on your channel
2. Have at least 4,000 hours of watch time in the past 12 months
3. YPP is supported in the country where you reside

Once you reach these milestones, you will become eligible to apply for the YPP. And here is how you can do that. In the YouTube Studio click on "Monetization", and you will be brought to the YPP application page. There are three steps you need to fulfill in order to become YouTube Partner:

1. Read and agree to the YPP terms of service
2. Set up a Google AdSense account and connect it to your channel
3. Wait for YouTube to review your channel and approve your application.

YouTube's policy promises you that the decision regarding your application will be made in 30 days. However, most of the channels that joined YPP testify that it took YouTube only around 72 hours to respond. YouTube reviews applications even during the weekends. A significant number of applications get declined, but don't let that discourage you. If you are not accepted to the YPP on your first try, improve your channel to fit YouTube's policies and try again. YouTube will allow you to reapply in 30 days.

YPP will allow you access not only to revenues from ads but also some extra monetization features such as:

1. Super Chats & Stickers: These are monetary donations of viewers during live streams. To become eligible for the feature you must be at least 18 and live in a country where the feature is available.
2. Channel Membership: This is a paid membership to a channel where creators offer exclusive content to their viewers. To become eligible for this feature you must be at least 18 and have more than 30,000 subscribers.
3. Merch shelf: This is additional space below your videos where you can display the merch you are selling. Again you must be at least 18 and have more than 10,000 subscribers.
4. YouTube Premium revenue: When someone who paid their monthly subscription to YouTube watches your video, you will get a percentage of that subscription.

Getting into YPP is only the first step in making money through YouTube, and it is worth it. If you create quality content that your viewers will like, you might even reach the status of a YouTube star!

Becoming an Affiliate

promoting a product in your YouTube videos and being paid for it is what affiliate marketing is. However, you can't just start doing it on your own. Putting links to the products you are reviewing in the video's description is not enough. First, you have to enter the affiliate marketing program with some of the businesses that offer it. There are many companies that want to do business with YouTubers, from Amazon to Microsoft, Loreal, or Maybelline. Once you sign up for their affiliate program, they will give you a unique URL that leads to their product, and that you can include in your video's description. This link will help the merchants keep track of the sales that came from your YouTube video. Each time a viewer clicks on a link in your video description, you will get paid. The brand you are working with might offer you a set price, or the percentage of the sale (the latter is more common). If you want to avoid applying to each brand, you can opt to work with affiliate marketing networks which will set you up with merchants willing to pay commissions. Clickfunnel and Affiliate are just some of these networks.

Affiliate marketing is a form of influencer marketing and it will require you to have a solid audience that enjoys your content and trusts you. keep in mind that items you are mentioning or reviewing to generate sales need to be in accordance with your youtube channel. If you are unboxing tech, and you gather an audience that is interested in tech, you don't want to sell them equipment for pets. You also want to affiliate only the products you actually trust. Don't ruin your image by reviewing and recommending a product that has low or no value to your audience.

If you wonder how and where you should include affiliate links, here is a quick guide that can help you:

1. The description of the video is the best place for the links, and you should always include them here. But sometimes, this is not enough as viewers might ignore the description. Make sure you encourage them to check the link out during your video. It can be as easy as saying "check out the link in the video description".

2. YouTube cards are in-video interactive boxes that let viewers click on them to find out more. These can be good places to put links as they are non-intrusive and subtle. They should be used only as an addition to the link in the video description.

Getting Sponsors

You don't have to have millions of followers in order to attract sponsors to your channel. Micro-influencers are prospering these days as the big brands came to realize that audiences are trusting them more than big YouTube stars. This is a good thing because it means you don't need to wait until your channel grows to extraordinary proportions in order to get sponsored. However, you do need to be patient. Nobody will sponsor a channel that is just starting. Sponsors make deals directly with content creators, without having the YouTube platform as a mediator. This means that YouTube will not push any requirements on your channel in order to get sponsorship. However, brands will have their own requirements because they cannot be associated with just anyone, same as you cannot. After all, your channel is your brand too. The trick is to find a good fit that will work both for your channel and for the sponsor.

There are three main things you should already be doing if you are a content creator looking into getting a sponsor.

1. Create quality content that is interesting, and that engages the viewers. Brands are always searching for high-quality content rather than the number of subscribers. You should also produce the content relevant to the brand that you are planning to work with.

2. Build your channel, and the brands will start searching for you. this doesn't necessarily mean you have to have lots of subscribers. A quality targeted audience is much better for brands than a large pool of viewers of different demographics. Build a community and engage your audience. Make them trust you and feel comfortable on your channel.

3. Follow the rules. Both YouTube and various brands will not be interested in working with creators whose content is filled or associated with violence, abuse, sex; in general inappropriate content. If you break YouTube's rules and regulations your sponsors would abandon you, and you are at risk at getting banned from YouTube itself.

There are two types of sponsorship: paid sponsorship and product sponsorship. It is easy to conclude that paid sponsorship is when a brand directly pays a flat fee to the content creator for advertising. Product sponsorship is where the content creator is provided with a free product in exchange for its promotion. Many influencers start with product sponsorship and are satisfied to receive the item or service they are promoting. However, paid sponsorship is more lucrative, and worthwhile.

Don't rely on a sponsor to approach you. There are things you could do to ensure sponsorship even if you are a small channel with the possibility to grow. Some sponsors are even happy to help their influencers grow their followers base, and make them into the face of their brand.

Leave your email. be sure to put your contact information in the About section of your YouTube channel. This way, sponsors who are in search of new influencers will easily be able to find you. it might be a smart idea to create a separate, business email to which sponsors can reach you. This way, the sponsorship opportunities won't get buried among the spam mail.

Reach out. If you already have some specific brands in mind, and you are sure that you can produce content relevant to them, be the first to contact them. Go to their website and you will find the contact information of their marketing department. make your email unique, make it stand out from the crowd as some famous brands get many such offers from various influencers.

Use influencer marketing platforms. There are brands that are actively searching for influencers, and it could be a good idea to use platforms such as famebit.com or inzpire.me, to make yourself available. You would need to have at least 1,000 subscribers to sign up and connect your

YouTube channel with your profile. These platforms will charge you, but only a percentage once you make a collaboration with a brand.

Selling Merchandise of Your Brand

Selling your own merchandise is the next step you should take, once you build your YouTube channel, and gain loyal subscribers. Your viewers love your content, they love what you do and they love you. They will want to support you, and they will want to own merch that is branded with your YouTube channel's name. This is very popular among the younger generations, just as people support their favorite bands by buying their t-shirts. Again, to successfully sell merch, you don't have to have millions of followers. As long as your subscribers are engaged, and love what you do, they will want to buy your products. You might get surprised by the fact that a YouTuber with 11,000 subscribers sells up to 6 pieces of merch every month. This means he is able to earn up to 70$/month. Top YouTubers earn between 6 and 8 million dollars per year, just from selling their own merch. If you are a small channel, you won't get rich from selling the merch, but it is a lucrative side hustle. As your channel grows, so will the sales. Soon enough, you will be earning an exciting amount of money. you wouldn't want to miss that. And it is very simple for a YouTuber to start selling his merchandise. Here is how you do it!

Choose the design and type of your merch. Come up with an interesting logo, popular slogans, and visuals that your subscribers will love. You should also decide the overall presentation of these visuals. Should they be large and central, or smaller, repeating patterns or substantial empty space? At this point, you should also think about the products you want to sell. What are they, and how do they appeal to your audience. In fact, before launching your merchandise line engage your audience and ask them what they would like to see in your upcoming store. Depending on the demographics, your audience might have different needs and styles. Consider their gender, age, and interests.

Find where to sell your mech. There are print-on-demand businesses out there ready to produce the merch for you. However, you have to be careful and choose well. many of them use low-quality, unsafe and unethical products. Some of them offer limited designs too and you won't have enough room to create unique visuals for your merch. It is important to do the research and only then decide where you will produce and sell your merchandise.

Select your products. At this stage, you should already have a pretty good idea of what you want to sell. Phone cases, pillows, cups, and T-shirts, are always a safe bet. But you want to be unique and distinguish yourself from every other YouTuber who is selling his own merch. Most successful YouTubers try to sell merch that is relevant to their content. Think about selling a yoga mat if you are a fitness instructor, or if you are in a beauty niche, mirrors are a good option.

Finalize the design. Now that you know how your mercy is going to look like, you can decide where to put your logo, how the slogans will fit in the best, and think about the colors you want your merch to be. Think about taglines, sizes, different designs, patterns, etc. There are various online tools that can help you design your merch, and sometimes the producers will offer these tools on their websites too.

Promote your merch. YouTube will offer you a merch shelf and you can opt to display your merch directly on your YouTube channel, under your videos. But there is more you can do to drive traffic to your store. Add links to your merch in the video description section, or in the comments. Make a custom link for your channel's art or in YouTube cards. You can also share your store on other social media platforms such as Instagram and Facebook.

Getting Funds

Most YouTubers don't seek monetization of their channel because they want to get rich. Instead, they use it as means to earn a living. And while the majority is satisfied with collecting revenues through ads or through sponsorship, affiliations, and influencing, some resort to crowdfunding and donations. Crowdfunding is amazing because instead of bombarding your audience with ads, and throwing products at them, you will give them exactly what they want; the high-quality content created specifically for them. Mostly creative people and artists prefer crowdfunding, which is basically collecting smaller amounts of money from a variety of donors, instead of having one big patron.

There are many ways to crowdfund your YouTube channel:

1. Patreon: a website designed to serve the artists and creatives. Patreon is created in order to help artists on a monthly basis. This crowdfunding platform also offers you to reward your audience for their support with early access, or behind-the-scenes access, exclusive content, merch, live events, etc.

2. YouTube's own Sponsorship button. Recently, YouTube launched this service allowing people to make donations to their favorite content creators. In exchange, creators will reward their viewers with exclusive content.

3. Kickstarter: is a very popular crowdfunding site, but it is not limited to artists. Although some famous movie creators used this platform to fund themselves, the sight is more popular among the people who want to start their own production line or business. Kickstarter is also oriented towards short-term projects, rather than supporting creators over a longer period of time.

4. Indiegogo: is amazing for small-scale production. Whether you are into music, movies, or games, there is a place for everyone who is into indie culture (it's even in the name of

the website). People are attracted to fund the projects on Indiegogo because they believe in their success.

Licensing Your Content

Once a content creator uploads his video on YouTube, he can choose Licence options; Standard YouTube Licence, or Creative Commons. Here is what you need to know about the two, and the difference between them. Standard YouTube Licence, by which you grant the broadcasting rights to YouTube. This means that viewers can access your content only through YouTube and that they have no rights to reproduce or distribute your content. But they can share, because clicking the share button, or copying URLs to other social network platforms will lead new viewers directly to YouTube. Creative Commons means that other people can use parts of your content and use it to create their own production. Creative Commons allows other content creators to edit, change or alter your original video, but they cannot own the copyright to it and they have to clearly mention the original holder of the copyright. If you choose Standard YouTube Licence, other content creators who want to use your work must ask you for permission. You can accept or deny them the permission as you please. Even big media companies will have to ask for permission.

Conclusion

This book is meant for anyone who wants to start using YouTube for more than just browsing through videos. Whether you already own a YouTube channel, you are an established influencer, or just at the beginning of your journey, now you have the knowledge necessary to further to get started and grow. Making a video and uploading it on YouTube is easy. But that is not even half the work you should be doing in order to succeed. Even if you're an experienced videographer, you might hit some bumps along the road, and turn to this book for a solution or inspiration. Everybody needs help from time to time, and this book is designed in such a way that whether you read it from cover to cover, or intentionally target separate chapters, it will help you. Feel free to return to it whenever you feel insecure, when you need to refresh your knowledge, or if you need new ideas.

From how YouTube started, to making money on YouTube, the book tries to cover all the important topics out there. So many focus on nothing but the videography and marketing aspects when a YouTube channel is so much more than that. You learned why it is important to choose a niche, and how to build a channel that can satisfy the needs of your niche's audience. You also learned what equipment you might want to invest in in order to deliver high-quality content, how to manage and grow your channel and how to record, edit, and optimize your videos. Now that you know how SMM works, you can bring your company to the next level by producing some amazing YouTube commercials and ads. And finally, you learned how to monetize your videos, how to get paid for what you are doing, either through the YouTube Partnership program or on your own, through sponsorships and/or Kickstarter projects.

This book is a solution to all the YouTube troubles you might encounter in your new adventure of becoming a content creator. It's purpose is to serve you as a comprehensive instruction manual that touches on every topic related to YouTube instead of cherry picking the most obvious ones.

As promised, this book touches on the topics that cater to all possible YouTube users. Whether you want to use the platform for marketing, or you want to become the next PewDiePie, you now have the knowledge how to do it.

Finally, take another look at all the inspirational stories of successful Youtubers, examples of extraordinary channels, and all the lists of ideas on how to promote yourself, how to collaborate, and reach out to future sponsors. If anything, the goal of this book is to push you forward, and make you stop wondering "what if". Of course, there will be lots of "what if's" along the way, but now you have the knowledge of how to deal with them! So, take the next step and "just do it!". After all, if you enjoy it, if you are passionate about sharing your experiences with the audience, there is nothing that stands in your way, so go on! We want to hear your name called out as the next big YouTube star!

References

10 Things to Know About Copyright and YouTube. (2016, March 26). Dummies. https://www.dummies.com/business/marketing/social-media-marketing/10-things-to-know-about-copyright-and-youtube/

Advertising Definition - Entrepreneur Small Business Encyclopedia. (n.d.). Entrepreneur. https://www.entrepreneur.com/encyclopedia/advertising

Anderson, M. (2020, December 24). *The 13 most popular types of videos on YouTube [Infographic].* IMPACT. https://www.impactplus.com/blog/most-popular-types-of-videos-on-youtube-infographic

Ang, C. (2020a, September 15). *Who's the Most Popular YouTuber in Every Country?* Visual Capitalist. https://www.visualcapitalist.com/worlds-most-popular-youtubers/

Ang, C. (2020b, September 15). *Who's the Most Popular YouTuber in Every Country?* Visual Capitalist. https://www.visualcapitalist.com/worlds-most-popular-youtubers/

Asmelash, L. C. (2020, April 23). *The first ever YouTube video was uploaded 15 years ago.* CNN. https://edition.cnn.com/2020/04/23/tech/youtube-first-video-jawed-karim-trnd/index.html

Attention Required! | Cloudflare. (n.d.). Canva. https://www.canva.com/create/youtube-thumbnails/

Baruah, B. P. (2015, September 22). *Why We Love YouTube (And You Should, Too!).* TO THE NEW BLOG. https://www.tothenew.com/blog/why-we-love-youtube/

Benator, M. (2015, May 5). *Can You Still Become 'YouTube Famous'?* Vox. https://www.vox.com/2015/5/5/11562306/can-you-still-become-youtube-famous

Bond, C. (2021, January 23). *The Complete Guide to Getting Started With YouTube Live.* WordStream. https://www.wordstream.com/blog/ws/2020/04/27/youtube-live

Brand your channel. (n.d.). YouTube. https://creatoracademy.youtube.com/page/lesson/brand-identity

Brown, L. (2021a, March 1). *How to Optimize YouTube Tags/Title/Description for More Views.* Filmora. https://filmora.wondershare.com/youtube-video-editing/edit-youtube-video-title-description-tags.html

Brown, L. (2021b, March 1). *Standard YouTube License vs. Creative Commons.* Filmora. https://filmora.wondershare.com/youtube-video-editing/standard-youtube-license-vs-cc.html

Bullock, L., & Bullock, L. (2019, September 3). *How to Create High-Quality Video Content on a Budget*. Social Media Today. https://www.socialmediatoday.com/news/how-to-create-high-quality-video-content-on-a-budget/562098/

Collaboration. (n.d.). YouTube. https://creatoracademy.youtube.com/page/lesson/collaboration

Cox, S. (2018, February 22). *Essential YouTube Equipment For Starting Your Channel - What Do You Really Need?* Filmora. https://filmora.wondershare.com/youtube/essential-youtube-equipment.html

Create an account on YouTube - Computer - YouTube Help. (n.d.). Google. https://support.google.com/youtube/answer/161805

Davis, P. (2019, September 26). *How To Stand Out And Build A Remarkable Brand On YouTube » Endeavor Creative | Brand Strategy for*. Endeavor Creative | Brand Strategy for Service-Based Entrepreneurs. https://endeavorcreative.com/youtube-branding/

Determine Goals for Your YouTube Channel. (2016, March 26). Dummies. https://www.dummies.com/business/marketing/social-media-marketing/determine-goals-for-your-youtube-channel/

Dhawan, E. (2016, March 23). *How You Can Use YouTube to Turn Your Passion into a Career*. Forbes. https://www.forbes.com/sites/ericadhawan/2014/12/17/how-you-can-use-youtube-to-turn-your-passion-into-a-career/#664b600f297c

Egan, K. (2020, December 24). *The difference between Facebook, Twitter, Linkedin, YouTube, & Pinterest [Updated for 2020]*. Impact Plus. https://www.impactplus.com/blog/the-difference-between-facebook-twitter-linkedin-google-youtube-pinterest

Engage Your Audience - Creator Academy. (n.d.). Creator Academy. https://creatoracademy.youtube.com/page/course/fans

Everything Marketing Entails. (n.d.). Investopedia. https://www.investopedia.com/terms/m/marketing.asp

Find your niche. (n.d.). YouTube. https://creatoracademy.youtube.com/page/lesson/niche

Free - Add Music to Your Videos | Adobe Spark Video. (n.d.). Adobe Spark. https://spark.adobe.com/make/add-music-to-video/

From PewDiePie to Shane Dawson, these are the 23 most popular YouTube stars in the world. (2019, June 18). Business Insider Nederland. https://www.businessinsider.nl/most-popular-youtubers-with-most-subscribers-2018-2-2/

Gardner, K. (2020, September 3). *Quality is in the eye of the beholder: new research on what viewers love*. Think with Google. https://www.thinkwithgoogle.com/marketing-strategies/video/video-production-quality/

Hardwick, J. (2020, March 25). *What are YouTube Tags and Which Ones Should You Add?* SEO Blog by Ahrefs. https://ahrefs.com/blog/youtube-tags/

Haughey, C. J. (2021, March 16). *17 Types of Video Content That People Actually Want to Watch*. Single Grain. https://www.singlegrain.com/video-marketing/10-useful-types-of-video-content-viewers-love/

Hook them with your channel trailer. (n.d.). Creator Academy. https://creatoracademy.youtube.com/page/lesson/trailers

Hosch, W. L. (n.d.). *YouTube | History, Founders, & Facts*. Encyclopedia Britannica. https://www.britannica.com/topic/YouTube

How to become a successful influencer, according to YouTube and Instagram stars. (2019, September 5). Business Insider Nederland. https://www.businessinsider.nl/how-to-become-an-influencer-on-youtube-instagram?international=true&r=US

How to earn money on YouTube - AdSense Help. (n.d.). Google. https://support.google.com/adsense/answer/72857?hl=en

Justin Brown - Primal Video. (2018, August 1). *YouTube for Business! How to GROW Your Business with YouTube*. YouTube. https://www.youtube.com/watch?v=TQRTrJDn82w

Lang, M. (2020, December 24). *15 best video editing software and apps for any budget in 2020*. Impact Plus. https://www.impactplus.com/blog/video-editing-software

Lorenz, T. (2019, May 31). *The Real Difference Between Creators and Influencers*. The Atlantic. https://www.theatlantic.com/technology/archive/2019/05/how-creators-became-influencers/590725/

Lynch, M. (2020, September 26). *Smart Classroom Furniture for the 21st Century Students*. The Tech Edvocate. https://www.thetechedvocate.org/youtube-valuable-educational-tool-not-just-cat-videos/

Martineau, P. (2019, December 4). *What's an Influencer? The Complete WIRED Guide*. Wired. https://www.wired.com/story/what-is-an-influencer/

Nazerali, S. (2020, September 3). *How YouTube influencers are rewriting the marketing rulebook*. Think with Google. https://www.thinkwithgoogle.com/marketing-strategies/video/youtube-influencer-marketing-rulebook/

Neil, S. (2017, November 29). *10 Oldest YouTubers in The World*. Oldest.Org. https://www.oldest.org/entertainment/youtubers/

Niazi, Z. (2020, May 18). *YouTube Ranking Factors – How to Rank Videos with YouTube SEO?* TimeZ Marketing. https://timezmarketing.com/youtube-ranking-factors

Oh, S. (2020, May 28). *YouTube SEO: How to Rank Your Videos From Start to Finish.* SEO Blog by Ahrefs. https://ahrefs.com/blog/youtube-seo/

P. (2018, July 31). *The Challenges of Building a Successful YouTube Channel.* Pingler Blog. https://pingler.com/blog/the-challenges-of-building-a-successful-youtube-channel/

Patel, N. (2020a, January 23). *How to Optimize a YouTube Ad Campaign.* Neil Patel. https://neilpatel.com/blog/how-to-optimize-a-youtube-ad-campaign/

Patel, N. (2020b, September 3). *9 Ways to Improve Organic Reach and Beat the YouTube Algorithm.* Neil Patel. https://neilpatel.com/blog/youtube-algorithm-organic-reach/

Patel, N. (2020c, November 11). *How to Double Your YouTube Subscribers (Without Buying Them).* Neil Patel. https://neilpatel.com/blog/the-real-secret-to-growing-your-youtube-subscribers/

Patel, N. (2021, February 12). *YouTube Marketing Guide.* Neil Patel. https://neilpatel.com/blog/youtube-marketing-guide/

Patton, D. (2020, April 28). *Avoid These 7 Common Video Editing Mistakes.* Welcome to the TechSmith Blog. https://www.techsmith.com/blog/common-video-editing-mistakes/

Price, A. (2018, January 15). *5 Tips for Creating Quality Video Content Even If You're Clueless How to Begin.* Entrepreneur. https://www.entrepreneur.com/article/306143

Reid, M. B. R. (2020, January 27). *How Video Editing Works.* HowStuffWorks. https://computer.howstuffworks.com/video-editing.htm

Renderforest LLC. (n.d.). *225 YouTube Video Ideas You Can Try Right Now.* https://www.renderforest.com/blog/first-youtube-video-ideas

S. (2019, December 9). *How to sell Merch on Youtube? 3 best strategies.* Sell Merch. https://sellmerch.org/welcome-back-to-my-channel-buy-my-merch/

Samuel, L. (2017, October 17). *YouTube Video Structure – What works!* Become A Blogger. https://iamlesliesamuel.com/25498/youtube-video-structure/

SEO Starter Guide: The Basics | Google Search Central. (n.d.). Google Developers. https://developers.google.com/search/docs/beginner/seo-starter-guide

Shopify Encyclopedia. (n.d.). Shopify. https://www.shopify.com/encyclopedia/advertising

Silva, C. N. (2020a, February 24). *YouTube for Beginners: How to Set up Your Channel.* Search Engine Journal. https://www.searchenginejournal.com/youtube-beginners-set-up-channel/349814/

Silva, C. N. (2020b, February 24). *YouTube for Beginners: How to Set up Your Channel.* Search Engine Journal. https://www.searchenginejournal.com/youtube-beginners-set-up-channel/349814/

Smith, B. (2020, August 3). *YouTube Ads: Everything You Need to Know.* AdEspresso. https://adespresso.com/blog/youtube-ads-guide/

Soare, D. (2018, December 7). *How to Choose The Best Niche for Your YouTube Channel.* Medium. https://medium.com/@diana_21435/how-to-choose-the-best-niche-for-your-youtube-channel-2e0fb5f465b0

Soliciting Crowdfunding and Donations for Your YouTube Channel. (2016, March 26). Dummies. https://www.dummies.com/social-media/youtube/soliciting-crowdfunding-and-donations-for-your-youtube-channel/

Sorrentino, D. (2020, July 23). *A straightforward guide to making money with YouTube affiliate marketing.* Brafton. https://www.brafton.com/blog/video-marketing/youtube-affiliate-marketing/

Southern, M. (2020, June 29). *Google Explains How YouTube Search Works.* Search Engine Journal. https://www.searchenginejournal.com/google-explains-how-youtube-search-works/373189/

Sullivan, T. (2018, April 18). *A Beginner's Guide to Taking Great Video on Your Phone.* The New York Times. https://www.nytimes.com/2018/04/17/smarter-living/beginners-guide-phone-video.html

Sweatt, L. (2020, November 30). *YouTube Partner Program: How to Monetize Your Channel.* VidIQ. https://vidiq.com/blog/post/youtube-partner-program-guide/

Team, H. I. W. (2019, March 5). *How does YouTube work?* How It Works. https://www.howitworksdaily.com/how-does-youtube-work/

The 5 YouTube Analytics Tools You Need. (n.d.). Brandwatch. https://www.brandwatch.com/blog/youtube-analytics-tools/

The Art of Improvement. (2018, November 11). *A Complete Guide to Goal Setting.* YouTube. https://www.youtube.com/watch?v=XpKvs-apvOs

The Latest YouTube Stats on Audience Demographics. (n.d.). Think with Google. https://www.thinkwithgoogle.com/data-collections/youtube-viewer-behavior-online-video-audience/

Top 10 Videography Tips. (n.d.). Desktop-Documentaries.Com. https://www.desktop-documentaries.com/videography-tips.html

Trounce, D. (2019, December 10). *7 Great Tools For Creating Your Own Video Tutorials.* Help Desk Geek. https://helpdeskgeek.com/free-tools-review/7-great-tools-for-creating-your-own-video-tutorials/

Types of Social Media Platforms & What's Right for You. (2020, December 10). Titan Growth. https://www.titangrowth.com/blog/types-of-social-media-platforms/

Video editing - Wikiversity. (n.d.). Wikiversity. https://en.wikiversity.org/wiki/Video_editing

Wagner, A. (2017, August 23). *Are You Maximizing The Use Of Video In Your Content Marketing Strategy?* Forbes. https://www.forbes.com/sites/forbesagencycouncil/2017/05/15/are-you-maximizing-the-use-of-video-in-your-content-marketing-strategy/#23b2d5c93584

What Is Social Media Marketing? (n.d.). Investopedia. https://www.investopedia.com/terms/s/social-media-marketing-smm.asp

wikiHow. (2021, January 13). *How to Upload a Video to YouTube.* https://www.wikihow.com/Upload-a-Video-to-YouTube

Write smart descriptions. (n.d.). YouTube. https://creatoracademy.youtube.com/page/lesson/descriptions

YouTube Ads. (n.d.-a). *Beginner's Guide To Video Insights & Metrics –.* YouTube Advertising. https://www.youtube.com/intl/en-GB/ads/resources/beginners-guide-to-video-insights-metrics/

YouTube Ads. (n.d.-b). *Online Video Advertising Campaigns –.* YouTube Advertising. https://www.youtube.com/ads/

YouTube is 15 years old. Here's a timeline of how YouTube was founded, its rise to video behemoth, and its biggest controversies along way. (2020, May 30). Business Insider Nederland. https://www.businessinsider.nl/history-of-youtube-in-photos-2015-10?international=true&r=US

Social Media Marketing Algorithms- Tiktok & Twitch: The $100,000/ Year Business Plan- Grow Your TikTok & Twitch Audiences & Create Passive Income Doing What You Love

Brandon's Business Guides

© **Copyright 2021 - All rights reserved.**

The content contained within this book may not be reproduced, duplicated or transmitted without direct written permission from the author or the publisher.

Under no circumstances will any blame or legal responsibility be held against the publisher, or author, for any damages, reparation, or monetary loss due to the information contained within this book; either directly or indirectly.

Legal Notice:

This book is copyright protected. This book is only for personal use. You cannot amend, distribute, sell, use, quote or paraphrase any part, or the content within this book, without the consent of the author or publisher.

Disclaimer Notice:

Please note the information contained within this document is for educational and entertainment purposes only. All effort has been executed to present accurate, up to date, and reliable, complete information. No warranties of any kind are declared or implied. Readers acknowledge that the author is not engaging in the rendering of legal, financial, medical or professional advice.

Table of Contents

Introduction 1
   What this book is not: 2
      Why I wrote this book: 2
   Why invest in TikTok and Twitch: 3
   The great promise to you: 3

SECTION 1: Understanding Social Media Algorithms 5

Chapter 01: Starting With The Roots: Everything You Need To Know About Algorithms 6
   Let's Talk About Social Media Algorithms 6
   Why is it a Big Deal? 7
      Why are they so important, and are they even necessary? 7
   Learning the Ropes: How Algorithm Works? 8
      Recommendations are based on the following: 9
   How Twitch recommends videos 10
   The Different Social Media Algorithms You Need to be Aware Of 11
   Facebook 11
   Instagram 12
   Twitter 13
   YouTube 14
   Four Key Strategies to Keep You Going 15

Chapter 02: Taking Advantage of Social Media Algorithms 17
   Social media active user data based on publicly available data up to January 2021 17
      Answering the Big Question: Can I Earn Through Social Media Platforms? 18
   Three Main Ways To Make Money Through Social Media Platforms 19
   Helping Hand from Your Audience 20
      Can't settle on just one audience? 21
      Avoid this mistake: 21

So how do you know if you're building the right audience? 21

You Have a Business? Boost it on Social Media Platforms! 23

Positioning Matrix Simple Plot 25

SECTION 2: Starting Your Trend on TikTok 27

Chapter 03: Get to Know TikTok 28

Key questions to ask yourself before launching into TikTok 28

Talking About Algorithms 29

Do I need thousands of followers to go viral on TikTok? 30

Content Creation: What Can I Put Out? 31

Go Live on TikTok! 32

To go live on Android and iOS, here's a simple step by step: 33

Why you should Go Live on TikTok 33

Using It for Your Brand 34

How to leverage TikTok 34

Chapter 04: Taking the First Steps 36

What's Your Niche? 38

The best performing niches on TikTok: 39

How to choose your niche: 41

Is Having a Pro Account Really Necessary? 44

Creating Your First TikTok 44

Kick-Off Your Content! 46

Chapter 05: Getting More Views 49

Here are a few tips on how to boost TikTok views: 49

Trends on TikTok matter 53

The most recommended trends on TikTok: 53

How to identify what's in and what's out: 54

Nothing Beats Consistency 55

When should you post? 56

Keep your video content interesting. 56

Some of the ways you can create exciting content: 57

Chapter 06: The Blue Check Mark 58

Verified: What is it For? 58
   How are badges given? *58*
The 3 Main Benefits of Getting Verified 59
6 Steps To Get That Check 61

Chapter 07: Monetizing your Content **63**
There's No Ad Revenue? 63
Getting Sponsorship from Brands 64
   Can you make a lot of money through sponsored content? *64*
Utilizing the Ad Commerce Tool 65
Gifts are Great! Virtual Gifts are Best! 66
   How this ultimately turns into cash: *66*
Sharing Referral Links 66
How to make money through affiliate marketing: 67

Section 3: Dominating On Twitch **69**

Chapter 08: What's Up with Twitch? **70**
The origins of Twitch: 70
From Hobbies to Social Experience 71
But Why Twitch? 71
How Do Algorithms Work? 72
Viewers versus Followings versus Subscriptions: There's A Difference 73

Chapter 09: Setting Up Your Studio **74**
Which Device Should You Focus On? 74
   • *Streaming from a PlayStation 4* *74*
   • *Streaming from Xbox One.* *75*
   • *Streaming from PC or Mac* *76*
Completing Your PC (For Those Who Need It) 77
   What you need to build a PC: *78*
   Tips for building your PC: *79*
What's Gonna Be the Setup on Console? 80
The 3 Essential Gears To Invest In 81
Outside the Four Walls 83

Chapter 10: Make it Look Professional 85
    Creating Your Profile 85
    Utilizing the Info Panels 86
    Befriend OBS 87
        The difference between Streamlabs OBS and OBS 89
    Make Sure You are Heard! 90
    Reach Out and Have Channel Moderators 91
    Make Your Streams Look Nice Using Overlays 93
        How to make your overlay more attractive: 93

Chapter 11: And We Are LIVE! 95
    It's Not Just About Streaming Your Games 96
        How to best interact with your new viewers in chat: 97
    But what if you really want to avoid talking? 97
    How to deal with having no viewers: 98
    Learn The Etiquette 98
    It's a Wrap! 99
    5 Important Tips for Beginners 99
    There's Always Some Space for Improvement 101
    Plan Ahead of Time 103
    Don't Stop Engaging 104
    Making Use of Your Vod 105
        An Avenue for YouTube Content 106

Chapter 13: Monetizing Your Content 108
    Start Being An Affiliate 108
    Next Step: Partnership 110
        How much can you expect to make as a Twitch partner? 111
    There's More! 111
    Make Use of Your Channel Analytics 112

SECTION 4: Growing Your Brand 115
Chapter 14: Engaging with the Community 116
    It Goes Both Ways 116

    Creating a Discord Server For Your Community 118

    Protecting Your Identity 120

Chapter 15: Connecting and Expanding **122**

    What kind of strategy works best? 122

    Don't Stop with Just Two. 123

    Collaborate with other Content Creators 125

        Why partner with the so-called competition? *126*

    The Power of Networks 127

    Grow at Your Own Pace 128

Conclusion: **129**

Resources: **130**

Introduction

Social media platforms have become the new norm for our society. Every smartphone has several apps installed where the consumer can connect, interact and consume social content and trending news with friends, family, and total strangers who resonate. Some apps come and go in a matter of months. Others never get any traction. A few, however, seem to have some magical formula that propels them seemingly overnight to stardom. From humble beginnings to billions of users, we've seen a handful of apps like Instagram become household names, and in recent years, two platforms have followed suit. I'm talking about TikTok and Twitch. These platforms have grown so much (in a relatively short time), it's impossible to ignore the opportunity they contain.

Most people used to hear "TikTok" and think about the hit pop single by Kesha, but for the teens of our current society, TikTok has an entirely different meaning. As one of the fastest-growing social media platforms, it is now considered a subculture for Gen Z. I think most people love TikTok because it's like a one-stop-shop for all things entertainment. It's a place where being raw, spontaneous, and different are fully embraced. I like the app because I think it takes creativity to a whole new level. You don't just create short expressive videos. There's the added bonus of editing, adding emojis, stickers, music, and so much more to the videos!

For anyone looking to create a passive income, build a solid personal or company brand, and for those who enjoy being on social media, these platforms are too good to pass up. I'm guessing you already knew that, which is why you picked up this book. Unfortunately, everyone else knows it too, which means people are storming these platforms trying to make it work. I don't know if you realized but knowing what to do and knowing how to do it are not the same. Many gamers, aspiring social media influencers, small business owners, and artists know they should be on TikTok and Twitch. Still, they are at a loss when it comes to practical implementation. Where do you begin? How do you grow your audience and brand? What kind of content works best? How do you eventually monetize your efforts? These are the questions this book attempts to answer in simple, digestible vocabulary that anyone can grasp.

If you've been looking for a simple guide that can teach you everything you need to know about TikTok and Twitch so you can build your online business and create passive income through these platforms, you're in the right place.

What this book is not:

If you're looking for a get-rich-quick formula or a magic bullet that will shortcut the effort required to succeed on social media, this book is not for you. You're also not in the right place if all you care about is a cookie-cutter system that will enable you to spam different platforms with the same content. For example, if you're lazy and all you want is to create the exact same content on Twitch and TikTok with the expectation that they will both work to grow your followers, then I'm sorry to disappoint. That's not what we are about here.

The ideas and hacks shared in this book are proven. They've produced incredible results for many people, but only because these people put in the work.

So, before you discredit this book's content, make sure you put in the work required. While it might seem to you as though influencers in your niche seem to be having an easier time as they explode their following/subscriber count, I guarantee you that it takes hard work, consistency, and perseverance to get the results you dream about.

Why I wrote this book:

The steps you're about to learn have helped thousands of other fellow entrepreneurs and me over the years. People who started from scratch with zero followers have thousands (some tens of thousands) of followers and subscribers just because they are committed to the same guidelines you will receive. They now generate both active and passive income thanks to their choice to establish a presence on these platforms. Some have dominated both Twitch and TikTok. Others only chose to go with one and still succeeded mainly because it was the right thing to do for their niche market. You'll learn a little later on why you don't need to dominate both accounts to reach your objectives.

Why invest in TikTok and Twitch:

Both these platforms are fun, laid back, and brimming with an active audience. There's so much potential for success. It's one of the most underpriced ways to gain attention and spread awareness about your product, service, or passions. These platforms are also growing rapidly. Check out these statistics.

The TikTok app was launched in 2016, and by February 2019, TikTok reached its first billion downloads. In a mere eight months, the app gained half a billion more. By April 2020, the video app had been downloaded more than two billion times globally, and it is still not showing signs of decline.

TikTok users spend an average of fifty-two minutes per day on the app. It is available in 155 countries in 75 different languages, meaning it covers a huge part of the global population. Influencers consider this platform to be the third-best platform for influencer marketing, right behind Instagram and YouTube, respectively. 41% of the audience are aged between 16 and 24 years old, with nine out of ten users log into the app multiple times a day. If that is your audience range, TikTok should be a no-brainer. But even if you only serve adults, here's an interesting fact (especially if your audience is in the United States). 26.5 out of the 500 million monthly active users are from the United States of America. Although the majority are teens, a growing number of adults (currently at 14.3 million) continue to engage on the platform.

On the other hand, Twitch seemed to have gotten a massive boost thanks to the 2020 pandemic. According to StreamElements and Arsenal.gg, there was a 50% increase in watch time between March and April of 2020. In the US, Twitch viewers are currently 41.5 million and growing. And although gaming is the core of Twitch, other categories are spiking, especially since it gives entertainers and performers a platform to connect with their audience and monetization opportunities. Music and Performing Arts nearly quadrupled its viewership from April 2019 to April 2020, so even if you're not a gamer, it's worth exploring and testing this platform.

The great promise to you:

While this isn't going to be a one-size-fits-all solution or a get-rich-quick scheme, I know you have the potential to crush it on TikTok and Twitch. By the end of this book, you will have a clear understanding of how to do it, even if you're completely new to social media. You will learn hacks that can help you grow with and without a marketing budget.

If you're still on the fence about investing your energy into this book, consider for a moment where you're at right this minute. Are you hitting your goals yet? Have you seen success with the tactics you've applied so far? Have you become frustrated with the more mature platforms like Facebook and YouTube, which have high competition and low organic yield? If you know something's got to change, then why debate this new investment? Jumping into TikTok and Twitch now is like having the opportunity to jump into Facebook when organic traffic was still a thing. Don't waste another minute of this precious time to grow something profitable on these platforms while it's still relatively easy. Learn everything you can from this book, implement religiously and trust in the process because success is inevitable for the one who perseveres in doing the right thing. Let's jump in.

SECTION 1: Understanding Social Media Algorithms

Chapter 01: Starting With The Roots: Everything You Need To Know About Algorithms

To succeed and sustain success on any social media platform, there's an essential term you need to learn and understand: Algorithm. Social media algorithms are what all social media platforms operate on these days. Most people shoot blanks when they hear the phrase social media algorithm. It's a mysterious puzzle that only a few seem to understand. Given how frequently the algorithms change, your content's health and reach depend mainly on your ability to grasp the founding principles behind algorithms. The good news is this chapter is written to guide you through this understanding so you can take advantage and exponentially grow your reach within TikTok.

Let's Talk About Social Media Algorithms

Before we can understand how the algorithms work, let's define what this term means. According to Merriam-Webster, an algorithm is a step-by-step procedure for solving a problem or accomplishing some end. Tech Terms offers a definition that brings it closer to our understanding and usage of this term by defining it as a set of instructions designed to perform a specific task. This can be a simple process such as multiplying two numbers or a complex operation such as playing a compressed video file. When it comes to social media, algorithms are used as the set of rules that operate in the background to sort out all the different posts in order to shape and match the preferences of their end-user. The basic premise is to provide the most enjoyable and personalized experience for the user in an automated and systematic way.

While programmers working on these social media platforms do their best to create efficient algorithms, there is always constant iteration of the system to ensure they continue to perform optimally and also to evolve their functionality. As such, we keep seeing new versions and upgrades of the algorithm, which often disrupts our posted content's reach and visibility. While programmers might believe they are doing the right thing to keep changing up the algorithm, for those of us, who are marketing and trying to grow our following, some of these changes can be devastating to our marketing efforts. Ask anyone who used to do their marketing on Facebook in 2012 how things used to be back then, and you'll see what I mean. But, such is the nature of social media. It evolves, and so must we. Presently, TikTok and Twitch algorithms are highly favorable to any newcomer hence the importance of jumping in to ride this organic wave.

Why is it a Big Deal?

Before algorithms became the norm for social media platforms, social networks simply displayed posts in reverse chronological order. So, a user would see the newest post from the people he or she followed. In fact, on Twitter, you can still experience this if you choose to set your feed to chronological order. After the introduction of algorithms, things started shifting. That's because the algorithm was now in charge of sorting and sifting through available content. Based on your preference as the user, it would show you only the most relevant ones and sometimes omit entirely what it rendered irrelevant. YouTube does a great job demonstrating how algorithms work. If you sign in to your account today, you'll see recommended videos, your history, and also any new releases from the accounts you most interact with. The algorithm digs into your behavior through elements such as categories, tags, and keywords. That same mode of operation is present on both TikTok and Twitch.

Why are they so important, and are they even necessary?

It's essential to learn about algorithms for the different channels you wish to dominate because they directly impact your visibility, channel growth, and ultimately your income-earning possibilities. This matters because if your content is being served to your followers and any new potential followers, you won't grow, and your engagement rate will also drop. Let me illustrate. A client shared his frustration before working with me. He had hired an agency to help him grow his following, and they did a great job taking his account from a few thousand followers to 30K within a few months. Unfortunately, his engagement rate dropped from 3% to 0.5%, and ultimately, he realized people did not see his content anymore. What was the problem here? The agency might have done a good job getting the young influencer new followers, but they lacked an understanding of how to play nice with the algorithm.

Consequently, it punished the account by cutting off reach and showing content to fewer people despite their increased posting frequency. All that could have been avoided if they had learned the ropes. That's what you're learning here, so hopefully, you won't experience the same frustration.

Learning the Ropes: How Algorithm Works?

The end result of an algorithm at work seems pretty straightforward and simple, but there are lots of complexities to learn about under the hood. It involves machine learning and data science. Don't worry, you're not about to die of boredom if these technical topics have no interest to you. There will be no difficult jargon or technical explanation. This is a crash course on how algorithms work for people who consider themselves tech-illiterate.

Since we established that an algorithm's end goal is to deliver the most relevant content to the end-user, the only knowledge you need to have now is around the set of rules or the criteria that the algorithm is fed. Some social networks are more open to discuss how they set their algorithms, while others like to keep all of us in the dark. My gut feeling tells me there are fundamental principles applicable to all social networks, best practices if you will that we can assume out the gates will apply to both TikTok and Twitch.

- Relevancy

Is your content relevant to your follower? If it is, the algorithm is more likely to recommend it to the user. How will it tell? It will base this decision on the user's history and preferences. For example, if you have a follower who often interacts with fashion content and you post an image that talks about fast fashion, that user is more likely to be fed that post.

- High-quality content

What determines high quality? The reaction and engagement of your audience. If there's a lot of activity on your content (likes, shares, comments, and reshares), the algorithms will read this as a signal that it should inform more people about your post.

- Recency

This signal is focused on your content being "fresh." The social networks want to feed the newest, freshest, and hottest posts to their community because they want to keep them engaged and thrilled. Human beings love novelty, and the algorithms have been programmed to feed this addiction of getting something new each time. So, if you're not posting fresh content regularly, it's going to be hard to have the kind of reach you desire.

Now let's look deeper into how the TikTok Algorithm works.

On TikTok, the "For You" feed (the main discovery feed you land on when you log in) is determined by the user's preference. That means I will see a different feed from you depending on the people I follow, where I often interact, and the categories I am interested in.

Categories and interests are chosen when you first join TikTok as the platform tries to learn more about your preference.

According to TikTok, "The system recommends content by ranking videos based on a combination of factors - starting from interests you express as a new user and adjusting for things you indicate you're not interested in."

Recommendations are based on the following:

#1: User interactions

That includes videos that a user likes or shares, accounts they follow, comments they post, and their content.

#2: Video information

The video information used includes captions, sound, and hashtags.

#3: Device and account settings

That includes language preference, country setting, and device type. These factors are included to optimize performance, but they also carry the least weight compared to the previous two factors.

It's also worth mentioning that the algorithm takes note of whether a user finishes watching a longer video. When a user watches a longer video from start to finish, they are more likely to receive similar content even if it's outside their country setting.

How Twitch recommends videos

For people who have been active on Twitch, they can profess to the massive shift that has taken place in recent years as the guys behind the scenes tried to make the platform easier to navigate. Twitch is rather complicated and doesn't necessarily work with a few algorithmic rules. What's more, is that we are dealing with live streaming videos. That makes understanding the algorithm and getting more reach way more complicated.

It used to be impossible to find the kind of content you want the instant you want it. All that has changed and continues to change thanks to machine learning. Their Twitch algorithm focuses on specific indicators, the most important of which is live concurrent chatters. This means that if you can have at least two active people chatting while you're live streaming, the algorithm will be triggered. The other thing that matters is the category you choose. Your chosen category must align with the kind of content you create so that as people join your stream, there is resonance. The better your content and the more accurately you categorize it, the higher the chances the algorithm will read your account as share-worthy.

Determining exactly how the TikTok and Twitch algorithm work will require some firsthand experimentation and listening to what these networks say about their platform. Sure, that implies a lot of trial and error, but the fact is, all of social media marketing is an ongoing process of experimentation which means trial and error is part of the game.

The Different Social Media Algorithms You Need to be Aware Of

In 2021, there are over 3 billion users worldwide across various social media platforms. The best social networks have to handle a lot of traffic and activity, so they all run on algorithms. Without some kind of systematic order, these platforms would have no way of sorting content, keeping their audience's attention, or selling advertising space to eager marketers. Even if you don't plan on running ads across various social media channels, it's worth understanding how different networks work.

Let's talk about the four major ones:

Facebook

Facebook's mission is to bring people together. They care about meaningful conversations and interactions between friends, family, and brands. To do this, they have an algorithm that is created to intensify the importance of viewership of local familial, friendly posts than salesy looking business-type posts.

Paid content, however, is set up a little differently but still revolves around consumer response, engagement, and relevance to the subject matter. Another aspect of their algorithm that few don't realize is that Facebook also sorts out spam content. So, it's not just about creating user-friendly content. It's also about adding value through your account and maintaining integrity. There are four prioritized ranking signals you should know about.

• Quality content - Facebook wants you to share relevant, helpful, and visually appealing content. So, if you want your content to rank better, go for high-quality images, create high-def videos or graphics animation that can improve your quality score so you can land more views on the newsfeed.

- Positive engagement - Facebook's algorithm is always in search of the most interactive content. If more people are engaging in your posts, you will gain more attention and reach. These positive signals include likes, comments, replies, mentions, and shares.

- Power of community - The next important factor is growing an active audience. The algorithm considers how often your followers interact with your brand's posts. You don't need a big audience, but you need a real one where people express genuine interest in what you publish.

- Collaborative conversations - I'm sure you've seen a rise in quizzes, polls, jokes, and other types of content that trigger conversations. Some accounts intentionally start controversial conversations to provoke their audience into engagement. As long as it's within your brand's integrity, feel free to be a conversation starter because the more people interact with your brand, the more the algorithm will push out your stuff to new people who don't know you. Anytime people leave long-form comments, links, or reshare your thought-provoking posts, the algorithm reads that positive signal and expands your reach. A fair warning here. Don't just create conversations for the sake of going viral or to get clicks. That kind of success will be short-lived.

Instagram

It's only natural that we also include the Instagram algorithm right behind Facebook since they share similarities, given that the same parent company owns them. You may think of Instagram as the baby sister (a very vain baby sister that is crazy about aesthetics and perfect-looking selfies). The algorithm here also focuses on engagement and interaction, but there are subtle differences worth noting.

- Current trends - Instagram's algorithm is crazy about "the hottest new posts." Anything about a week old is "too old" on this platform. The fresher your content, the better reach you'll have.

- Relationship interaction - Signals like being tagged in a video or photo, getting a mention, or engaging with someone in a direct message are what the Instagram algorithm uses to determine where to rank your content on the person's feed. The more often you engage with your followers, the more likely they will see your new content.

• Individual interest - We cannot ignore the emphasis Instagram gives on personalizing our feed. They don't want to show me MMA posts if I already expressed interest in music and fashion. So, the algorithm looks at my past behavior to predict what content to place on my feed. If I interact mainly with business accounts, media forms, certain hashtags, or specific personal accounts, my content will come from those sources. Hence, it goes without saying that you need to be more active and engaged on your brand account if you want to show up on your followers and a new audience's feeds.

• Real accounts with verifiable followings

The idea of buying fake followers so that your account can look prominent caught fire very quickly. Why? Because too many of us love shortcuts. Pay for fake followers and bots to build yourself up into an influencer, and everyone will believe you're a big shot, right? Wrong! Actually, no one believes you're a big shot when you have 50K followers and only two likes on all your posts. What's more, the algorithm can detect an account that's stacked with fake engagement signals. Instead of wasting money buying followers, read this book and my Instagram marketing book and put in the work to grow a genuine and real audience around your brand.

Twitter

Twitter likes to prioritize content that is focused on the latest hot news around the world. The algorithm is hot for anything hot this minute. Other signals affect the algorithm, including the relationship between users, but ultimately, fresh hot content consistently ranks up. Here are some signals you need to know.

• Rich Media - If your tweet contains images, polls, video, or GIFs that are relevant to the tweet, you're likely to see a bigger reach. People also seem to engage more with these forms of media, so make sure you use the right file size and make the text match the media content.

• Receny - On Twitter, trending topics always get high priority on the feeds. And if you post something that gets immediate engagement, the algorithm sees that as super important and pushes for more reach.

• Hashtag

Twitter is very different from most other social networks because of its "text message" style and the platform's small character limit. For this reason, hashtags are a big deal. The hashtags organize tweets into searchable keyword categories. Then the algorithm picks the hashtags with high search volume and pushes more of the content within that hashtag.

• Relationship with your followers

As with other platforms, Twitter values the interaction between you and your followers. If your fans tend to comment and retweet your content, your relevancy score increases. It also means you get priority on their feed.

YouTube

YouTube is both a social network and a search engine, so it's worth learning a thing or two about how they rank content. The platform continues to evolve and mature, and they are tightening down on clickbait videos that provide little value to their consumer. Here are some signals you should know about if you want to start uploading your videos from TikTok or Twitch to YouTube.

• Authentic and original content - YouTube doesn't like spammy, repurposed content. If you're not committed to creating something original and valuable to your growing audience, the algorithm will not favor you.

• Keywords - Before you post a video, make sure you do some keyword researching so you can include the right terms you think your audience will be searching. The algorithm will determine which video to recommend in a viewer's search query based on things like your video's title, description, etc.

• Channel Authority - The YouTube algorithm will rank you based on factors like viewing time, shares, thumbs-ups, linking your channel to a website, and high-resolution thumbnails on all your videos. That, in turn, gives you a specific channel quality score that positively or negatively impacts your reach. The higher your score, the better, so if you'd like to master YouTube channel building, I encourage you to check out my other published book on YouTube marketing.

Four Key Strategies to Keep You Going

#1: Focus on sharing engaging content that reaches your target audience

The only way to signal to any algorithm that you are worth being ranked at the top of people's feeds is to create content your audience understands and loves. If the material is not attractive, no engagement will occur. Make sure you invest some time doing market and audience research. A user's psychology on TikTok is different from that of the same user on YouTube or Instagram. Ensure you get these subtle nuances and dish out content that reaches them where they are in the manner they prefer. What am I trying to say? Know your audience, and you will beat the algorithms across any social network.

#2: Post fresh content frequently but get to know the right amount for each platform.

Social media platforms are noisy. It's safe to say posting one piece of content a month will get you nowhere regardless of how good your content. You need consistency and frequency. And you also need to understand the nature of the beast you will be handling. We'll talk specifics on TikTok and Twitch and what experts recommend later in the book. But a good rule of thumb on most social networks, especially Instagram and Facebook, is to post between 1-2 times per day. However, if you're on Twitter, you probably want to make that once per hour or once every three hours. Why? Because the nature of Twitter is to give a short lifespan (about 18minutes) to each tweet so content can remain fresh and hot. Experts recommend posting 15 times a day on Twitter, once a day on LinkedIn and Facebook, and twice per day on Instagram.

It's also important to keep in mind the most active timings for your audience. Depending on their location, they might be active in the morning, afternoon, or early evening. That might be while you're working or sleeping (if you have an international audience), so you'll need the help of a scheduling system like Buffer or Hootsuite to ensure you post frequently and at optimal times. Here are some standard recommended timings to experiment with on the main social platforms:

Facebook: The best time is between 1.00 PM and 3.00 PM Tuesdays and Fridays.

Twitter: The best time is between 1.00 PM and 3.00 PM Mondays, Tuesdays, Wednesdays, and Thursdays.

LinkedIn: All day long on Tuesdays, Wednesdays, and Thursdays.

#3: Use captions to drive more attention and engagement

This particular strategy is especially effective on Instagram. Most people invest time and resources capturing that perfect image but then waste it all by adding a single sentence or word and a bucket load of hashtags. What a waste of precious real estate. Both your audience and the algorithm will stand to benefit if you invest time to create thoughtful words that help you tell the story, inspire or reflect on the chosen image, GIF, video, or graphic. When the audience is happy, the algorithm is happy, making you happy as more and more people are served your beautiful posts.

Chapter 02: Taking Advantage of Social Media Algorithms

By 2021 the number of social media users exponentially grew, with 490 million new users joining various social networks in January 2021. That's about 13% of annualized growth or roughly 15.5 new users every second! As it stands, 53% of the total global population uses social media (4.20 billion), and I'm guessing that number will continue to grow, especially during the pandemic season. I think it's safe to say that you are using social media already. That could be why you got curious about building your brand and marketing yourself because you realized the great opportunity social media possesses. Current data shows your hunch is spot on, and it is worth going all in and pursuing your current social media objectives. But one thing to bear in mind is that creating a presence on more than one social network is worth considering.

The typical user has an account on more than eight different social networks and spends an average of 2.5hrs daily using social media. Now, let's assume this person sleeps about 8 hours per day. That would mean about 16% of their waking time goes to social media. Doesn't it make sense to interact with that person as much as possible? As a marketer, you want to ensure that wherever they invest those 2.5hrs of their day, your content will be there to engage them. That brings me to my first suggestion. If you have interests or hobbies you would love to share with the world (cooking, gaming, working out, arts & crafts, wine tasting, etc.), consider sharing these across more than one social network. Let's take a look at how the big social networks have distributed audience attention.

Social media active user data based on publicly available data up to January 2021

1. Facebook has 2.7 billion monthly active users.
2. YouTube has 2 billion monthly active users.
3. Facebook Messenger has around 1.3 billion monthly active users.
4. WhatsApp has around 2 billion monthly active users.
5. Wechat has around 1.2 billion monthly active users.
6. Instagram has 1.221 billion monthly active users.

7. TikTok has 689 million monthly active users.
8. Quora has around 300 million monthly active users.
9. Pinterest has 442 million monthly active users.
10. Telegram has 500 million monthly active users.
11. Snapchat has 489 million monthly active users.

Given this data, would it make sense to set up both a TikTok and YouTube/Instagram/WeChat account to complete your marketing activities?

Answering the Big Question: Can I Earn Through Social Media Platforms?

The answer to this question can be pretty controversial. Some people say it's too risky or even impossible unless you have a website and deep pockets. The thing is, every business is risky, so let's not use that as an excuse for discarding the idea. In a Forbes article, TikTok revealed their top seven highest-earning stars who made serious money in the previous year. Topping that list was Addison Rae Easterling, who earned a whopping $5 million in 2019. Many experts estimate that TikTok creators are on the trajectory of earning one million dollars a post very soon, but of course, all of that is speculation. We cannot state with accuracy how much TikTokers are getting paid for sponsorship opportunities, but we do know people like Loren Gray, Baby Ariel, and Zach King are at the top of the TikTok Rich list. Content creators don't make it a habit of adding price tags to their sponsored posts or announcing their partnerships' value, especially not on this platform. Still, there is no denying that earning a ton of cash is definitely possible for anyone who can build a large enough audience and get the attention of brands with big budgets.

Still on edge about making that passive income a reality?

I believe anyone with the right mindset, the right message, and the right work ethic can make social media work for them. But if you want to learn how to earn on social media, you need to understand some basics. For example, do you even know what the process looks like?

Social media monetization involves creating a systematic process that generates revenue from your ever-growing audience. That entails having a strong social media account and an engaged and growing audience. Audience targeting and nurturing is therefore defining factor on whether you succeed or not with your monetization efforts. If you know what people you want and what you're going to offer them that they will find valuable, you're in a much better position to tailor your product or service to their needs and generate revenue. Great social media monetization is centered on a win-win philosophy. Given the statistics I just shared of billions of users online, you deserve to connect with, serve, and get rewarded by an audience who sees value in your brand.

Three Main Ways To Make Money Through Social Media Platforms

Depending on the platform you chose to be on, there can be various ways to generate passive income, including affiliate marketing, becoming a consultant, and selling informational products. But for TikTok, let's focus on the three best strategies that are proven to work.

#1: Influencer marketing

Every social platform has influencers. These influencers often get approached by companies to promote their products, services, or the brand itself in hopes of generating sales. TikTok is doing a great job creating and growing an environment for massive influencer marketing opportunities. For companies looking to gain brand exposure and engagement, working with influencers seems to be a great strategy for various reasons. First of all, instead of spending weeks or months analyzing the app and its audiences to determine what content will be interesting, these bigger companies prefer to work with an influencer who has a decent following, videos with high engagement, and a visible track record of reaching TikTok audience. It's also a great way to limit the time and resources needed to create their videos because they can get the influencer to create quality content for them. So, this can be an excellent opportunity for you, but you will need to have an audience and demonstrate your ability to create great content.

#2: Sponsored content

Sponsored content is premium content that a sponsor will pay you to create and distribute on your social media account. Sponsored content is an ad, but it usually doesn't feel like it because it naturally fits the environment. For example, if you're a gamer and a gaming company hires you to sponsor their brand and a particular video game, that would qualify as a sponsored ad. It wouldn't feel intrusive for your viewers because you already create content around video games in the same genre. Sponsored ads are great, and companies love them because it adds to the user experience instead of disrupting it.

It makes the brand feel trustworthy and credible because they place it alongside other things your viewers will enjoy, and you, as the account owner, are responsible for the execution of the content. This type of content is mutually beneficial because you get funded, and the brand gets access to your audience, who could potentially turn into buying customers. The mechanics of this are simple, and if you do an excellent job of sharing sponsored content, you can earn a great income from it. Take the example of Loren Gray, who in 2019 earned $2.6 million after landing a major Revlon deal where she creates content for the company's TikTok account and Revlon-sponsored posts for hers.

#3: Selling your own branded merchandise

Another passive income opportunity is selling your own line of products. These can be as simple as T-shirts and coffee mugs to entire makeup line products, all of which have proven very profitable on TikTok. You do, however, need to have a wildly popular account with lots of engagement. You should approach selling products the same way you would any other business venture. Do your research, be smart and make sure you're profitable as early on in the game as possible.

Helping Hand from Your Audience

Before you can hope to generate any passive income or sponsorship and partnership opportunities, you must focus on building a healthy-sized audience. Your audience is the key to your success. That means you need to understand who you are creating content for and what they most resonate with on TikTok. If you don't invest the time to find that sweet spot, you'll unwittingly land on the wrong side of the TikTok algorithm.

There's only one rule of thumb to concern yourself with when it comes to growing an audience: Choose an audience you care about.

The content you create to attract these people to your account will have to be of high value and high volume. One content randomly created cannot help you grow an audience. This process must be methodical, and it will require effort on your part, so you need to really care about what you're doing and the people you're doing it for. Otherwise, you'll want to quit a few months in. If you care about your audience, you'll be motivated to continue to create content even if no money comes in. And as this audience grows and falls in love with all that you do for them, opportunities will start to present themselves.

I encourage you now to make a list of all the potential audiences you care about that you can see yourself helping for the next few years with no return.

Can't settle on just one audience?

If you realize you want to talk to more than one audience, that's okay. Simply pick one to get started with. For example, if you're into gaming and would like to attract different segments of video-loving people, go with the one that is closest to your current situation first. The broader audience can come in later once you've gained momentum with this more niched audience that most resembles you.

Avoid this mistake:

Don't build an audience full of people who don't want to or can't afford to buy a product. For example, if you're a beauty makeup artist and want to become popular on TikTok, the best audience would be young ladies who love makeup. The worst audience would be creating an audience of minimalists or a young male audience who follows you just because you're pretty and make cool dance videos.

So how do you know if you're building the right audience?

First, you need to consider what your audience cares about and what they'd be willing to spend money on. There's no need to build an audience of extreme sports teenagers if your passion is playing video games. Similarly, if you build an audience of gamers, trying to sell them sports merchandise is probably not the best idea. That's why you need to understand the audience profile as much as possible. Invest some time to research basic demographic and psychographic information. I'll show you how...

Fire up a Google doc and start creating your audience personas. Let's start with demographics.

- Age
- Location
- Gender
- Income
- Education level
- Ethnicity
- Status

Figure out the demographics that are important to you. For example, if your audience is college students, then marital status and children probably shouldn't matter to you. If you're selling make up the gender should matter. The purpose of this is to define your ideal persona so that you can create a strong content strategy that they'll be interested in. Once you have all the details, move to psychographics.

Psychographics is about figuring out what your audience thinks and believes.

- Why do they want to learn about your niche?
- How do they like to learn/be entertained (depending on what your channel will offer).
- What common questions do they have about your niche?
- How knowledgeable are they about your niche?
- How important is your niche to them? Do they approach it as a hobby or part of their job?

As you answer these questions, do your best to think from your audience's perspective. Do it right, and you'll be ready for the next phase, i.e., Positioning.

How to position yourself for success on TikTok and Twitch

Positioning is how you present yourself to your audience to make sure your audience associates your account or brand with a particular aspect of what you already know they value. That's why this comes only after you feel like you know and understand your target audience. Your job should be to position yourself to a specific segment or group of people by creating content in a way that they want, but no one else is providing. For instance, there are many different subcategories within the gaming niche, such as reviews, walkthroughs, game news, etc. So, the best approach as a beginner looking to build an audience and ultimately a brand is to choose one of that subcategories to be the central theme of your account. If you're only doing walkthroughs, you can either go specific and only focus on a particular game (e.g., Tomb Raider) or do walkthroughs for various games in the same genre. Note that the former might end up being limiting in the long run because you might run out of content too soon.

The bottom line is you want people to associate your account with something specific immediately. That's the easiest way for you to imprint yourself and stay top of mind. And just as a side note, you don't even need to be amazing at playing the game. In a recent Google Consumer Survey, viewers often cited the "reactions" and "commentary" of the YouTube creator as a big attraction factor for this kind of content. One respondent said, "It's a shared experience with a favorite creator."

An excellent example of this is Conan O'Brien's Clueless Gamer series. It's worth mentioning that he really sucks at playing. But his commentary, observations, and reactions are just epic! He adds a lot of value to the experience and offers a great laugh, so his audience keeps growing and coming back for more. So, if you're worried that you're not that good at playing, think again. As long as you've targeted the right people and you add value through your personality, you'll be just fine. And if you're still at a loss with finding your position, check out the positioning matrix that I've added for your convenience at the end of this chapter.

You Have a Business? Boost it on Social Media Platforms!

If you have an existing business, social media is a powerful tool to leverage. The advantages are too numerous to mention here but let's start with the main ones.

• Building brand authority and credibility.

When people see your brand active on social media especially replying to customers and posting original content, you appear more credible. Interacting with your fans and customers demonstrates that you care about serving and satisfying your customers, and that promotes brand loyalty and causes people to want to talk about your brand more.

The plus side of having people talking about your brand and doing mentions on social media is that it helps you beat the algorithms. Not only does word spread about your brand, but it also enables you to avoid suffering the rage of ever-changing algorithms.

- New growth opportunities

Social media is one of the best places to find growth opportunities. A lot can happen when your brand is visible and thriving online. You'll find people reviewing your products, tagging you, creating user-generated content all for free. You'll also find volunteers who want to become your brand's ambassador and other companies pitching partnership ideas because they recognize how strong your brand and audience are. The possibilities are endless when you leverage social media, and you've got a great product or brand.

- More inbound traffic

If you're not on social media, then it's likely your inbound traffic is limited to the people who are already familiar with your brand. Unless you're running direct ads to your site, it's going to be tough getting substantial traffic to your website. So, if you have a website (whether you have a brick and mortar business or an eCommerce store), it's imperative to build a solid social media presence. Each social media profile you add to your marketing strategy is a gateway to your website. Each post is another opportunity to acquire new prospects who could turn into customers. So even if you only have TikTok content, think of how you can start syndicating that fresh content to as many other platforms as possible - as long as it matches your target audience.

- Brand Evangelist

Having your own brand/product evangelist can boost your revenue. Social media is a great place to gather enthusiastic and vocal people who love what you offer and spread great stories about using your product or experiencing your service. By nature, these super fans tend to create more super fans. By creating an online environment on social media where these individuals can receive special treatment (fun interaction, product testing, etc.), you'll create evangelists who will draw in more attention, leading to revenue and opportunities.

Regardless of where you choose to boost your business, make sure to do it wisely because it makes all the difference. Go where your ideal audience hangs out.

Positioning Matrix Simple Plot

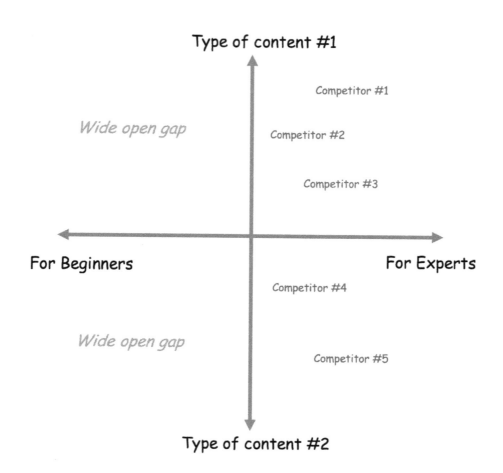

Step One. Identify differentiators.

Have a brainstorming session where you come up with all the things your audience might find valuable. Don't overcomplicate this. Just think of what your audience may like or dislike. Write everything down on the same Google Doc that contains client persona information.

Examples of common differentiators are Easy vs. Hard; Beginner vs. Professional; Brief vs. Step-by-Step; Short vs. Long.

Step Two. Identify your competitors.

Competition in the marketplace is a good thing because it means there's a need/demand for what you have to offer. It won't be too hard to identify the top contenders in your niche. You can do some hashtag search on the social media platform on which you want to establish your presence and use Google and Ubersuggest to see who is dominating online to learn from them. Try to find 5-10 competitors.

Step Three. Plot your competitors

Now that you know your top competitors, pick two of the differentiators you identified in step one and create a basic matrix with those differentiators as the axis labels.

Next, I want you to go through the list of competitors and figure out how they fit on this scale. Plot each of them and notice where the gaps are. The aim is to find at least one significant gap that you could fill. That becomes your ideal positioning spot.

What happens if there are no apparent gaps?

It's easy. Pick a new set of two differentiators and repeat this process.

SECTION 2: Starting Your Trend on TikTok

Chapter 03: Get to Know TikTok

What is TikTok?

TikTok is a short-form video-sharing app that allows users to create and share 15-second videos on any topic under the sun. The kids love the app, but there's much to learn for most people over 25 years. Initially, the platform was called musicl.ly until 2017, when it merged into TikTok. This Chinese-owned app (Douyin in China) bought Musical.ly and integrated the two into a single platform (at least in the international market) called TikTok. By 2020, TikTok had become the most popular new social media platform in the world. A mix of music, lip sync videos, and micro-video content, TikTok is extremely popular with Gen Z (32% of all TikTok's active users are teenagers). TikTok is home to many lip-synching videos but what makes it stand out and continue gaining popularity is its act-out memes backed by music and other sound clips, which get endlessly reproduced and remixed among its young users. There are countless tunes (pop, rap, R&B, electro, and DJ tracks) that serve as background music for the 15-second video clips.

What makes TikTok unique is that it's still not dominated by celebrities or even micro-celebrities. Instead, the feed is often saturated by everyday users (amateurs) doing something cute, funny, or clever with a tacit acknowledgment that "yes, I am making a fool of myself, and I hope the internet finds it funny" underlying much of the content. Most of the content on TikTok is weird, addictive, and unique to the platform. Whether it's from Will Smith or some unknown teenager, many of the best performing videos would probably not do well on any other social platform. Yet, on TikTok, it just works!

Key questions to ask yourself before launching into TikTok

Although TikTok growth is enticing, not everyone should be on TikTok right now. So here are a few questions to answer to help you determine whether this app is right for you to build your brand:

#1: Is your target audience younger than 35 years old? If yes, this would be a great social media platform. As you saw in the statistics, the majority of the users are Gen Zers and younger Millenials. It might change significantly in the future, but for now, this is where the kids like to hang out.

#2: Do you have visually appealing and demonstrative content?

#3: Are you an artist, musician, or gamer?

#4: Is your brand's identity leaning more toward fun, casual with a "cool kid" vibe?

If the answers you come up with validate that getting into this platform is right, then go all in!

Talking About Algorithms

There have been many rumors and speculation about the TikTok algorithm, much of which makes the platform sound super complex and hard to dominate. All that is about to change because not too long ago, TikTok headquarters finally opened up about it, and you're about to learn the facts as learned from the experts!

First up, let's talk about how TikTok determines what shows up on your "For You" feed and, for that matter, what will show up for your audience. According to the platform, when you upload a video, the For You algorithm shows it first to a small subset of users. These people may or may not be existing followers of your account, but TikTok shows it to them based on their past behavior. If they respond favorably (sharing the video, watching it in full, etc.), TikTok then offers it to more people with similar interests. That same process repeats itself, and if the positive feedback loop continues long enough, the video could go viral. Of course, the opposite is also true. If the first sub-segment doesn't show signs of enjoyment, the content is delivered to fewer users limiting the video's potential reach.

The For You is, therefore, the best place to go to find new content. That's where you want to end up more often than not, if at all possible. According to TikTok, "The system recommends content by ranking videos based on a combination of factors - starting from interests you express as a new user and adjusting for things you indicate you're not interested in, too."

Bet you're wondering what these "factors" are. Here's what we know for sure:

- User interactions

User interactions refer to the videos you like and share. It's also the accounts you follow, the comments you post, and the content you create for your account.

• Video information

Video information includes details like the hashtags you use, captions, sounds, etc.

•Device and account settings

That refers to things like country setting, the device you're using as well as language preference.

The TikTok recommendation system will weigh all the factors mentioned above to ensure each For You page is unique to the user based on their level of interest. TikTok also explains that they have strong signals and weak signals that help them determine where to rank content.

Strong signals include how long a viewer watched the video, whether the person shared it and if they followed the creator who uploaded the video after watching it. If someone watches your video start beginning to end, the algorithm takes that as a strong indicator to show more of your content. And even if you're not in the same country, your content is more likely to show up on their For You page. Weak signals include language preference, the device being used, and whether the consumer and creator are in the same geographical location. There are also a few negative indicators that TikTok looks for, including whether a user taps "Not Interested" or if they chose to hide content from a certain creator.

Therefore, we may assume that For You page videos are ranked based on the likelihood of a user's interest in a piece of content. That's why you need clarity on your audience and a great content strategy that will get them hooked. More on content creation later. For now, let's address another ubiquitous question among new content creators.

Do I need thousands of followers to go viral on TikTok?

The good news is you don't. TikTok has confirmed you don't need to be a superstar to go viral on their platform. While a video is likely to receive more views if posted by an account with a large follower base, it is not a prerequisite. TikTok stated that "neither follower count nor whether the account has had previous high performing videos are direct factors in the recommendation system."

Take a deep breath and celebrate your future success because, according to TikTok, even if you have zero followers, you can still get attention if your content is interesting to the target audience. This is one of the reasons TikTok is pretty special. You might be on your first post, and you still have a chance of appearing on the For You page of potential followers!

Content Creation: What Can I Put Out?

Before you can put anything worth viewing on TikTok, you need to understand the interface. When you first open the app, you'll see two feeds adjacent to each other. The first is called "For You," and this is where discovery and exploration usually happen. It's mysterious, and we all love it because showing up here can make or break your aspirations of becoming a TikTok superstar. Most users spend 75% of their time on the For You page. The For You page usually has content that is tailored to your interests. The more time you spend here, the more personalized this content will be. But you'll also find popular content that may soon go viral because the algorithm likes to test and see what you're more likely to engage with. Next to the For You, Page is your "Following Feed." This is where you'll find all the content of the people you've chosen to follow. If you want to know the best content to put out, perhaps a great option would be to follow brands in your niche that are not necessarily direct competitors.

The type of content you can post on TikTok continues to evolve. Although it started as a lip-syncing platform, there has been a significant expansion in various categories, making it easier for people with diverse passions and interests to still succeed on the platform. Here are the main types of content that perform well on the site.

#1: Creating videos based on trending hashtags

You could search for trending hashtags on TikTok (we'll cover this a little more in the next chapter) and then create videos around the same theme. Instead of reinventing the wheel or wasting time trying to figure out what your ideal audience wants, you can simply copy what's already working. Make sure, however, that whatever you create is better quality and more interesting to your audience than existing videos. That will increase the probability of getting more views, shares, and new followers who enjoy the theme of the chosen hashtag.

#2: Cute Animals

Cute animals doing humorous or cool things will get you lots of followers. People are simply addicted to cats and dogs doing funny things or simply just looking cool. In fact, you can find plenty of cute animal accounts already succeeding on TikTok. So go ahead, if you're a cat lady or an animal lover, share that passion with the TikTok audience.

#3: Do the album cover challenge

This type of content is seriously growing as more and more content creators come up with humorous questions and convert them into videos. It works by first showing your question and then answering it by posing as a famous song's cover photo. The title of the song usually answers the question posed. Some TikTok users have taken this trend seriously, using costumes and elaborate makeup to resemble the album cover as closely as possible. The trick to getting this right is to be as specific as you can with the song choice. So, give some serious thought to the scenario and question you want to record. An example of this is a video I saw from @peytoncoffee, who created this kind of content by posing the question that her mom asks.

Mom: "what's the earliest you get off TikTok?"

If you watch the video, you see her recreating the album cover for Halsey's song "3 AM".

#4: Dance videos

Dance videos are super popular on TikTok. If you're an aspiring dancer, this is precisely what you need to put out as often as possible. I've seen many creators showcasing their talent and even doing group dance performances to attract attention on the platform.

But even if you're not a great dancer, you can use your personality and some creativity to entertain people, and you can still succeed at going viral with this type of content.

Go Live on TikTok!

TikTok live has become increasingly popular for content creators who want a more intimate experience with their followers and those who want to start monetizing their brand. Unlike other social media platforms, going live on TikTok doesn't just happen. You need to meet specific criteria before that button can show up for you.

• First, you must have 1,000 followers in your account. Without that, you don't even see the option for going live.

• You need to be at least 16 years old. Although anyone from the age of 13 can sign up, you can't access the live feature unless you're 16. For those who would like to activate the feature of receiving gifts from followers during live streaming, you will need to be at least 18 years old.

If you meet the above requirements, then you're ready to start live streaming on the app. The mechanics of going live are pretty straightforward. What is less so is the actual content that you will share on your broadcast. So before going "Live," invest some time outlining what you're going to share, the title of it, and a little description that will help people know what the video is about and what to expect. Whether it's a cooking class, dance-off, or just sharing your thoughts, you need to be thoughtful and strategic with your content creation so your audience can keep coming back for more.

To go live on Android and iOS, here's a simple step by step:

#1: Open the TikTok app and log in if necessary.

#2: Touch the +(plus) button at the bottom of the screen.

#3: Press the "Live" option under the record button.

#4: Title your live stream and add a description so that viewers can get hooked and join.

#5: Click "Go Live" to begin.

#6: Tap the "X" button when you're done streaming to end your broadcast.

Why you should Go Live on TikTok

If you're still on the fence about using the Live stream feature, it might be helpful to learn of a survey conducted by Livestream.com in which 82% of the respondents shared that they prefer live video from a brand to social posts. 67% of viewers say the quality is the most important factor when watching a Livestream. So going live will continue to be a huge trend across all social media and especially TikTok. It's going to help you gain more exposure and grow your brand authentically and rapidly.

Using It for Your Brand

For new brands coming into the platform who already have an existing product or service, I like to think about TikTok as being similar to Instagram, except it's purely for videos. It can be a powerful branding tool when used appropriately, and yes, it can generate lots of business. The best part about TikTok is that it is easy to make creative, funny, entertaining, and inspirational videos for the TikTok community. And even if you suck at dancing, making a little effort on this platform will go a long way in grabbing users' attention. One thing to remember is that TikTok isn't a serious platform, so if you want your brand to thrive, your content needs to be light-hearted, fun, and visually pleasing. Lots of big and small brands are doing well on TikTok. Just check out what brands like Pepsi, Nike, and even Universal Pictures are doing if you want a little inspiration.

How to leverage TikTok

Some of the best brand promoting content I've seen is through the creation of "TikTok Challenge" campaigns. A brand creates a challenge and even provides new music clips for users to interact with. The winners get big prizes as a reward for their attention and participation. For example, fashion brand Guess partnered with TikTok on a campaign targeted at Millenials and Generation Z. In early September 2018, as TikTok users opened the app, TikTok directed them to the #InMyDenim challenge that urges them to post videos with the hashtags. Although this type of challenge didn't have any prizes up for grabs, thousands of people still participated.

Another great example is Chipotle's #GuacDance challenge which urged guacamole fans to show off dance moves dedicated to avocados. This Mexican Grill reported record results for this TikTok campaign with 250,000 video submissions and 430 million video starts during a six-day run. The promotion resulted in Chipotle's biggest guacamole day ever, with more than 800,000 sides of the condiment serves. Avocado consumption jumped from 68% to 18,500% for National Avocado Day.

Both these examples demonstrate the viral power of TikTok. Challenging other TikTok users to participate in an activity is a key driver of viral growth. Every existing business serving the Millennial and Gen Z demographics would do well to leverage the platform in this way. For smaller brands without such huge marketing spend or brand recognition, you might want to create a challenge with some enticing swag that these cool kids can get as a reward.

Chapter 04: Taking the First Steps

Now that you're well acquainted with the TikTok platform's mechanics, it's time to get practical. The starting point should always be your account set-up. In this chapter, we want to launch and establish your account the right way. We are starting with your profile.

Step One: Begin with Your Profile

Let no one tell you differently. First impressions do matter. On TikTok, your profile must much the psychology of the users and the nature of the platform. So, if you think you can just slap on your Twitter or Instagram profile on there, think again. We need to approach the TikTok platform in a whole new way.

The main objective here is to create a profile in a way that attracts viewers, grabs their attention, and entices them to follow your account. A few things you'll want to think about now include:

- The username you want to use.

- The profile photo.

- The word choice you use to describe yourself, your brand, and how you want to be perceived by the community.

Your profile bio is your big chance to introduce yourself to every potential follower because the short video format leaves very little room for introductions. So, you have to make sure it's intentionally created.

The first thing you need to do is show your followers who you are and what you do. They might be able to guess a little about your brand and who you are based on your video content, but we don't want to leave that impression up to chance. The character limit on TikTok is super tiny (80 characters), so you need to ensure you stay under that limit without compromising the message's quality.

I want you to fire up your Google document or a private journal and start writing sentences that boil down precisely what you want people to know before they decide whether or not they want to follow you. Use captivating, simple, and engaging language that puts across your brand's value and uniqueness.

Example of a good one-liner for TikTok: Fashion/Lifestyle & Beauty Blogger. AZ ☐ Follow me on IG for daily looks.

Exercise: What is a sentence that best describes your brand and your "Why"? I call this type of sentence a One-liner. Write different variations touching on various aspects that you might want to share on your TikTok, then go for the one that feels right before moving on to the second step. You could even ask a few friends to vote for the best one.

The second thing is to add an emoji or two into your descriptive one-liner. From the various sentences, you wrote above, pick one that feels best and spruce it up with some emojis. Why? Because TikTok is fun, casual, and entertaining. An emoji that helps you emphasize your brand's personality is a must-have. You can also use emojis to highlight what your brand does without taking up much real estate space. For example, if you're an eCommerce brand selling clothing for teens, you might include a t-shirt ☐ emoji. Get creative with this and use emojis purposefully.

Exercise: What emojis can help you enhance your one-liner and give people an insight into your brand? Add it to your one-liner now before moving on to the next step.

The third thing to do with your profile is to add a good call to action in your bio. Tell new visitors and potential followers what you want them to do next or how you wish them to interact with you. For example, if you're a gamer on Twitch, let them know when they can join a live game. If you have a travel blog, include a CTA (call-to-action) to direct followers to a blog post link. If you have an eCommerce, add a link to your best-selling merchandise there.

Don't feel pressured to send people outside of TikTok if you're just getting started. You can also simply ask them to follow you on TikTok or send a message. The important thing is to train your new audience into receiving actionable instructions from you.

Exercise: What CTA works best for you and your brand now? Write it down and make sure the relevant link is included if you want to redirect people outside the platform.

The fourth thing is to decide on a handle name for your account. I don't want this to be the first step because it may evolve by the time you're done creating your one-liner and thinking about your niche. Now that you are closer to determining your niche, which we'll get into shortly, you might already have some ideas of your handle name. That is the name that people will see and use to find you - @exampleaccount. It's essential to think through what you want to call your account because it should be an easy name for your audience to recall, and it should reflect your brand personality and purpose. If you're still uncertain about your handle name, leave it until after you've settled on your niche and then go with a name that matches what you want to be known for.

The last thing you're going to do is add a link to your bio.

TikTok gives you space for a link on your bio, which is excellent for driving traffic to other pages you wish to promote. There are few ways to make sure you're getting the most of this valuable piece of real estate. First, you could send traffic to a single URL. This can be your most recent blog post, a landing page to download some free goodies, another social media profile you wish to boost, or any other page you want to promote. The other thing you could do is promote multiple links through a link in the bio section. Url.bio is the best option if you opt for this because you can offer your followers numerous options when they click on your bio link. That enables you to share all necessary links, including all the other social media platforms you're on and your online store if you have one. This service also enables you to track the traffic so you can see which links are performing best with your audience. One of the reasons I like this method is that it saves the hassle of editing and creating new links whenever you want to promote a different product or service.

Please note, however, that it's okay if you're unable to add a link to your bio at the moment. Some people (depending on the device) seem unable to access this capability. Suppose you're unable to add a link to your bio. In that case, I encourage you to access the TikTok Testers program, where you can receive instructions for accessing the various Beta versions of TikTok as they release them.

What's Your Niche?

TikTok operates a lot on "what's trending and cool," so it makes sense that by copying the content that's going viral and gaining a lot of views, you can start building an audience. But there is another way to build your audience, and that is through a niche.

What is a niche audience?

A niche audience is a focused subgroup of a broader target market. It's a specific group of people with particular needs, and in your case, you'll want to go for a niche that you know you can serve well. Users across social media love discovering niched accounts because they know they'll get more specialized content that feels personalized to their exact needs. If you can pick the right niche and post valuable content, you can quickly become the go-to expert on TikTok. If you think about it, cooking is a target market, but it's pretty broad. Homemade Spanish cooking recipes is an example of a niche within cooking. People who love Spanish food will immediately resonate with your account. Such an account is more likely to gather like-minded people who share a passion for homemade Spanish food leading to a lot of interaction because it genuinely appeals to them.

So, if you start your new account specializing in Homemade Spanish dishes, TikTok is likely to push your content to users who have expressed interest in cooking. Those most interested in Spanish recipes are more likely to click and watch your content on their For You page. In fact, the small group of individuals passionate about this form of cuisine are likely to watch the full video and click on your account profile to see if there are more Spanish recipes.

If they continue to find more and more on this niche topic, turning them into followers will be a natural by-product. Whenever this user desires a homemade Spanish recipe, guess where they'll go first?

Examples of niche accounts on TikTok include:

drcody_dc uses his TikTok account to promote his chiropractic clinic. That's a niche audience. It's doing well for him as he shares small clips from his sessions with clients showcasing how he can help. That demonstrates his expertise in the field and does indirect marketing because anyone who needs a chiropractor will think of him first.

The best performing niches on TikTok:

- Lip-syncing

The most popular niche on TikTok (in fact, the genre that launched its success online) is lip-synching. Most people use TikTok to make videos of themselves lip-synching to their favorite songs or scenes from their favorite movies. The key is to add a unique flair and your personal twist to this competitive niche.

• Dancing

TikTok is all about music and dancing, so it makes sense that the most famous niche with a ready-built audience will be viewers who love to watch people dancing. You can be a professional or amateur dancer. Heck, you can even be doing dance-offs to famous songs with your grandma, and people will still love your content. There are lots of popular accounts of regular people "trying" to dance to famous tracks. It's hilarious, and viewers seem to enjoy the authenticity of such content.

• Comedy

This has to be my favorite part of TikTok. I enjoy catching Trevor Noah's comic rants about politics and our society in general. Kevin Hart spent his first several months literally creating content on TikTok where all he would say is "let's do a TikTok video" to whoever was around him. And he would comically shoot the entire 15-second video "trying to do a TikTok." Most of it was so funny. It didn't even matter that there was no substance to the content. Thousands of people still viewed and liked his videos. You can make clips of yourself either testing out jokes or just doing something funny. You don't need to be a famous comedian or have a Netflix comedy special. If you can make people laugh, hit record and let the show begin.

• Fashion

Are you naturally great at putting outfits together? Are you currently in school studying fashion? There's an audience waiting for you on TikTok. People love seeing daily outfits and getting fashion advice. If you like being a little edgy and creating "cool" looks that you would wear if you were part of a certain movie, this is definitely a niche for you.

• Cooking/baking

If you enjoy cooking, this can be a great niche to get into. You might already have a YouTube cooking channel, so this would be a great addition, but instead of long videos of preparing and cooking the entire meal, you simply make short segments and snap them together over some cool music. Then you link the recipes in your profile!

- Arts and crafts

This is another growing niche on TikTok. People enjoy watching videos of how to draw or craft something, especially the process entailed to get to the final product. You can do it with painting, sketching, sculpting, pottery, or anything else you're passionate about. Make it a montage or do a time-lapse of yourself drawing or making something and post it into your account. The creation process can be the entire content which makes things feel more intimate and authentic. Then you can send people to your shop or wherever you showcase the final products.

- Fitness

Although fitness is broad, we'll consider it a niche, and it is trending on TikTok. Share your tips on getting toned arms and sculpting a six-pack, or share your extreme sports passion with people, and you'll soon be amassing a loyal audience.

How to choose your niche:

- Identify your skills and passions

"I'm not good at anything. How do I choose a niche?"

That is a common question, especially for young people who aspire to be influencers while still in school. It's easy for an existing brand or social media influencer to join TikTok and immediately identify their target audience. They just need to look to their existing customer and follower database. But if you're just starting out and you don't have your hard skills honed, how do you approach this? By starting where you are.

Where you are is the perfect place to begin. Start by identifying all the things you've been interested in since childhood. What do you enjoy doing most? What makes you skip lunch and forget to pee because of how engrossed you are in the activity?

Identifying all the things you currently do just because you enjoy it and building an audience around that increases your odds of success because you're likely to keep creating content consistently even without an audience.

Which comes first - the chicken or the egg?

On TikTok, the answer is that content comes first. If metaphorically speaking, the chicken represents your audience, and the egg represents the revenue, you need to produce a ton of content before any of that. Yes, there will be crickets, and hardly anyone will see that content, but you still need to produce it. That's the only way to ultimately attract both the chicken and the egg. And since you already know that it has to be an ongoing effort of good quality content that your potential followers will find appealing, you need to go with something that you enjoy so you can have the enthusiasm and commitment that will produce great material.

Make a list of everything you feel passionate about or everything you wish to learn. Perhaps there are skills you'd like to develop.

David is an excellent example of this. He absolutely hated school. Graduating from high school and getting into college was a burden and the only reason he did it was that he didn't want to disappoint his single, hard-working mom, who had to take up two jobs to put him through school. When we started his TikTok account, he struggled a lot with this concept of picking a niche. He had never excelled at anything before. To his mind, building an audience around a skill felt impossible. But David remembered that he enjoyed building his toy cars as a young boy from scrap metal. And throughout his middle and high school, he spent his free time playing with magnets, making toy car models from recycled materials, and taking pictures of nature.

So, at first, he started posting content of what he was creating behind the scenes. He also took a free photography class and started documenting that journey on both Instagram and TikTok. After a few months, he focused more on his toy cars from recycled materials for TikTok and his amateur photography tips on Instagram because his audience on TikTok seemed more responsive when he put out simple DIY videos of his toy cars.

It's only been a year since he started his daily posting, and his site has grown to 970,000 followers. David learned that it's not about being an expert or having top skills. It's about finding something you already enjoy doing and sharing that with the world.

- Begin by experimenting

I always say to newbies that the best way to find a niche is to embark on a scientific experiment. Evaluate your passions, strengths, and what you genuinely think your audience will love to watch. A handful of these different categories should be the main themes for your content. As your TikTok account starts to gain traction, monitor the category that seems to get the most interactions.

• Narrow down based on audience feedback

Once your account has grown and you have a decent-sized audience, consider narrowing it down to a specific category. Since your initial experiment started by going for themes that you naturally like, switching down to a single theme shouldn't be too hard at this point because you'll be working with content that you enjoy creating and your audience loves to watch. That is the ultimate sweet spot of picking a good niche.

Susan is a 14-year-old girl who cracked TikTok and landed the status of influencer almost by accident. Or was it? Susan had a private account on TikTok for a year or so, just like all her school friends. When the lockdown hit, she decided to create a public account which she now uses to share sewing videos and tutorials under the nom de plume Fashionflip.

Within six months, the account had 127 videos which attracted 37,500 followers and over 730,000 likes. Her fan base is between 7years and 9years old. Before setting up the public account, Susan wasn't an avid sewer. In fact, she only acquired a sewing machine to help pass the time during the long pandemic where she had to isolate herself from her friends. Her nanny taught her the logistical basics, like how to thread her machine and run it. Adding her creativity and insights gained from watching YouTube videos, Susan was able to produce adorable stuff, which her audience obviously loved. She said she just experimented and kept learning and iterating along the way. Her audience appears to be novice sewers who prefer Susan's simpler repurposing videos over complex multi-part sewing tutorials. Many of her followers started sewing after watching her videos, and they frequently tag Susan in their products which Susan says is such a treat.

This is the power of TikTok. Users usually flock to the app and browse the "For You" page, which feeds them content similar to videos they've watched in the past. Because TikTok's algorithm focuses more on interest than anything else to determine what a user will see, sticking to a particular niche is crucial to one's success. Susan was smart enough to figure this out for herself. As a consumer, she would often watch videos from specific hashtags. Using the app first as a consumer, she identified that creators who use well-chosen tags in their videos tend to accrue more views, likes, and followers. That's precisely what she did when she launched her public account months ago. Susan shares that she will never post a sewing video on one day and a dance video on the next. That would just confuse her audience and dilute their adoration of her account. "I make very specific videos so that people who want to see them will find them. That's how you get followers."

Susan is spot on. And so, while it may seem to be a chance or an accident that she's already an influencer, her simple strategy makes us aware of the critical ingredient that you need before moving forward.

Is Having a Pro Account Really Necessary?

You're now aware of what TikTok is and the immense opportunities it can offer you and your brand, but have you heard of TikTok pro? A TikTok pro account is an extension of the basic TikTok account. It's more of an analytical tool where you can better understand what your followers are looking for, what they are most interested in, and so on. If you're just using TikTok for fun, then it's not really necessary. But if you're keen to build a brand, influence, and ultimately monetize your efforts, this tool will be immensely helpful. The TikTok pro will help you track down the number of views weekly and monthly so you can understand your best-performing content and traffic source in detail. By the way, this is currently a free feature, so if you already have an account, here's what to do.

Launch your TikTok application.

Go to your profile page and select the "privacy and settings" tab.

Tap on "Manage my account" > select "Switch to Pro Account" and follow the onscreen instructions.

Once you make the switch, you'll start to see a new "Analytics" button in the options. That's where you can analyze how to attract and retain audience attention and engagement.

Side note: If you currently have a private account, making this switch will make your account public. So, you may want to create a separate public account like Susan and use a pseudo name just like she does if you wish to get a pro account.

Creating Your First TikTok

Before you can publish your first TikTok, you need to set up an account. Let's get that done first by setting up your TikTok account. If you already have an account, you can skip over to the next part.

Download the app on the smartphone if you haven't done so and sign up with Facebook, Gmail, Twitter, or create a new username and password. By default, TikTok assigns all users a unique username made up of random letters, so let's change that. Remember the handle name you were to think about? Here is where it comes into play. Set your new handle, and let's start exploring the app.

Once you're logged in, you'll be taken to the homepage. That is where you edit your profile with the information we created earlier and your profile pic. To edit, tap "Me" in the bottom right corner > "Edit Profile." Now you can change your TikTok picture profile. This can be a static image or a video. When it comes to a picture profile, the best practice is to use something that aligns with your handle name, the bio, and what your brand represents. The next thing to do is to copy-paste the bio one-liner that you came up with earlier, as well as the links you'd like to include on the account profile. You can also add your Instagram and YouTube accounts if you want. Once you're happy with the account set up, you're ready to create your first TikTok. Let's go.

Filming your TikTok

Step one. Tap the + button icon at the bottom of the screen. As soon as it opens, it will be in selfie mode.

Step two. Choose video length and template. Under the record button, you have the options of 60s or 15s, depending on how long you want the content to be. The templates give you TikTok's premade video templates in case you don't want to start from scratch. For those who will have the option to go live once they meet the criteria, this is also where the button will be that will enable you to start a live broadcast.

Step three. Next to the record button, you also have the "Effects" icon that lets you access TikTok's built-in video effects. Tapping that will open up a long line of AR filters and other special effects that can augment your face or your surroundings. Don't feel pressured to use any video effects, but I will tell you that using these can make your video fun and appealing to a new audience. Let people see that fun side of your personality. Certain effects are usually trending on TikTok. I recommend spending some time daily on your "For You" page to see which ones look best. You can add an effect before or after you've filmed your video, but there are a few that you can only get before shooting. Play around with this to familiarize yourself.

Step four. TikTok is famous for its music library. Sound matters a lot on this app. Every trending or viral content has a great sound, so you need to invest some time figuring out your sounds. To do this, tap the "Sounds" icon, and you'll be able to browse different categories like trending, top 40, and viral sounds.

Pro tip:

Instead of wasting time trying to figure out what sound to use, go to your For You page, find the sound you like, and then tap "Add to Favorites" to save for later or tap "Use this Sound" to use immediately.

Step five. Film or upload your video

Now it's time to either hit record or upload a previously recorded video. Make sure the content delivers value and that you're happy with it. Then it's time to decide how you'll edit. Some content creators will use the features provided by TikTok, while other use external editing tools. For in-app videos, there are several features to play with. All features are located on the right-hand of the screen. Flip the camera to either be in selfie or subject mode, change the speed of your video, film in slow motion or speed it up from 0.3x to 3x, turn on the "Beauty" filter to smoothen out skin and give a nice glow, select the timer option to turn on an auto-record countdown so you can film hands-free and on and on. There's quite a bit to play with here. Once you've chosen the desired settings, you can hit record.

If you'd like different shots in each video or if you wish to record in sections, simply hold the record button for each segment, let go, and then press again for your next shot.

For pre-recorded content, simply upload content by tapping the "Upload" button in the bottom right. You can repurpose specific content from your device and even adjust your clips' length or select multiple videos.

Kick-Off Your Content!

Before making your video live to the audience, you'll want to do some light editing and consider a few best practices. As soon as you finish recording or uploading your segments, hit the checkmarks to switch to TikTok's video editor. That's where you can add text, adjust video clips, record voiceovers, and more. Some best practices here include:

• Adding text

Adding some text to your video provides additional context to your viewer. Tap the "Text" button on the bottom of the screen, where you'll get the option to choose from a variety of font colors and styles. You can also set text duration and use the sliding scale to decide when you want the text to appear or disappear on your video.

- Record voiceover

You have the ability to custom voice over your video by tapping the record button to record audio for your video. These are great if you're shooing a tutorial or educational content. Uncheck "Keep original sound" if you'd like the voiceover to be the only audio on your TikTok video.

- Edit video clips and volume

You can apply unique voice filters to your audio, for example, electronic or shake. You can also adjust the volume of both your added and original sound by tapping the Volume button. This could be helpful if you messed up some parts of your audio.

- Add sounds, stickers, effects, and filters

Just like on Instagram, you can add any filters, stickers, GIFs, and effects that you like. It's your chance to share more of your brand personality. If you didn't add sounds yet, now is the time to pick a tune that will boost your video content. Once you're happy, click Next.

It's time to kick off your first TikTok video. Tap "Next" in the bottom right corner, and you'll be redirected to the final page, where you can add a caption, hashtags, and even tag others. Don't skip over this part because your marketing strategy depends on writing great captions and using the right hashtags.

The captions:

On TikTok, you can write up to 150 characters, including any hashtags you want to add. Your captions should be compelling, short, and complimentary to your video. You can also include some key phrases or keywords that tell TikTok exactly whom to put your video in front of.

The hashtags:

We will be talking more about hashtags in this book, but for now, I want you to realize that picking specific hashtags that your ideal audience is probably searching for is the right approach.

The more niched down, the easier it will be for people to discover your content. Make sure they relate to the content in the video.

The cover photo:

This is one of the last things you'll want to choose but make sure it's done intentionally. The cover photo is what shows up on your TikTok profile, so it's essential to select something eye-catchy. You can also add some text to encourage your audience to click on the video.

Chapter 05: Getting More Views

On any social media platform, getting views on your content is significant. It shows social proof that you are someone of value and your brand has been accepted in that particular community. So, it should come as no surprise that TikTok and Twitch require some clever thinking in order for you to gather as many views on your videos as possible. If you've pushed out some content and you're wondering how to start increasing video views, this chapter is for you.

Keep Your Friends Close

The most important thing you can do once you start posting content is to engage in the community. Posting a video is only half the job. The other is getting proactive and connecting with people in TikTok and other social media platforms where you have an existing audience. If you have zero followers online, keep your focus on interacting with other accounts that are putting out great content and leveraging your phone book and offline social circles. That includes friends, family, old schoolmates, and anyone you regularly connect with.

The more invested you can be in engaging your followers, the easier it will be to retain their attention and attract new people. Accounts where no one responds to comments struggle to have high engagement because other users see it as a sign that the owner doesn't really care. The bottom line is that when it comes to audience engagement, people need to know you genuinely care about connecting with them and not just promoting your brand.

Here are a few tips on how to boost TikTok views:

#1: Find other brands to comment and engage with

If you're just starting out, this should be part of your daily routine. The more you engage with existing users and their brands, the more known you become. Open up a Google sheet and do some research to find the top ten accounts that align with your brand and have a healthy audience engagement. Remember to choose a brand that shares a similar audience to the one you want to serve. Then be generous with your time and insights. Comment on their content where relevant, ask questions, interact and offer your ideas with other users to build more engagement for that account. As you do this in a non-promotional way, people will start to notice you and might be inclined to check out who you are.

#2: Use proper tags

When used correctly, hashtags can give you incredible results for your TikTok viewership. You need to add a handful of relevant hashtags that tell more about your video genre. To do this, use the symbol "#" followed by a phrase or keyword related to the video. Whenever users search for or come across that keyword, they will be directed to your video content, thus increasing your video's visibility and views.

#3: Collaborate with friends

If you're just starting out, it won't be easy to get existing influencers to collaborate with you. That will come with time and reputation. But you can always form collaborations with your friends. Even if both of you have small followings, you're still doubling your viewer list by creating content and posting it to each of your accounts. Make sure, however, that the content you make is well thought out and beneficial for both audiences. Try to make it as interactive and exciting as possible.

#4: Post multiple times a day

Unlike most other social media platforms where posting more than once becomes spammy, these platforms promote you more when you actively post. Users on TikTok are accustomed to seeing lots of action from their content creators. By consistently posting at least twice a day, people will feel a sense of connection with your brand, and that will lead to more engagement and viewing of your content. It shows you're serious about your work on the platform and sets you on the path of becoming a TikTok influencer.

#5: Create original and high-value videos.

This cannot be emphasized strongly enough. You need great content. It must be high quality and purposeful otherwise, you'll drown in the ocean of TikTok videos. Instead of copy-pasting, stealing, or even mimicking other people, invest some time making authentic videos that mean something to you. That way, when users come across it, they can sense you have a lot more to offer. That's how they'll keep coming back for more.

#6: Ask questions or make a quiz video

Another way to get more views for your video is to create interactive content. Most of the content on TikTok is passive, whereby the audience simply watches and gets entertained. You could spin your content differently by regularly creating quiz videos, polls, and even posing questions and inviting them to share their answers either by commenting or shooting their own video. It's an excellent way for users to voice their opinion and for you to land more views and followers. Just make sure the questions are relevant to your brand and the interests of your ideal audience.

Pro tip: Ask open-ended questions so that people feel engaged and loved. You can also ask questions around their interests or what they would like to learn about. That might also help you create better content in the future.

#7: Create challenges and participate as well.

People love participating in TikTok challenges. By creating your own challenge or participating in those already initiated by others, you can increase your videos' views. It helps launch you as an active member of the community and a creator in your own right.

Keep Your Enemies Even Closer

To compliment audience engagement and your commitment to connect and build a connection with new and potential followers, we also need to talk about strategic ways for you to measure what's working, so you don't waste time on things that don't. That's where benchmarking comes in. Benchmarking is a tool that can be used to measure your performance. It's a tool you can use to figure out what's working, what you need to do more, and what you must stop doing. This process involves establishing best practices, evaluating your position within your niche and on the TikTok platform, and creating a strategy to ensure you stand out from your competitors. So that means you will need to dig into what your competitors are doing to make sure you're doing it even better. This shouldn't be confused with competitor research. While competitive analysis is nice to do and mainly attempts to mirror what others are doing, it is, for the most part, a quick-fix attempt that some might even consider spying. Benchmarking, however, is continuous and is essential if you want to maintain a competitive edge amongst your peers. It's about keeping your focus on the audience you're serving and figuring out what they love best and what they need, not just copy-pasting everything your competitor does. For example, if you realize your competitor is fast at creating videos and usually focuses on producing trending content to leverage that hashtag, but they also have evergreen content that does reasonably well, you don't just want to start copying their trending videos approach. Instead, you're going to dig deeper and observe the content that gets the most engagement and what the audience seems to enjoy more. Perhaps with the trendy videos, they do get more views because of the hashtag, but you might realize that there are more comments with evergreen content. In that case, it would make more sense to invest time creating high-value evergreen content similar to the top performers because the audience clearly shows they want more of that stuff.

In order for you to set the right benchmarks, especially if new to social media, here are a few things you need to do:

• Create a process for yourself if you don't already have one. This will help you recognize gaps as you build your audience and post content.

• Develop a way to plan, monitor, and measure your content so that down the line, you will have something to reference as you establish your new benchmarks.

• Write down benchmarking objectives and scope.

• Decide on the primary metrics you're going to monitor. What will you measure? How will you know you're growing? What does success look like for you?

• Identify research sources and initiate data gathering so you can have a different reference point that will enable you to spot the gaps in your growth.

If you're wondering how to find data that you can use for your process, not to worry, here's a 2020 benchmark report by Conviva that shares helpful insights on how top brands are utilizing the platform and what those efforts reap: (https://www.conviva.com/research/conviva-TikTok-guide/) The report is over thirty pages long and delves deep into sports, television and other big brands but here's an overview that might give you some inspiration.

#1: The top 20 sports media accounts average 1.6 million followers. They also average 61,231,565 likes. Each of these accounts has posted an average of 535 videos on TikTok, with an average of 109,162 likes per video as a result.

#2: The top 20 television accounts average 1.5 million followers. They average 17,714 likes on average and have posted 222 videos on average as well. Their average likes per video are 135,610.

#3: The top 20 pro sports leagues account average of 1.2 million followers. They average 20,300,886 likes in total. These accounts have posted an average of 629 videos, and they have an average of 70,421 likes per video.

#4: The top 20 news and media accounts average 750 000 followers. They average 754 followers with a total of 12,301,922 likes on average. Each of these accounts has posted an average of 248 videos, and they have 49,181 likes per video on average.

Understanding what best practices are and how top brands are performing can help guide you on the kind of benchmarking objectives to have. If you're going after a smaller niche, get the top ten performers on TikTok and find the average total likes, the average number of videos, and the average number of likes for each video. That should get you started on the right path.

Trends on TikTok matter

Unlike any other social media, trends are a big deal. Both individuals and company brands should pay attention and participate whenever possible. It's an excellent opportunity to seamlessly end up on someone's feed, build that initial connection, and make your presence known without being too pushy. When you follow the latest trend on TikTok, it literally expands your brand's reach. Why? Because TikTok's algorithm gives preferences to trending videos. Besides, users enjoy exploring various interpretations of an ongoing trend. They'll often binge-watch video after video of new accounts and people they've never heard of just because they care about that particular trend. That can quickly lead to the discovery of your brand and new followers.

If you're not a fan of the term "trend," then think of it as getting into the ongoing conversation. By participating, you tap into the algorithm. It gives you that credibility within the community that you are "one of them" and your account is relevant. In marketing speak, it's a top-of-funnel awareness that is critical when looking to grow a brand that ultimately drives revenue. While it's difficult to drive sales through trends, it's a lot easier to drive awareness, engagement and to be crowned "the cool brand" when you ride trends on TikTok.

The most recommended trends on TikTok:

- Dances
- Sounds
- TikTok challenges
- Songs

TikTok Challenges

TikTok challenges can be organic or paid. They are usually a combination of three elements: Text, sound, and movement (usually a choreographed dance). Anyone can start a TikTok challenge, but the most successful ones are often from individuals with many followers, influencers, or brands that have invested in TikTok advertising.

The key to an excellent TikTok challenge is the sound. There are many cool sounds on the platform, but you can also create and upload your own sound or find ones uploaded by influencers and other TikTokers. Most of the sounds on TikTok are pulled from movies, viral YouTube videos, and music, including chart-topping hits and indie songwriters.

Innovative businesses and aspiring influencers usually find popular existing TikTok challenges to jump into so they can ride that wave and gain new followers and potential customers. All they need to do is create a high-quality video based on a trending challenge.

Remember to think outside the box and get creative with your concept if you choose to do this. It needs to be really entertaining to grab the audience's attention. If you're participating in an organic TikTok challenge, make sure to use the same audio clip as other challenge videos.

How to identify what's in and what's out:

#1: Spend time daily on the app

You need to be using the app to figure out the best trends. That first-hand experience is priceless and will enable you to participate in things that are authentic to your brand. Scroll through your feed, explore the For You page and pay attention to everything you see and hear.

#2: Investigate causes or topics you like

Are you into sustainability or recycling? Then do a quick search to see if there's a demand for that topic and whether something is trending that you could join. You should also check out current social and cultural events to see what's what. For example, there was a lot of content related to Black Lives Matter and the COVID-19 pandemic. Countless TikTok trends emerged from these social issues. If they resonate with your brand and you have something to share, that's your cue.

#3: Research the music

By this, I mean finding music that is being played a lot on the platform. The For You page is perhaps the best to help you identify which music is trending. If you hear the same song over and over again, that's a signal you shouldn't ignore. See if you can create your own interpretation or remix of the music or perhaps integrate it into your content. As long as it aligns, go ahead and do it.

#4: Explore someone else's TikTok

Since we know how specialized TikTok is, your For You page might become limiting because you will only see trends based on prior behavior. Get a friend's phone or a family member to share their For You page. You might be shocked to discover trends you'd never encounter on your own.

Nothing Beats Consistency

A question many content creators ask is, "how often should I post to become successful on TikTok?" The answer is simple: As often as you can, create high-quality content. If you can only make one great content a day, then post one epic content daily. If you can create more, then I recommend posting between 1 - 3 times per day.

Here's the big secret, though. You need to be consistent with your content creation and posting. Sporadic, unpredictable posting will work against your efforts of becoming an influencer. People need to get accustomed to seeing new stuff from you either daily or multiple times a day. This may sound like it's too much, but you need to realize that many of the millions of active monthly users on TikTok are creating content as well. That means you're competing on a daily basis with users who are just as hungry for success as you are.

By picking a posting frequency and committing to it, you give your audience something consistent to look forward to. Think about your own preference. Don't you prefer following accounts that regularly publish fresh content? Have you ever followed someone you really liked on social media who then suddenly disappeared and stopped posting? If you're like me, that feels very disappointing, and it definitely alters the authority you once gave that person. That's why you should be consistently posting on TikTok so that as new followers come, they get a daily reminder that you're a worthwhile and authoritative content creator. And it keeps you top of mind with your already existing follower base.

When should you post?

You need to experiment with this to identify what your niche audience prefers but based on benchmarks and market surveys, we can assume the best times to start testing are Tuesdays at 9am, Thursdays at 12 noon, and Fridays at 5 am. If you're posting on Saturdays, consider doing it at 11 am, 7 pm, or 8 pm. On Sundays, the best times to post are 7 am or 8 am in the morning and 4 pm in the evening.

Keep your video content interesting.

If you want to stand out from the crowd and amass a large, engaged following, you need to earn that attention. The content you create will determine how people perceive you and how quickly you can rise to influencer status. Do me a favor, head over to your TikTok account right now, and search for Zach King, Will Smith, The Rock, or Gary Vee. Notice how different all these accounts are. But the one thing they all have in common is that they produce high-quality content-rich with substance that their audiences find extremely interesting. Now, these guys have teams helping them and enough of a marketing budget to go high-end with their production. But that doesn't mean you can't create something your audience finds equally attractive.

The first thing you must do is decide that your account will not have useless posts. Never post something for the sake of maintaining consistency. Once you've committed, it's time to get serious about creating your content strategy so that you never run out of ideas. For your audience to see your account as enjoyable, you need to make fun, easy to interact with videos tailormade to your niche. In other words, unless you are a professional magician launching your career, don't worry about being perfect. Don't worry about complex concepts. Instead, learn from many of these successful social influencers and the many stories I already shared of regular individuals who passionately share their journey as they learn and do silly, simple, fun activities.

Let's revisit one of the most successful TikTok challenges - Chipotle's #GuacDance Challenge. On a platform like TikTok, where hashtags and challenges dominate, this brand did exceptionally well and set new records with a simple campaign. The dance challenge involved the Guacamole Song from children's entertainer Dr. Jean. All people had to do was share a dance inspired by their favorite Avocado topping! How simple is that? And yet, it worked. Over 250,000 submissions!

The less serious you are on TikTok, the better. People want to see your personality and "humanness" than your status or pro skills. That's one of the things that makes this platform unique. Instead of trying to be perfect, think instead about your audience and what they find interesting, then align it with your brand values.

Some of the ways you can create exciting content:

• Create content for your audience

It doesn't matter how much you love a particular topic. If no one else is interested in it, you won't go very far because the marketplace will reject you. To increases the chances of showing up on the For You page and to continue attracting new followers, think about your audience. What would your ideal follower like to see and share with his friends? Once you have some followers, get into the habit of regularly creating polls to help you learn what they are interested in watching.

• Trigger emotions

Social media is all about getting emotional and personal. When you can spark strong emotional reactions from your users, your content is likely to perform better. Many studies show that emotions like happiness, sorrow, anger, and gratitude have the power to engage people and make them share digital content. But use this technique wisely and make sure it's aligned with your brand values.

• Add a little humor

If you like being funny or enjoy adding humor to your life, bring that to your content. Your brand is serious, but your content on TikTok doesn't have to be. Funny videos grab users' attention and promise you a fair portion of shares, so if this is a strength of yours, lean into it some more.

Chapter 06: The Blue Check Mark

The coveted blue checkmark. Ah, how glorious the search for this symbol of social stardom and influence. There's no denying, it is an excellent boost for your brand and makes you appear more legit and authentic. But do you understand the psychology behind it? Sure, there's the fact that having a blue checkmark helps protect you from impersonators and people stealing your precious work. Besides that, everyone wants it (who isn't a movie star, celebrity, pro athlete, or big brand) because of perceived value. By having this blue badge, people immediately assume you're some kind of a VIP, and everyone likes to hang around important people. Psychologically, people are more inclined to follow you after watching one video if they see that checkmark.

How does one go about acquiring such a holy symbol on TikTok, and why do they have it anyway?

Verified: What is it For?

The account verification symbol is there for a simple purpose according to TikTok - they want to help users stay informed about who they are really following, especially when it comes to celebrities, professional sports teams artists, and official brand pages. They want people to know whether the account is the real deal rather than a fake or fan account. The verification badge helps to confirm that an account belongs to the user it represents. It's an essential way of creating clarity within TikTok's community to build trust among high-profile accounts and their followers. I mean, if you think about it, without the blue badge, it would be hard to tell whether the account you're following was JLo's fan club, an obsessed girl pretending to be JLo, or the real Jenny from the block. You can usually spot it next to a TikTok's user account name in search and on the profile as the coveted blue checkmark.

How are badges given?

Several factors go into getting that blue checkmark. Before we talk about the best way to get one, let's talk about the scams and tactics you should avoid:

Scam #1: Do not buy a verification badge.

This is one of the worst ways to get this blue checkmark. Not only is it illegal to buy it, but most of the options are also shady and no guaranteed to work. You might spend your money (some people charge up to $10,000) and still not get the badge.

Scam #2: Do not buy followers expecting to get verified

Having a large following doesn't automatically qualify you for a badge, especially when those followers are fake. In fact, you may have noticed some accounts get verified even though they don't have large followings or celebrity status. We'll talk about why that happens shortly, but the main point here is you cannot get away with fake followers on TikTok because the platform considers a lot more than just the number of followers you have.

The main factors that TikTok considers are whether the account is unique, active, notable, and of course, that it adheres to their community guidelines and terms of service (make sure to read those when you join the platform). That being said, you may have spotted some accounts that are verified even though they aren't owned by celebrities. Often these are accounts belonging to individuals who migrated from musical.ly. If the person had a "crown" during their time as muscial.ly users, they would likely be rewarded with that blue checkmark now that they made the switch to TikTok. The platform also tends to give the blue badge to accounts that are likely to be copied to protect the account owners and their content.

One thing TikTok wants to emphasize is that having a badge isn't a form of endorsement. Although it seems like they only give checkmarks to public figures, big brands, celebrities, and publishers, there are certain things you can do to increase the likelihood of getting verified as the real deal. By the end of this chapter, you'll learn the six steps you can take starting today.

The 3 Main Benefits of Getting Verified

Why would you want to make the needed effort to get verified?

#1: It will increase your content exposure and video views

When people come across your account on the search and spot that blue tick, they are more likely to watch your content and even click on your account to learn more about you. It comes back to that paradigm of "celebrity status" and being the chosen one by TikTok. That symbol naturally causes people to assume you're worth watching. That increases your video views as more and more people share your content. Add to that the fact that verified accounts have a priority of 1 whereas regular accounts have a priority of 0, and it's easy to see why your videos will show up more on feeds and the For You page.

#2: Generating a bigger following

The blue checkmark will generate interest from the general public with the probability of increasing followers. Why? Because that blue badge is a symbol of trustworthiness and celebrity status. It shows people that TikTok vetted you and approved you and the content you produce. This suggests to potential followers that they can expect high-quality content that is spam-free. The other aspect of this is that it increases your perceived value and importance. In other words, people assume you must be a "big deal" because you have that badge. Users are more likely to think you are worth following if you're noteworthy enough to be verified.

#3: More visibility when it comes to searches.

If your username is a common one, finding you on search will be super hard because many users may already have variations of it. But if you have the blue checkmark, you always show up at the top of the search result because you hold priority 1. As a result, you become easy to find whenever people are searching for your account. And sometimes, people will discover your account as they search for someone with a similar handle just because your account ranks higher in the TikTok search.

Ultimately, growing in this way will open up new opportunities for monetization as big brands might favor working with you instead of your competition. As a content creator, getting that "Popular creator badge" or the "verified account" badge isn't going to be easy. Still, it will be worthwhile, especially if you plan on making money through this platform. Livestreaming is one of the ways your followers and growing fans can start supporting you with "gifts" and stickers. It's also easy to establish your affiliate marketing income stream if you choose to follow that monetization path. The more people perceive you as an authority, the easier it becomes to leverage that influence and monetize it.

6 Steps To Get That Check

#1: Create a good content strategy

Don't rely on moments of insights where great content ideas come to you. Although that's great when you get inspired to create something, you should always have a solid content plan running in the background to ensure you have an abundance of content from the moment you publish the first video. A great content strategy comes from understanding your niche, what your audience wants, the best trends to jump into, and identifying themes that help establish your brand credibility. Search for top-performing hashtags in your niche, join relevant challenges and create content out of that and also, check out my list of best performing video content for video ideas to help you get started.

#2: Be consistent with your posting

Consistency is the one thing that will demonstrate to your audience and the TikTok platform that you are noteworthy. Once you have a content strategy in place, producing and publishing content daily won't be so much of a burden, especially if you use tools and software to stay organized. If you commit to publishing a TikTok daily, then do it without fail. Stick to a schedule that works with your lifestyle. Ideally, you want to do it multiple times a day (shoot for three videos) but don't put out meaningless content. If you want to rise to the influencer level, you need each video to be valuable for your audience. As people get used to expecting your videos multiple times a day, they'll interact more with your account and increase your watch time, which is super crucial for growth.

#3: Engage with other users

Equally as important as posting is actively engaging on the platform with other users and content creators. You do this by liking other people's content, leaving thoughtful comments, sharing their work, and even giving shout-outs and tagging the people you talk about in your videos.

On your own account, you need to make sure to respond to each and every comment. Make people feel valued and appreciated. You could also come up with challenges for your followers or invite them to do duets with you so you can interact more. This personal and high-level engagement will dramatically increase your account's engagement rate, and TikTok guys are bound to take notice.

#4: Demonstrate consistent and steady growth

Suppose you want to increase your chances of receiving the blue checkmark. In that case, you need to make a lot of effort toward growing the number of people who follow you daily and the amount of time users spend on your videos. A good daily aim as a beginner should be around 500 new followers each day. That will get you on the right track to influencer states and the verification badge. Eventually, you can double that. The more people follow you and watch your videos, the more growth your channel will have. If you start having views of close to a million per month in a few months, you'll definitely get noticed by TikTok. It also increases the chances of going viral with some of your content. Viral content is the main bloodline of TikTok. It demonstrates that you can create videos that will go a long way in entertaining and holding other users' attention on the platform. That's ultimately what TikTok is after - to captivate and delight their users.

#5: Get media and PR coverage

Consider creating some PR for yourself because what I noticed is that it's easier for your account to be verified if you're being featured on other well-known magazines, television, radio, etc. If you are on Forbes, CNBC, local tv, etc., it shows TikTok that you're a person of influence. That gives them a reason to elevate your position on their platform as well. You should also consider taking part in public projects or events that can help you get noticed by the media.

#6: Collaborate with others

Round up your friends or find TikTok creators in your neighborhood and collaborate on some dances or challenges. Viewers love this type of content, especially if you find the right group and create something entertaining. It also increases your chances of going viral as your content gets more exposure.

Bonus Tip: You should also consider getting verified on other social media accounts. Whether it's Facebook, Instagram, or any other platform, being verified there seems to help you get verified on TikTok. Make sure these accounts are connected to your TikTok account.

There is no straight path to getting verified, and none of us have much control over how it happens. Even if you happen to know someone who works for TikTok (like I happen to), they will tell you it's not as black and white as many of us would like. Therefore, while it is a great goal to have, don't get hung up on it. Your brand's growth and success aren't directly tied to having the blue tick. You can still become a highly popular and well-respected presence on TikTok even without the blue checkmark. So, focus on producing amazing content, engaging with your audience, and just let the rest take its natural course.

Chapter 07: Monetizing your Content

If you're new to social media and the world of online income and passive income opportunities, then you're probably still confused about how posting content on social media can equal bills paid at the end of the month. A few years ago, the only way to pay the bills was to get a regular nine-to-five job. If you want extra income, you needed to add a second shift or work two different jobs. Thanks to social media and platforms like YouTube and Facebook, people have new ways of earning extra cash and making their dreams come true. And I mean regular people! If you're wondering how this is all possible and how you jump in, this is the chapter for you.

We are going to focus on TikTok's monetization opportunities which you should know right off the bat are different from other social media platforms like YouTube. To make it work for you, a strong strategy is essential. Part of establishing a solid strategy is to realize that TikTok doesn't work like Instagram, YouTube, or any other established platform when it comes to monetization. Things are still pretty much like the wild wild west on the TikTok platform, so you need to approach it with some creativity.

There's No Ad Revenue?

TikTok doesn't have a creator ad monetization. But don't let that throw you off. Most of the money on this platform is made through the fan support you get while growing the account. The more people love you, the easier it becomes to receive donations/gifts and even open up opportunities for influencer marketing which we'll discuss shortly.

The platform isn't built explicitly around monetization and providing income streams to creators. However, it's still very commercial-friendly, and it continues to evolve. New opportunities for generating income are popping up each day. Unlike YouTube, this platform doesn't exactly offer monetization of their videos through placement ads, but that doesn't mean you can't make lots of money on this thing. Suppose you want to get paid on TikTok. In that case, you're going to have to diversify your monetization sources and get TikTok brand deals. We will go through the various ways you can monetize your account once you have a decent-sized following. The more followers you have on TikTok, the easier it is to generate income actively and passively. That includes getting sponsorships from brands, live streaming, referral or affiliate links, and so much more. Now, there's also the opportunity to be part of the Creator Fund.

What is the creator fund? According to TikTok, it is a fund that content creators who meet certain criteria can apply to be part of where they can earn money simply for producing excellent content. There are currently $70 million funds available to thousands of creators across the European launch markets, i.e., the United Kingdom, Germany, Italy, France, and Spain. TikTok is still raising the fund so they can continue to open up this opportunity to more European countries and reward content creators for their hard work and creativity. Of course, this is only open to a few content creators in a particular part of the world so let's not focus too much on this as a means to earn your money just yet. Instead, let's discuss the real moneymakers.

Getting Sponsorship from Brands

Sponsorship is when a brand pays you to promote and generate awareness around their products and services. It's part of influencer marketing which I talk about at length in one of my other books. On TikTok, however, there is no set standard price since the app is relatively young in the market. Neither the influencers nor the brands can accurately predict the performance of content and the results that it can yield. Therefore, although one can earn lots of money from this, it is still up for experimentation. Each creator seems to have their own way of approaching sponsored content. Take Bernath as an example. He is charging a base price with an additional "X" number of dollars per million views. For someone like him (lots of his videos go viral on TikTok, and he also has a large audience on Instagram), this price structure seems reasonable to brands. Another TikToker (Skylar) charges $25 per 25,000 followers, and that seems to work for him as well.

Can you make a lot of money through sponsored content?

Loren Gray earned $2.6 million within a year with just over 45 million followers. I think it's safe to say - you can make a ton of money on TikTok. It's possible, but not everyone will.

If you've got a big following on TikTok with a growth trend of viral videos, brands will be eager to sponsor you. But there are a couple of things you should do first. You need to stop focusing on getting brand deals and making money and instead focus on your fans. Understand the nature of the platform. People are there to genuinely connect. It's supposed to be a "real" social app. That's why there is less editing and filtering of videos. So, if you want brands to notice you, get more REAL. Be proactive with your followers, interact with them and show them that you care. Once you start growing in follower count (at least 10,000), you can start thinking about brand deals.

The other thing you need to do is create a press kit that you can offer brands when you start reaching out. Let them know about the growth of your channel, how content performs, the follower count and demographics, a list of other brands you've worked with, any case studies you might have, the specific services you offer, and a little more about yourself and why you want to work with the brand. Be creative with this press kit, and make sure it rocks!

One more tip I want to share when it comes to getting the attention of brands is to create organic (non-sponsored) content about the brands you love. Demonstrate that you have the influence and the ability to drive sales. Likes and shares are great, but if you want them to come knocking, show them that you can deliver. That's rather hard to do on TikTok because it's not yet easily mapped out like on Instagram, which is why I suggest creating content by yourself to prove that you can do it. Once you create content, upload the videos with a linked ObsessedWith.it page where your fans can shop everything you recommend. Then call out your links and encourage subscribers to buy. That will earn you commissions, and you can then use the sales records as proof to entice brands to sponsor you.

Utilizing the Ad Commerce Tool

This is a new tool that TikTok introduced first to the U.S and will continue to roll it out elsewhere, so if you're reading this and don't see the option available where you live, be patient. It's coming. But what is this ad commerce tool? It's a self-service advertising tool where users can add affiliate links to help with promoted content. You can use this tool to gain commissions from sales generated through your videos. There's also the added feature of being able to showcase goods during a Livestream so your viewers can shop in-app.

Gifts are Great! Virtual Gifts are Best!

One of the easiest ways to start generating some money is through TikTok gifts. There are several types of in-app currencies (known as gifts), and to get some, your audience must purchase TikTok coins. There are different bundle options. The bigger the bundle, the better the discount will be. I encourage you to buy some TikTok coins just to experience what your viewers will go through when they want to send you a virtual gift. Once the coins are bought, they can be exchanged for various unique virtual gifts (Panda, Italian hand, Love Band, Sun Cream, Rainbow Puke, Concert, I'm Very Rich, Drama Queen).

If your viewers enjoy your content, they can support you by sending gifts in various amounts and forms. During a live stream, everyone watching the video and the person who created it will be able to see the username of the one giving the gift and the type of gift they have given to the creator.

Once you receive the gift on TikTok, it is converted into a diamond on your profile. Diamonds are used to measure a content creator's praise and popularity and cannot be bought with money. Hint. You need to collect as many diamonds as possible.

How this ultimately turns into cash:

Diamonds turn into cash once you reach a certain threshold. The minimum withdrawal is $100, and the maximum weekly withdrawal is $1,000. Payment is usually via PayPal or one of their preferred verified payment services.

Sharing Referral Links

For most people, TikTok is just an app for kids. And that's kind of true, but there's more to this story than meets the eye. Let's do a little marketing math here. Around 40% of the overall TikTok audience is between 16 and 24 years of age. The app has approximately 800 million monthly active users spread across 155 countries. And in the United States alone, there are an estimated 80 million monthly active users. That means you have a potential audience of about 300 million (give or take a couple of hundred thousand who might be younger than 16) that can buy something from you. That's where affiliate marketing comes in. It is literally a gold mine if you're a savvy affiliate marketer and you know how to match the right product with your niche. For example, if you plan to sell home loans or B2B services, I will say this is not the platform for you. But if you're into gadgets and gizmos or fashion and beauty, TikTok users are there in abundant supply.

This is by far the best and easiest way to generate both passive and active income. Depending on the range of products you set up, you could be making anywhere from a few thousand a months to tens of thousands each month. Talk about financial freedom!

What is affiliate marketing? It's the process of selling a product you don't own for a commission or referral fee. Think about it like this: You buy a product you absolutely love and realize they usually pay a referral fee for anyone who sends the company some business. You create content for your 100,000 followers and share your experience with the product, then you tell them to go try it for themselves. Through the unique link that you share with them, many of them head over to the company's eCommerce store and make a purchase. As agreed, the company (which tracked your special link to know how many sales came through you) sends you a sweet little check at the end of 30 days or so for $10,000 as a thank you for sending over 250 new buying customers for their $50 product.

How to make money through affiliate marketing:

The most important thing is to have a big enough audience in the niche products you want to sell. You can either use organic or paid advertising. If you have a big advertising budget, then you can use the second option. For most people reading this, organic reach is the way to go. Let's see how to make that work.

With organic traffic, as long as you're pushing out great content and growing your following, you will see people clicking on your links. That's why you need to set up the following referral links:

• Add an affiliate link of the desired URL to your profile information.

• Promote a coupon code or URL in your video that sends them to the page you want people to go to.

- Add an affiliate URL to your content description.

- Redirect that TikTok traffic to another social media profile, e.g., YouTube, where you can lead them to your affiliate site.

#1: Adding an affiliate URL on your profile:

Remember, this only works if you have a business or pro account. If you want to have multiple referral links set up, then consider using Linktree.com. It's free and allows you to add as many links as you need.

Pro tip: Don't add direct affiliate links. Experience has taught me that blog posts or any other kind of valuable content performs better. So, ensure the affiliate links are contained within the content you offer in the front end.

#2: Use Coupons and Promo codes:

Many affiliated products often have discounts and promo codes that you can easily leverage to get your followers to shop through you. Using the coupon can be as simple as mentioning it in the video content or in the description.

#3: Add a URL to your description:

You will need to copy and paste the link into your video content description, so it might feel monotonous. Still, I've seen many big influencers doing it, so it makes sense to add it as well. At the very least, it increases the chances that someone will not miss getting the link to your affiliate site.

#4: Redirect people to your desired social media platform:

This isn't as straightforward, but it actually works, especially if you have a good following on the other social media platform. Suppose you have more content on the products you want people to buy. In that case, it makes sense to send people to that YouTube or Instagram channel so they can move a step closer to making that purchase as they learn to trust in your credibility. Adding a social media account is actually pretty simple. Just tap on the "Me" icon at the bottom of the screen on the app, then tap "Edit Profile" and simply add whichever profile you want.

Section 3: Dominating On Twitch

Chapter 08: What's Up with Twitch?

Twitch is the leading live streaming platform, and its growing popularity is a testament that people love watching videos, especially live videos (which is Twitch's specialty). Think YouTube but in this case, purely live videos. Most people, however, don't know about Twitch, and that's okay. This platform is dominated by gamers who host and share eSports events and challenges on the platform.

What Do I Do Here?

If you're wondering why you should consider this platform to build your influence, then perhaps realize that there are 15 million active users and growing. That means you can create a pretty healthy audience size for yourself and gain lots of influence. Combine this influence with TikTok, and you could literally have any kind of income and lifestyle you desire. But as with all social media platforms, strategy matters.

Now, if you're reading this and thinking, "I am not a gamer. This can't be for me!" That wouldn't be the first time I hear that statement, and I'm here to confirm that you don't need to be into games and sports to thrive on this platform. You can find all kinds of videos on Twitch. Recently (especially since the pandemic), more categories have started growing in popularity, especially music, cooking, creative arts, lifestyle, make-up, and DIY content.

The origins of Twitch:

Twitch started as a spin-off of Justin TV back in 2011, and as it grew in subscribers, Amazon decided to purchase it around 2014 for $340 million. The platform is designed to help content creators demonstrate their skills, connect with their audience in real-time, build niche communities, and, oh yes, make money doing something they love. On the platform, creators are known as "Streamers," so you'll see me use that term a lot in this section. There are many ways to make money on Twitch but before we get to that, let's cover the basics of how it works and why you should join today.

From Hobbies to Social Experience

Not a fan of MMO-style games or any gaming adventures for that matter? No problem, there's plenty of room for you to explore, share and grow a tightly-knit community around your hobbies, especially if you love music, talk shows, travel, arts, and food. Are you a musician or starting a local teen band? Twitch can be great for enabling you to share your passion with the world. You just need a little creativity and take into consideration what your fans would be interested in seeing. Perhaps you could Livestream band rehearsals, practice sessions, behind the scenes working in the studio, jams, and improv sessions with other artists, or you could do some live Q&A. If you're a DJ, consider live streaming during your mix and scratch practice. Think along the same lines if you're passionate about cooking, art, doing make-up, and so on.

A good rule of thumb is to approach live streaming as something you would do anyway but with the added benefit of sharing it with your niche tribe. Of course, as you Livestream, you will need to engage and interact with the audience, but we'll cover that shortly.

But Why Twitch?

The biggest reason Twitch live streaming is so appealing (aside from the obvious monetary opportunities that come with it) is that it enables you to have an immediate brand to audience engagement. In most other platforms, you will create content, but there's no real-time engagement, so in many ways, you're working with a monologue instead of a dialogue. When it comes to live streaming, however, the dialogue is immediate. With every live streaming effort, you make people show up, and they interact with you and give you instant feedback. It makes you have that real sense that you are doing all this work for "real people," which is easy to forget on other social media platforms. That live chatting, commenting, and feedback is very reassuring and motivating for a new content creator.

The other thing you get is that sense of freedom of reaching and building a real-time connection with anyone anywhere. Your location doesn't matter at all. You could be broadcasting from your tiny bedroom of your small town that none of us ever heard of, and yet we would all come to know and love you and your content. All you need is internet access. You can also create as much content as you like. Demand is always there for more videos. In fact, in the United States alone, the number of digital video viewers is expected to top 232 million over the next few years. Half a billion people are already watching videos on Facebook daily, and according to networking giant Cisco, live video will account for 13% of all video traffic by 2121.

How Do Algorithms Work?

Twitch holds an ocean of "live" content, which by default makes it more chaotic and harder to sort out since everything happens in real-time. Still, compared to YouTube and Facebook, the algorithm seems to be pretty straightforward. Maybe too simple? There have been many complaints from streamers who felt the platform favors larger channels, making it hard for smaller ones to grow in terms of audience and revenue. But things have shifted a lot recently.

Previously it was only listed highest to lowest number of views. Now they're a bit more sophisticated on the platform with the "recommended for you" feature helping users find the streamers who are currently live that are similar to the people the audience already follow and watch regularly. I suppose it makes sense to have a totally different algorithm because it focuses on "live" content. So, the best thing to do is to show viewers the best options they have as soon as they log in. Their main aim is to help viewers stumble upon the right channel and the right community at the right moment when the streaming is going on.

To do this, Twitch uses a form of machine learning that lets the machine work out for itself what viewers are interested in. The system is directed toward certain "features" of streams that we mentioned earlier in the book (audience chat and engagement, etc.) and uses it to determine how important the content is. The more people chat in the channel, the more the algorithm will push for more people interested in the same category to join in and catch the live stream. The AI often categorizes a channel either as "chatty" or "not chatty" and determines which viewer to recommend which channel to as soon as the user logs in. It also takes into account time lapse. If the streamer has been on for a while and you log in, you're likely to be recommended someone who is just starting their streaming or one who is just a few minutes in. In other words, it tries to match the timing of the viewer and the streamer.

Viewers versus Followings versus Subscriptions: There's A Difference

A viewer is a person who watches your Livestream. This person can be a first-time visitor, a follower, or a subscriber. A follower is someone who consciously chooses to support your channel by following you. There is a purple icon with a heart at the top of your channel whenever you stream content. If a viewer finds you, watches for a little while, and decides they like your stuff, they can show their support by clicking on that heart which turns them into a follower.

If they really want to show your support and take things to the next level, then the follower can turn into a subscriber. Subscription is a much higher form of support because it involves financial investment. In fact, subscriptions are one of the ways streamers make money on Twitch. When a person subscribes to your channel, they essentially agree to make a monthly payment on Twitch, of which you will get a cut. In turn, the subscriber would receive special benefits that aren't available to followers of the channel. Your subscribers will have various options to choose from. Tier 1 is $4.99/month, Tier 2 is $9.99/month, Tier 3 is $24.99/month.

Chapter 09: Setting Up Your Studio

Before you can start streaming on Twitch, building an audience, and generating income, you'll need to set up your Twitch account and your studio. The actual streaming aspect is pretty straightforward, but the initial setup will require some effort and careful planning. If you haven't done so already, head over to Twitch's official website, click the purple "Sign Up" icon in the upper-right corner, enter your desired login credentials, and hit the button at the bottom. Once that's done, you can click your username in the top-right corner for access. Before you start producing content, I recommend reading the Twitch community guidelines to familiarize yourself with acceptable conduct.

Streaming on Twitch is possible on several devices, including PC, Mac, Tablet, Xbox One, PS4, among others. Let's take a look at the most recommended ones.

Which Device Should You Focus On?

- *Streaming from a PlayStation 4*

PS4 is one of the simplest devices to use for a Livestream. You don't need any external or additional software, and you could even use a PlayStation camera as the microphone and "facecam" for all your broadcasts. That simplifies the number of equipment needed to set up your studio. Here's what to do:

First, you need to play a game.

Open the game you plan on streaming before changing any broadcast settings. Once you've launched the game, press the "Share" button next to the touchpad on your PS4 controller to open up your broadcast settings.

Next, you should change settings to your preference and then start streaming! Select "Broadcast gameplay," and you'll see an option to stream via three different streaming services. Select

Twitch, and the service will provide you with a streaming key. Then, go to twitch.tv/activate and enter the key. Your PS4 should be ready to start streaming in a few minutes.

From the "Broadcast gameplay" menu, you can also change your stream's title if you like, adjust the quality, and choose whether to use your camera and/or microphone.

Note: If you have a PlayStation Camera and want to use it, make sure it's plugged in and check to ensure it hasn't been automatically muted from the quick menu on your console. Otherwise, you won't be able to use it once you start streaming.

If you're satisfied with the settings, press "Start broadcasting" and share your passion with the world.

• *Streaming from Xbox One.*

This option is just as easy as PS4, but you will need to take care of a few more technical issues. For instance, if you want to have a "facecam," legacy Xbox One owners can use the Xbox Kinect. You need the Kinect because it's the one that is compatible with Xbox One's Twitch app. Once you have it, pair it with a headset s you can record your voice because Kinect's microphone isn't that reliable. It often cuts out intermittently during streaming, so having a separate headset plugged in usually solves this problem.

The first thing to do is launch your game. Just like with PS4, you need to load up a game before starting the stream. Install and open the Twitch app and sign in with your credentials. You'll then receive a unique stream key to gain access. Activate this key at twitch. tv/activate on either your mobile device or computer. Twitch immediately detects the game when it starts the stream, which will make it more discoverable for potential audience members.

The next step is to edit your stream's title and quality level before you go live. You can also move your Kinect's camera display to one of the corners of the screen. Finally, click on "Start Broadcast" to commence streaming. You'll see a display count at the bottom of your screen showing the number of viewers watching the game.

• *Streaming from PC or Mac*

Streaming from Windows or Mac OS is trickier than the first two options because most systems don't come with any sort of built-in software for gaming. If you have the budget, consider getting subscription-based products like XSplit, which helps you control every aspect of your broadcast. For beginners, however, the best starting place is to download Open Broadcast Software (OBS). It's a free software that works with both Windows and Mac OS.

Another option for beginners, if you don't want a hassle with the setup, is to use the Twitch Studio app, which is currently only available on Windows. Assuming you want to settle for OBS, here's what to do.

The first step is to download OBS.

First, click on your username in the main Twitch interface and hit the "Creator Dashboard" link. Locate the three bars in the top left border of the screen to reveal a drop-down menu with a list of other options you can choose from. Look for the "Streaming Tools" option. That will take you to a page with several download links to various streaming applications like OBS. Find OBS in the list and click down or simply head to their main website, where you can choose the version you need to download.

The second step is to set up your streaming. Click the "Output" tab after clicking on "Settings" in OBS and ensure that your video bitrate is set to about 2,500. That should allow you to stream content at 720p, but you can increase this number if you want to broadcast at a higher resolution. You should set the audio bitrate at 128. If you're running Nvidia graphics card that's a few years old, you can make use of the built-in NVENC encoder. Otherwise, you'll want to stick with OBS's default software x264 encoder. Once you're happy with the settings, click "Apply" to confirm and save changes.

The next thing to do is to enter your stream key.

For this, you'll need to go back to the creator dashboard, click on "Preferences," and then select the "Channel" option from the drop-down menu. That will take you to a page with your Primary Stream Key as well as other options. Find the stream key area and then press the copy button next to it. If the stream key gets shared somewhere else unintentionally, you can always reset it here. Now, take that stream key and paste it into OBS by clicking "Settings" in the bottom right, then "Stream." Once done, click "Apply" to save changes.

Now it's time to set up your game and plug in your microphone. Take a look at the Audio Mixer area in OBS. It should already have at least the volume bar set up for your desktop. In OBS, locate the "Settings" button in the bottom-right area of the application. That will open up a window where you can navigate down to the Audio tab. This is where you can add or remove audio devices as needed. Ensure the Desktop Audio is set to the correct piece of hardware and then locate the Mic/Aux audio options. Once that's done, open the game you want to stream and take a look at the Sources menu towards the bottom of OBS. Find the + button at the bottom, and it should reveal a list of items when clicked. The easiest way to capture gameplay is to use the "Display Capture" option. That allows you to capture an entire desktop screen. If you want to avoid sharing too much of your screen, consider selecting the "Game Capture" option.

Finally, you are ready to stream your game. Hit the "Start Streaming" button in the main OBS screen, and you'll instantly begin broadcasting from your Twitch account. When done, click on Stop Streaming.

Completing Your PC (For Those Who Need It)

Now that you know how to set up your live streaming on Twitch, let's talk about the different options you have available if you'd like to do it through a PC but don't currently own a good one. You see, when it comes to PC, you will need to invest in a high-quality one if you want a truly immersive gaming experience. If your budget allows, then you could always just buy one, but for those who can't afford to blow their money on something expensive, here's an affordable alternative. Build your own PC.

The amount of money you spend on the computer parts will vary depending on the purpose and your budget. If your primary intent is to spend as little money as possible, you need to match a store-bought desktop or laptop's performance. If your main intent is to get a high-performing beast without breaking the bank, then you'll need to go for the best possible performance in all of your PC components. In that case, you should expect to spend a little more money, but the result will be a powerful PC.

If you're hesitant because you worry it might be too hard, don't worry. I got you covered. Let's run through the equipment you will need and how to go about building a great PC without going broke.

What you need to build a PC:

• Motherboard

It is the first component to think about. The motherboard dictates your PC's build (physical form factor and size), and it also determines what other pieces of hardware your computer will need. Your motherboard's choice establishes the power of the processor it can handle, the memory technology (DDR4, DDR3, DDR2, etc.), and the number of modules that can be installed. It also determines the storage form factor (2.5-inch, mSATA, or m.2) and storage interface (SATA or PCle).

• Central Processing Unit (CPU)

The CPU is the engine of your computer. It sets the performance expectation for the entire build. Memory and storage fuel the processor, which controls every data transaction within the PC. When you're determining which CPU to install, pay attention to the gigahertz (GHz). The higher the GHz, the faster your processor. However, more GHz also means the CPU will consume more energy, leading to higher system temperatures that require better airflow or heat dissipation within the computer, so that's something you must consider.

• Memory (RAM)

The third important aspect is choosing your RAM. Adding memory is the easiest and fastest way to amplify your computer's performance. It gives your system more space to temporarily store data that's being used. Almost all computer operations rely on memory, including having several tabs open while streaming your content, typing and composing an email, multitasking between applications, and even moving your mouse cursor. To say that you need to pick the right RAM is an understatement. The more things you're doing with your PC, the more memory you need. Even background processes like system updates can draw from your RAM. Consider these two things: compatibility and how much RAM your system can support before choosing the best RAM.

You want to make sure you've identified the kind of module your system uses by identifying the form factor (the physical form of the module - generally desktops use UDIMMs, laptops use SODIMMs) then figure out the memory technology (DDR4, DDR3, DDR2, etc.) that your system supports. When it comes to figuring out how much RAM your system can handle, think about the kind of system you're building. If you buy 64GB of RAM and your computer can only handle 16GB, you're essentially wasted 48GB because regardless of how big the RAM is, your computer will not utilize it past its limit. So, in other words, know your limits before choosing the memory.

- Storage

Your files and data are saved long-term on your storage drive. This data is either on a hard disk drive (HDD) or a solid-state drive (SDD). Hard drives generally offer more storage space, but solid-state drives are essentially the in-thing because they are faster and more energy-efficient. SSDs are, on average, six times faster and ninety times more energy efficient. Why? Because hard drives use mechanical moving parts and spinning platters, whereas SSDs use NAND flash technology.

- Case, Fans and Power Supply

The materials you choose to use here will depend on the kind of computer you're building. If you're creating a high-powered performance workhorse, you'll need a robust power supply to make it run efficiently. You'll also need optimal internal airflow and fans to expel hot air that could potentially damage the system. Buy some Zip ties to help manage the cables inside your rig and consolidate the cables as that will improve airflow.

Tips for building your PC:

The exact process of setting up your PC will vary depending on the Owner's Manual, so I recommend following the instructions diligently. The act of installation isn't complicated, but there is the potential for errors. That's why you must stick to the detailed step-by-step instructions. I also encourage you to wear an electrostatic discharge (ESD) wrist strap to protect your system's components from the static electricity that's naturally present in your body. Alternatively, you can ground yourself frequently by touching an unpainted metal surface. It's also helpful to keep a can of compressed air to remove any dust or fine debris from the interface as you install the processor, memory, and SSD.

- Tips for installing the memory.

The easiest hardware to install is the RAM. Locate the memory slots on the motherboard, hold the memory modules on the side to avoid touching the chips and gold pins. Then align the notches on the module with the ridge in the slot and firmly press the module until it clicks.

- Tips for installing the HDD or SSD

If you're looking for lots of memory at a lower cost, then a hard drive is probably your best option. The kind of SSD you purchase may require a specific installation procedure, so again, read the instruction manual. Still, in almost all cases, it involves attaching the drive to the storage interface, then fitting it into the drive bay.

If you followed the instructions for installation from your provider perfectly, your system should be ready to launch in no time. Hit the power button and make sure the monitor and keyboard are connected to the PC. You should see a screen appear where you can enter the system BIOS. If you have a disc or flash drive with an operating system (OS), put it into the appropriate drive, boot up, and you can install the OS. Congratulations, you are now the proud owner of your new PC! Let the gaming sessions begin!

What's Gonna Be the Setup on Console?

If you'd like to stream gameplay from your console, there are a couple of things you must know. First, some consoles like Nintendo Switch just don't have native streaming apps like the earlier mentioned Xbox and PlayStation, so the only way to do a Livestream is to use a capture card.

A capture card is a physical device that links your console with your PC and a TV, allowing you to stream your game into a piece of software like OBS, XSplit, or Elgato Game Capture. The software then broadcasts or records your gameplay and audio to Twitch.

There are many capture cards that you can choose from, but the most recommended is the Elgato HD60S. It's cheap and works wonderfully. The installation is also pretty fast and self-explanatory. It's also worth noting that some games on PlayStation can be blocked from streaming and recording. Many companies like Atlas (Persona 5) and Bandai Namco (Dragonball series) have included in-game functions that stop their titles from being streamed after a specific time period. Unfortunately, you won't know when that happens until after. Since you cannot disable this feature, it's best to find a more sustainable solution for your streaming, especially if you want to make this a full-time career.

If you'd like to use your computer set up to stream on Twitch, there are some recommendations to consider.

- Your CPU Intel Core should be at least i5-4670

- Your memory should be minimum of 8GB DDR3 SDRAM

- Your operating system should be Windows 7 Home Premium or newer

By going for the setup of a capture card, keep in mind you will also require the additional investment of a PC. The Elgato costs more than $100 at retail and depending on whether you buy or build your own PC, you could potentially spend several hundreds of dollars (if not a few thousand) just to set up your streaming.

The 3 Essential Gears To Invest In

In a world of countless livestreams, you want to set yourself apart on Twitch because of the content your produce and the look and feel of the content. That's why you need to invest in these three must-have pieces of equipment:

#1: Video Camera

Twitch audiences enjoy watching both the game in session and the streamer playing the game so investing in a good quality webcam is necessary. Whether you're celebrating a victory, engaging with viewers, or throwing a full-blown rage fit, your growing audience will keep coming back for more when they can see you in high quality without interfering with the view of the game. Hook up a camera, and you can pull its feed into your chosen software and overlay the game stream.

Consider getting a Logitech Streamcam (1080p, 60FPS). It has autofocus abilities and a multitude of settings to make your studio set up top-notch. You can use it in both landscape and portrait mode. Mount it on a tripod or on top of your monitor, and you're good to go.

An alternative to using a webcam would be getting a DSLR (e.g., Elgato Cam) or any other digital camera you fancy.

#2: Audio

You definitely need a high-quality microphone and pre-amp set up for your streaming. Any streamer worth their salt needs a great mic to enable them to talk and engage with their audience while working their gaming magic. The mic you choose should block out surrounding noises and focus on your voice. If you're into Elgato's lineup of products already, consider getting the Elgato Wave:3. It has an internal pop filter and an intelligent clip guard technology designed to stop your audio peaking even if you get a bit shouty while capturing audio. The highlights of this microphone come when you pop it on a boom arm and dive into the Elgato Wave Link Software. This free software comes with a microphone and allows you to do some really clever things with your audio. For instance, you can add audio sources to it, including Spotify, game audio, Discord chat, and more. That means you can customize the listening experience and easily monitor what your audience will hear when you go live on Twitch. The best part, of course, is that it's compatible with Elgato's Stream Deck, making it easy for you to tweak, monitor, and control audio on the fly.

Alternatively, if your budget allows, consider going for Shure SM7B. This is a studio-quality microphone renowned for its capture capabilities, rich sound, and capable background removal. Unlike other standard microphones, this one doesn't come with a USB connection, so you'll need to get a pre-amp as well as something to power and control the microphone (GoXLR). The Shure SM7B microphone combined with a Go XLR pre-amp gives you all the power you need to sound like a professional and excellent on the fly controls for adjusting things like game, voice chat, and music audio levels while you stream. The best part is you can block out irritating background noises like the whirr of your PC's fan, air conditioner, etc.

Of course, the kind of microphone you choose should be based on your budget and the equipment you're using. Make sure you purchase something that is compatible with your devices.

#3: Deck Switcher

Although this is an additional cost to your investment budget, getting a deck switcher will help simplify your life as you stream content, and if you get the right one, it will help you add more flair to the gaming experience. A deck switcher is essentially a control button switch that enables you to move from one deck to another seamlessly. The one that comes most recommended is the Elgato Stream Deck. This small control panel with 15 customizable physical buttons enables you to control multiple things without leaving the game or messing around with commands elsewhere.

For example, you can press the easy-access button that disables your Webcam or mutes your microphone if you need to gobble some food or talk to a family member who's just wandered into the room. You can even set a mute and deafen button for Discord so you can temporarily stop your friends from being heard while you talk to your audience. If you find that you're getting certain questions asked regularly, then you could craft a reply and send it to chat with the press of a button. This stream deck also gives you the ability to clip a stream, place a highlight marker for future editing, play an advert, delete the current chat or change the current chat mode to follower only, emote only, or slow chat. All that and so much more at the touch of a button. Getting a deck switcher may not seem like a necessity but trust me after you've had one, you will never want to go back.

Outside the Four Walls

Have you been wondering whether it would be possible to stream from a mobile device? Good news. With the Twitch app, you can easily do mobile broadcasting. All you need is some decent bandwidth and a commitment to providing a quality, entertaining and informative gaming experience.

Streaming from a PC or gaming console is sure to give you high-quality visuals during a broadcast, but that doesn't mean you shouldn't take advantage of mobile streaming abilities. Whether you're on the go or unable to invest in the types of equipment mentioned earlier, your Twitch influencer project can still make progress if you have an Android device and iPhone or iPad.

There are two ways to broadcast from a mobile device. You can either install an app compatible with your operating system or install computer software that lets you cast the screen of the device you intend to use for streaming. The easiest option is, of course, to download the Twitch app. You can get StreamLabs or Mobcrush to stream from your mobile device directly to Twitch.

If you choose StreamLabs, you'll need to log in with your Twitch account. In the upper right corner of the window, you'll see the Stream icon. Tap on it and wait for a dialog box to appear with the notification that everything displayed on the screen is being recorded. From there, simply tap on the "Start Now" option.

For Mobcrush streaming from your iPhone, you will need to enable the Screen Recording option in the Control Center menu. You also need to make sure that the Access Within Apps option is enabled so you can grant Mobcrush permission to record your activities as you play.

To start a broadcast on your Android, tap the broadcast icon and give your stream a title. Select the right category, e.g., IRL, Talk Shows, Creative, Music, Social Eating, then rotate your phone to landscape and start streaming!

Chapter 10: Make it Look Professional

Twitch is one of those unique platforms that allows you to watch content without an account, but if you want to get the most of this platform and especially if you are starting your channel, the very first step is to sign up and set up your channel.

Creating Your Profile

There are a few ways you can sign up, i.e., through Desktop or mobile. On your desktop, you can sign up for an account by going to Twitch. tv and selecting from the top-right side of your browser window the "Sign Up" option. That will open up the option to sign up for a new account where you can fill out the form by giving your preferred username, password and by sharing legal information like your date of birth.

On mobile, you first need to download the Twitch mobile app, then launch it and tap the "Sign Up" button. When signing up for an account on mobile, you will be able to sign up using your mobile phone number or email address. Once you've completed the signup form, you'll get a six-digit code known as a one-time password (OTP) sent to your email or via SMS, depending on the option you chose.

Coming up with a username

It's imperative to give some serious thought to your username as this will be what people see in Chat and how they will access your channel. Twitch is very strict about usernames, and they often shut down accounts that violate their rules and guidelines. But it's more than just picking a name that isn't offensive. It's also about being creative and using this as a branding tool so that people can remember your channel. The easier it is for people to remember you, the more likely they are to search for you the next time they want to watch your content.

Another aspect of this is adding some key branding elements like a good profile picture and a customized Twitch banner that helps viewers understand what your channel is about.

Once you're done following the instructions for signing up and verifying your account, you're technically speaking ready to launch your channel. Of course, at first, you will have no content. But even before you start streaming, you want to familiarize yourself with the dashboard and some of the platform's fundamental features.

Utilizing the Info Panels

A twitch info panel is used as a call to action or an info banner under your live stream. It's a great way to provide some more information about your stream or to direct viewers outside the platform to a specific page. The recommended Twitch panel size is 320 by 160 Pixels. There are several different types of info panels that you can use to attract subscribers and followers, including:

• Schedule Panel - This Twitch panel shares your streaming schedule with viewers. That shows people that you're serious and consistent about putting out fresh content and gives them an incentive to follow you and show up at the mentioned time. Consistency is key when you want to grow a large following and become successful on Twitch so let everyone know when you will be live!

• About Me Panel - This graphic has a summary of your channel and stream. Use it to introduce yourself to your first-time viewers.

• Social Media Panels - These are self-explanatory. They are great for cross-promoting your brand and getting users to follow you on other social platforms as well. Most viewers will have other accounts, including TikTok, Snapchat, Instagram, Facebook, Clubhouse, etc. You don't need to include every social media platform though, simply use the most relevant social channels you frequently use.

• Discord Channel Panel - This is good to have only if you've got a discord channel. It will help you build an engaged community of viewers and gives you another way to interact with your fans outside of Twitch. We'll talk more about Discord and how to set it up later in the book.

• Donation Panel - This panel allows you to create a donation button so that people can support your creative efforts. It will redirect people to an external website where they can "buy you a coffee."

• Sponsored Panel - Although this kind of panel won't be of value until you have growth on this channel, it's still nice to become aware of it. Sponsored panels are a great way to make money. These panels promote a brand or business that sponsors your channel. The panel sends people to the sponsor's website, and you get paid for driving traffic their way.

• Stream Merchandise Panel - This panel is used to sell and promote your own products. It gives your merchandise greater visibility and drives direct sales, which is another great way to earn an income while streaming.

Best practices:

• Use your brand color when creating the graphics.

• Make sure the text isn't too much. Keep things short, clear, and concise.

• Keep the image file size under 2.9 MB to meet Twitch's requirements.

• Maintain consistency and be relevant with the panel graphics that you use.

One of the main reasons Twitch panels are a must-have is that they help you customize your channel's branding, enabling you to stand out from everyone else in your niche. It also lets viewers know why they should tune in or follow your channel, which ultimately attracts only the right kind of audience.

Befriend OBS

In a previous chapter, we introduced the term OBS (Open broadcast software) as one of the easier options to stream on your Twitch channel. Still, given how new this terminology might be for beginners (which many reading this book will be), I think it best to invest a little more time understanding and befriending the OBS. Please note that this information isn't exhaustive, and I don't claim to be a professional at any of these features or software. I am simply sharing what I've picked up over time as I continue to grow my channel and brand on Twitch.

So, what exactly is Open Broadcast Software? It's a production-level software that allows you to display multiple cameras and even desktop screens during a stream. You can control microphones, media, and so much more. You can do real- source and device capture, broadcasting, encoding, recording, and scene composition. In other words, it's the point where your inputs and outputs merge.

The best part is OBS is free to use and works with both Windows and Mac OS, and if you're feeling generous, you can always donate something to continue supporting the fantastic OBS Studio software. While OBS can feel pretty daunting for beginners, it can also be a great ally when you learn how to use it.

What does the OBS do?

It can help you do real-time audio-video mixing, and it also gives you the choice of per-source filters such as noise gate, noise suppression, and gain. With OBS, you can add screen recording in between your videos or as part of your video by providing a small space on the same screen. You can pause between your live sessions to display a pre-selected banner or video to our audience during breaks. You also have the ability to display screen recording to your audience during your live sessions and also allows you to share your screen.

How to set up OBS to stream on Twitch

The first step is to connect your OBS to Twitch by selecting it from the streaming services drop-down list. On your Twitch TV dashboard, select Settings > Stream Key > Show Key and just follow instructions and prompts, then copy and paste the Stream Key into the Stream Key box in the broadcast settings menu in OBS. Then click Apply.

From here, you need to set up the layout of the stream. You can do this by adding a live webcam feed, nice images, a banner around the edges of your stream, or even a social media handle for your favorite platform so viewers can follow you there as well. OBS has two windows: scenes and sources. Each scene comprises multiple sources, from the game capture window to your live webcam input and more. You can create multiple scenes for different games and load them up by selecting them from the scene menu. When starting out, just keep things super simple and create a single scene for all games. Once you've made your scene, you need to add sources. To add your game source:

a. Click the Plus icon in the Sources menu and select Game Capture.

b. Give your game capture a title to make it easy to recognize it later on.

c. Customize the capture settings. Be mindful of the mode you choose. You can set it up to automatically capture any full screen application, capture the foreground window when a hotkey is pressed or set it up to manually select which window should be captured. If you're using a game capture card, this is where you would select that. Once you're happy with the settings, click OK to save and add the source to your scene.

If you'd like to add some personality to your streaming, I recommend adding your Webcam to the live feed. To do this:

1. Click the plus icon in the Sources menu and select Video Capture Device.
2. Give your Video Capture Device a name, e.g., Webcam.
3. Select your Webcam from the Device drop-down and tweak any other settings if needed.
4. Click OK to add the Webcam to the scene. If you need to move your camera input or resize it, just click on it and drag the corners to adjust accordingly.

You can also click and drag to adjust and move it from one side to the other.

For images (especially info banners), you can easily add them directly to your OBS by going to the Sources box, then clicking Add > Image. Name the source so you can locate it again next time. Click Browse on your computer to find and add it. Tweak the settings (you'll see various options) and click OK to add the image to the Livestream. Like the Webcam, you can move it around by dragging and dropping it wherever you want it viewed.

If you also want to add text to your stream, the process is similar. Click the Plus icon in the Sources menu and select Text (GDI+). Enter a name for your text box (the name that will be on the source, not what people will see). You can customize the font, size, color, opacity, and more to get the desired effect in the text menu. Click OK to close and save the text. To adjust the text's position, choose "Edit Scene" and simply drag and drop the text to the desired location.

Once everything is set up, and you're happy with it, it's time to go live. In OBS, you just need to click Start Streaming in the bottom right corner of the main OBS window, and that's it!

The difference between Streamlabs OBS and OBS

Streamlabs OBS and OBS are the most common and widely used broadcast software. They are both free and pretty great to use for streaming, so which one should you go for? Let's look at the key differentiators:

• OBS is a high-performance software that delivers the ultimate user experience, but it lacks certain features and functionality. In other words, if you're into bells and whistles, you won't find them here unless you develop them for yourself.

• Streamlabs OBS is like the much-needed upgrade to OBS that certain streamers have sought. It is essentially the same OBS code revamped with a better user experience. Unfortunately, it works best on Windows, so if you have a Mac OS, you're better off using the standard OBS.

- Streamlabs OBS provides various themes and advanced features to create a unique experience for the streamer. There are dozens of themes to personalize your stream. It also comes with alerts, widgets, built-in text-to-speech, layouts, and so much more. As you may have inferred, these aren't available in the standard OBS.

Make Sure You are Heard!

When Twitch viewers tune in to watch your live stream, they expect to hear your voice and the music and sound effects from the game you're playing. They expect it to be a pleasant experience, and that implies you need to ensure that sound quality is on point. So, let's talk about how Twitch advises you to set up your audio, as well as some additional tips.

When you launch Twitch Studio for the first time, you'll get the first-time setup prompts that you need to follow. The first one is setting up your microphone. Your default microphone will be automatically selected, but you can change the mic at any time if you're using a specific device. You can also change other settings by clicking on the personalize button.

Next, you want to navigate back to the Twitch Studio screen, where you can see your Chat, Activity Feed, and Scenes. In the bottom left corner, you'll see the bar for your microphone. To add an audio source, click on the Audio Mixer icon with three lines. Then click the (+) Plus icon to add another available source if needed.

If you want to use a capture card to broadcast, you need to add the device's output as a source for your Main Screen Share or any other Screen Share layer. Not all capture cards are compatible with Twitch Studio, so here are some of the most recommended ones by Twitch. For Windows, you can use Elgato HD 60S, HD 60S Plus, HD 60 Pro, HD 4K Pro, Screenlink. You can also use Razer Ripsaw and Ripsaw SD or Avermedia Live Gamer Extreme 2 (GC551), Live Gamer ultra (GC553), Live Gamer Portable 2 Plus (GC513), Live Gamer Mini (GC311), Live Gamer HD 2 (GC570), and Live Gamer 4K (GC573A). For Mac, you can use Elgato HD 60S Plus and Screenlink or Avermedia Live Gamer Ultra (GC553), Live Gamer Portable 2 Plus (GC513), Live Gamer Mini (GC311).

Besides getting these basics right, you also need to consider the kind of mic you're using, the recording space, and your OBS settings. What do I mean?

Getting the right microphone doesn't need to be expensive, but you need to invest in something that will make you sound like a pro. You can get a condenser mic like Blue Yeti, which has a larger range and is more sensitive to loud noises, or a broadcast mic which is often easier to work with. Regardless, you will need to position it properly. The microphone's position will determine how you sound on the receiving end. Consider putting approximately 1-6 inches away from your mouth.

If you're using a headset, never place the mic directly in front of your mouth because most people don't want to hear you breathing. Instead, put it right around or under your chin.

You also need to remember that every game is different, so you need to test your audio levels before each session. To do this by yourself, just test settings before you start the actual Livestream by recording a preview of your stream and then playing it back so you can hear what viewers will hear once you go live. Using your OBS, you can do this by clicking Start Recording. Let the game run a few minutes and talk into the mic a few times. Then when you feel like you have enough material, click Stop Recording. Find the recording by going to Settings > Broadcast Settings > File Path. That is where all recorded sessions will be saved. Play it back, and if it sounds fantastic, then you're good to go.

Reach Out and Have Channel Moderators

When you're just starting out, it's going to be easy to manage both the live streaming content and the work involved in engaging with your audience on the chat. However, as things evolve and your channel growth snowballs (assuming you follow and apply everything taught in this book), you'll get to a place where handling the chat activity will become overwhelming. And that is a good problem to have. How do we solve this issue? Simple. Reach out to the most active viewers (someone you resonate with) and invite them to be your channel moderator or mod, as often called in Twitch vocabulary.

A mod is someone who can help you, monitor, clean up and engage with your growing audience so that you can focus on doing what you do best - create epic entertainment. What should you look for when picking a mod?

• A good moderator is reliable and service-oriented.

This person is actively engaged in the chat long before you ask them to be a mod. They enjoy answering people's questions regarding your channel even before they know you, and they seem to be good at responding to comments.

- A good mod is trustworthy.

Not only should your moderator be reliable, but he or she should be trustworthy and should believe in the same values you do, as that will make it easier for them to carry out the rules you give them on the general conduct of the channel. As they clean up comments, eliminate spam and handle tough questions or critics and comments regarding your brand, things will go smoothly if they believe and value the same things your brand stands for. So, make sure you pick someone you genuinely feel connected to.

How to make someone a mod:

There are two ways to make someone a moderator. First, you can type in the command /mod USERNAME in your chat while they are in your channel. That should automatically make that person a mod. The other option is to click on the person's name in the chat. You'll see the possibility of promoting them to mod. Click on it, and they instantly get the upgrade with the green sword icon next to their name.

Do you need to pay your mod, and how many do you need?

Mods are generally not paid, but you could offer them perks or gifts during holiday seasons or work anniversaries. Things like gift cards, game codes, special stream perks, or other individual presents are commonly accepted.

When it comes to mods, there really isn't a standardized answer. Twitch recommends adding them as needed, which makes sense because the bigger your viewership, the more comments you'll get on your chat, and the more help you'll need. Twitch recommends five active mods for every 200 viewers once you start to see five messages per second. If you don't want to start with a human mod, you can always experiment with a stream chatbot that enables you to pre-customize certain rules so they can automatically delete things like hate speech, spam links, etc. With a chatbot, you can have hundreds of different replies. In fact, some programs such as Nightbot offer dynamic replies, which is perfect if you only want an automated moderator while your channel is still gaining momentum.

How to reach out to your audience:

If you're ready to bring in some human moderators, I suggest creating a Google Form with a few questions to ensure you're picking the right people. Post the link to the document in your Discord or profile and let people know you're looking for mods. If you've already spotted someone from your community that you feel would be ideal, then reach out directly and ask if they'd be interested in an interview. Do not just pick someone because they donate to your channel. Make sure it's someone who genuinely loves engaging with people. If you have real-life friends or relatives who enjoy socializing, then it's worth asking them too.

Make Your Streams Look Nice Using Overlays

All successful gamers on Twitch put a lot of effort into creating that customized look to imprint their brand on their audience. This is usually done through the use of overlays. An overlay is a graphical design that consists of varying graphics that appear along with your gameplay footage during a stream. Usually, the overlay is a transparent PNG image that is overlaid on top of the Livestream content. The graphics are positioned around the edges of the screen so that the center remains unobstructed. Still, depending on your brand image, you can always create one that suits your particular taste and the layout of the game you're playing.

You can include a unique color scheme, mascot logo, or stream information such as current music track, top donators, recent subscribers, and so much more on your overlay design.

Why do people invest in Twitch overlays?

It's the easiest way to stand out from the crowd of fellow streamers. It's also a cool way to show off your personality and enhance the game's visual experience for your viewer.

How to make your overlay more attractive:

Choose designs that align with your brand and personality, as well as the games you play. If you are colorful, playful, and energetic, then go for brighter color schemes creative design themes. If you're playing genres such as MMORPGs, MOBAs, and so on that feature complicated UIs, you're better off choosing minimalist overlays which are hidden to avoid obstructing key in-game information. If, however, you're playing First-Person-Shooters and Battle Royales, then you can get more creative since you'll have more real estate to work with. So before investing in an overlay, think about the games.

There are many free sources on the web to get some pre-made overlays, and if you're just starting, that might be a good option. Once you've established yourself, however, I suggest getting a custom-made overlay, especially once you play around with a few and identify one that really suits your channel. Consider visiting Nerd or Die, Twitch Overlay Maker Placeit, Ghost Rising, Zerging, WDFLAT, Haunted Twitch Overlay- visuals by impulse, and Own3D Club: Free

Twitch Streamer Community. Just Google any of these names, and you'll gain access to the free overlays each platform offers.

Now, I bet you're wondering how in the world to get that overlay showing up on your stream. For this, you need to be streaming using OBS or XSplit software on your PC or Mac. Then it's as simple as adding an image layer and selecting your files. Then you can have it as a border around your Webcam or the full 1080p experience taking up the entire frame of your screen. While transparent PNG is the most common file type, you can also use GIFs and JPGs. Just note that JPGs will not be transparent, and GIFs will not have the high-quality resolution that a PNG offers.

Chapter 11: And We Are LIVE!

At this point, you have ticked all the boxes on your checklist, and you should be feeling pretty excited because you can launch your live streaming and start growing your brand. But before you go live, you want to make sure those details that could make you come across as unprofessional are well covered. Make sure you do a final check to ensure your channel branding is on point, your Twitch profile represents the brand image you're trying to create, and that you've practiced with your streaming software.

Your First Live Stream

Besides the hardware and software, you also need to create a Twitch channel trailer, set up chatbots and alerts, decide on a schedule for your stream, and practice talking to chat. You should also plan out some time to interact with other streamers who already have an audience. Use this opportunity to network, build relationships and create opportunities for collaboration. There's lots of evidence supporting the fact that new streamers do better when they network with other broadcasters. I would say before doing your live stream, you need to be active on at least five channels that you can invite to come to support your first Livestream and cheer you on.

Before your live stream, you also want to make sure you've practiced the gameplay and that you've developed sufficient techniques through study and practice. If you think you can just wing it and become successful on Twitch, then you're sorely mistaken. You must understand the game well enough that you can be entertaining to watch while playing it. Game rehearsal is crucial before your first stream, and once you do start streaming, make sure you've planned it out well enough, so you don't run out of entertaining content a few weeks down the road. Ideally, you want to ask yourself:

what content will I stream?

How long will each stream last?

Who will be gaming with me, if at all?

How often will I go live each week?

What goals do I want to hit with each stream that I can track?

All these questions help you create a clear and measurable plan beforehand so you can stay focused, organized, and on purpose with your content.

The last quick check you need to make once you feel confident about doing your live stream is to make sure your design elements are on point. You need to have a profile picture, Twitch overlays, Twitch banners, Twitch panels, Twitch emotes (if you plan on becoming an affiliate), and your overall profile design should be congruent with your brand image and ready to go. We've talked about these different aspects of your channels in previous chapters, so please go back and re-read that if you're not sure how to create these. Assuming you're ready, it's time to head over to your dashboard and let the magic begin. Always remember to title your stream in a way that will attract viewers to click through and watch your game. You should also remember to add tags, choose the language and game/category so that people can discover your content. The next thing is to go to settings to make sure you've selected archive broadcasts. That will automatically save your broadcasted streams to the "videos" tab on Twitch. This is important because you want viewers to be able to watch VODs (videos on demand) whenever they miss your live stream. If you want to limit commenting, you can do so by clicking on the "Followers-only" mode in your settings. Now you're ready to stream!

The step-by-step breakdown for newbies (recommended by experts):

#1: Restart your PC before streaming.

#2: Open your streaming software, e.g., OBS or Streamlabs.

#3: Prep the background music.

#4: Test audio for sound quality as well as your video to see how the lighting is.

#5: Open your Twitch chat ready to go. If you have a mod or are using a bot, make sure they are prepped and ready to go.

#6: Grab some water, light snacks, and that you're sitting somewhere comfy.

#7: Hit the start streaming button and go live!

It's Not Just About Streaming Your Games

A question I get asked by new streamers is, "can I stream without talking?" If you've been wondering the same, I'll take out the guesswork and tell you that you can absolutely stream without chatting on Twitch. In fact, there are certain scenarios where not talking is probably best. For example, if you're doing a tournament and you need to be hyperfocused or if you're streaming music - chatting isn't recommended. And by streaming music, I mean something intense like you playing the drums or piano. In this case, the viewers will get that you can't possibly play your instrument, make good music, and still read the chat. But on any other occasion, I discourage it because here's the thing. Twitch isn't just a place to play video games. It is, after all, a social platform. People come to Twitch to make friends with like-minded people.

So, if you want to grow your channel and attract more viewers, chatting is a big part of what you must be willing to do. Radio silence as you play your game will hurt your channel's growth and success because most people coming to view your game also care about interacting with you in some way. Many Twitch viewers value the community aspect because it's like a bonding session for them over a game they love or aspire to play.

How to best interact with your new viewers in chat:

You need to make sure your chat is set up so viewers can see it to the right-hand side of your stream. You can also integrate the chat into your overlay to make it look more professional. There are widgets in Streamlabs OBS that can help you do this. Also, now is an excellent time to create a list of vulgar terms that you feed the AutoMod so that it can filter any spam or unwanted messages. Decide whether or not you want to add chat delays to give your mods time to filter out negative messages and whether users without verified email addresses are allowed to chat. All this is done in the settings area. If the preparation is done well, the rest will flow.

All you need is to have viewer questions ready that will enable you to create dialogue and also a script to help you welcome new viewers and followers. It's going to be up to you to maintain that high positive energy that will get people to understand what kind of streamer you are and how they should behave when interacting with your channel. This is especially true in the beginning when you're growing your audience. Be sure to set the tempo, be clear about your rules and guidelines and constantly interact with your chat. In terms of topics for discussions, I strongly suggest avoiding politics, religion, or any sensitive topics that usually create too much heat and bad energy in the chat.

But what if you really want to avoid talking?

There are a few things you can do on those days when you really don't want to talk, e.g., when you're feeling sick or had a long day at work.

• Announce on your title that you will not be talking on the stream. That way, people tuning in will immediately come with the right expectation, and you won't end up with complaints and bad comments on your chat.

• Let people know on the title that you won't be reading or actively responding to the chat. If you're fighting a cold, you could even make fun of that and let them know so they can understand why you're not actively engaging. If you're having microphone issues, you could also share that. Again, both these ideas help you communicate ahead of time so that people come in knowing what to expect.

• Set the chat to followers only, sub only, or emotes only. That allows you to filter your discussion, so you get less spam and only talk to people who really matter.

One thing I encourage my more introverted friends to do is to activate followers-only mode so they can adjust the chat to accommodate people who've been following them for a specific period of time. For example, you could open it up to people who have been following you for at least two months. I will, however, insist that you train yourself to chat because it's going to be impossible to gain new viewers and followers if you never interact with the larger community.

How to deal with having no viewers:

When you start your live stream, you'll likely have no viewers unless you're fortunate enough to have friends and family who really want to support your channel. So, what should you do in this case when the chat is empty? I think giving commentary on your gameplay even if no one is watching is always a good idea. If someone was to pop into the live stream for the first time and find you adding commentary, goofing around, and making fun of yourself, they are more likely to engage you and start some chat activity. Have you ever been to a social gathering and you saw this person who was just standing alone in the corner? Then you thought about saying hello but decided to go over to the group of guys laughing across the room? Why do we tend to gravitate toward those who seem to be more open, friendly, and fun-loving? Because it's easier to join in and create a dialogue where one already exists. The same is going to be true on Twitch. People will click on your Livestream, and if you come across as that aloof, silent kid on the corner who just wants to be left alone, they will leave. And that will make it hard for you to grow your viewership, followers, subs, and account in general.

Learn The Etiquette

Twitch is a social platform that's based on sharing common interests, especially around gaming. It's up to you to establish the energy and behavior that will be acceptable and representative of your brand. How you interact with viewers, fellow streamers, and the image you put out will determine how others treat and perceive you. Establish your own set of rules and guidelines that people should adhere to when interacting on your channel. When you visit other streamers, make sure you demonstrate that same etiquette level you want to see on your channel. So, if you don't like people coming to your stream to self-promote or spam your chat with links, make sure you never do that on another's channel. It's also not a good idea to see fellow streamers are rivals or competitors that you can just steal content from. Don't steal or copy. Be your own original streamer so that people can see what makes your channel unique.

What I encourage you to do is to invest time in the community visiting other channels that you enjoy so you can get inspired and motivated. And when you do network, do it because you genuinely want to be friends with that particular streamer. Do it because you want to surround yourself with successful, like-minded individuals who do what you want to be doing further down the line. Another good habit to get into is to reach out to channels that are similar to you in size and scope so you can support each other and grow together. Mutual respect for both streamers and viewers is essential to your success. Many people on Twitch want to feel like they belong to a certain community so treat others as you want to be treated and become the example. Then your people will naturally gravitate toward you.

It's a Wrap!

Now that you're all set and ready to stream and chat and everything in between, let's make sure you also end with a bag. The end of your stream is an important part that requires a little thought because you want to make sure the viewers can continue interacting with you. You can do some shout-outs for your social media accounts or other fan pages that you may have where people can come to interact with your post the gameplay. If you were doing a collaboration or are planning on doing one soon, make sure to give that a shout-out too and let people know when they should show up for that event. Let viewers know when the next stream will take place and any additional info that you feel would be relevant to them. Encourage those who enjoyed watching you for the first time to at least follow and maybe even reach out with their questions or ideas. If you didn't have time to give shout-outs to new followers or subscribers and you'd like to do it, the end part of the stream can be a great way to praise and acknowledge all the new people who supported you during the stream. Be creative with this, have fun, and test out different endings to see which feels most natural to you.

5 Important Tips for Beginners

#1: Have a clear goal in mind

Why do you want to stream? Is it just a hobby? Do you want to make this your full-time career? What exactly do you wish to get out of it? If you don't have clearly identified goals, you won't know whether you're making any progress because you're like a guy driving a car with no destination. Sure, he might be going west, but west to what destination exactly? Have the main goal and subdivided into smaller ones that you can track. For example, if your main goal is to be a full-time gamer earning seven figures in the next ten years, you can certainly break it down to smaller goals for the next year, leading to that long-term goal. That can include starting and growing your audience to X number of followers and subs in the next 12 months.

#2: Make the most of your social media

Although it would be great to think that all you need to succeed is to buy the right gaming equipment, set up your Twitch channel, and start producing epic content, and the rest will fall into place. The fact is, you have to be more proactive with attracting an audience because that is the lifeblood of your gaming success. And the best way to attract an audience is to leverage social media because that's where your potential fans are hanging out when they're not on Twitch.

Developing your social presence and building awareness about your brand on the channels you most enjoy is a must. You don't need to be on all platforms, but I encourage you to consider YouTube, TikTok, Twitter, Instagram, and Facebook as all these social platforms have large, engaged audiences who love gaming. TikTok is, of course, the easiest place for you to grow an audience from scratch. Still, if you naturally enjoy being on any of the previously named networks, I suggest setting up an account there as well so you can have at least two active social media platforms. That gives you a place to let everyone know when you go live, which increases the chances of getting more viewers. It also allows you to communicate with your fans and fellow content creators. That will boost your credibility, build up your identity and establish your brand online. One thing you can do is create compilations of funny moments or game highlights that you can share on these social networks.

#3: Collaborate with other broadcasters

The more social you are, the easier it will be to connect with and build relationships with fellow content creators. Then you can cross-promote each other's content and even use dual streams so you can play a game together while streaming. It is a great way to tap into each other's communities.

#4: Stick to your streaming schedule

It's important to create a streaming schedule and train your viewers into expecting to tune in and connect with you at a specific time each day or week, depending on how often you go live. Once you manage to create this pattern, you must stick to it. That creates a habit in the journey of your viewers and gives them something to look forward to. When getting started, try different slots throughout the day to see what is more comfortable for you and what yields more average viewers. Once you identify this pattern based on data, not guesswork, commit to streaming at that same time each week.

#5: Communicate, entertain and engage your viewers

You have about ten seconds to grab someone's attention on Twitch, and if they don't like what they see and hear, they'll just click away. People will come expecting to be entertained, so make sure you deliver. Communicate clearly, be authentic and leverage your quirky traits. Talk about your strategy, your train of thoughts, and how your feeling throughout the game. Be verbal so people can feel immersed and engaged. That's how you'll grow the channel.

Chapter 12: Improving Your Stream And Getting More Viewers

Anyone can start a streaming channel on Twitch, but not everyone will succeed at turning that hobby into a lucrative full-time job. Those that are fortunate enough to do it have a couple of things in common. The main underlying one is their commitment to creating the best possible stream each time they go live. How do you climb up to the ranks of the best streamers on Twitch? By adopting the same frame of mind, they have. That begins by ensuring that each stream is better than the last.

There's Always Some Space for Improvement

Regardless of how good your last stream was, make it a point to continuously up your game. There are many ways you can keep improving your stream from both a technical and quality perspective. The easiest is, of course, with your content. The more you learn and practice your gameplay, the better you'll get at streaming live. If you can get so good at playing your games, you might start to find innovative ways of approaching the game that your viewers are likely to find enjoyable. That might involve taking a bit of a risk as you step outside the norm and establish your unique approach to the game. But as long as you're smart and you've practiced well enough, it could easily help you stand out amongst other streamers, and it will train viewers to expect better content from you.

When it comes to the technical bit, you should continue to educate yourself on how you can tweak your OBS settings to get better quality and more optimization depending on the PC and microphone you're using. A few things you should know here include:

- Streaming FPS games or any other fast-paced games are better off in 900p@60fps instead of the standard recommendation (1920 X 1080@60fps). It's going to give your viewers better quality and less pixelation during fast movement.

- To get a more efficient bitrate usage that will give you better overall stream quality navigate to the OBS advanced settings and activate "Enable network optimizations."

Aside from the nerdy technical stuff, you can also improve your stream's appearance. First impressions really matter, and you've got ten seconds to make a great impression. So, you want to tweak and upgrade your aesthetics continually. Here are some pointers when it comes to making things more appealing:

- Use quality graphics and sounds and try to maintain a consistent look and feel.

Even if at first you start with free or cheap graphics for your branding, be clear with the overall look and feel that you want for your channel so that even when you start investing in custom designs, people don't experience a huge shock. Think of the overall color scheme, the sounds, and the style of your transitions, and then do your best to find free stuff that matches what you want to create. As you grow, you can always purchase or get someone to design something of higher quality, but if you outlined the original brand personality properly, the upgrade would be received very positively by your viewers, followers, and subs. If you want to purchase some cool graphics on a budget, consider checking out Fiverr, which has creators who design exclusively for streamers and are likely to produce something epic that matches your budget.

- Don't use over-the-top overlays. Tacky designs won't help your brand. Yes, lasers and flames are cool and theoretically sound like a good idea, but clean aesthetics make for a better viewer experience. Less is more in this case. You don't want things that take up 30% of your screen as that will be disturbing to the eye, and most people will suffer from visual fatigue.

- Use emotes and emote extensions such as FrankerFaceZ and BetterTTV to add some flair and excitement. People love cool emotes. What exactly are emotes? These are Twitch's emoji glyphs that people can insert into their chat communications during a Twitch stream. They are an integral part of the Twitch streaming community's culture and identity-building process, so you want to use them to establish your brand's personality. Unlike standard emojis that you might find on WhatsApp or other social platforms, these emotes are diverse and have the power to add more expression. They can also be sent as standalone polyps without any text to signify a certain moment during the stream. I also like to use them as a mini ad for my channel by encouraging my followers and mods to use my emotes. That way, as other viewers see them circulating around, they might feel enticed to join the community and subscribe as well. There are both free and custom-made emotes. To make custom emotes, you need to be a Twitch affiliate or Twitch partner.

- You can also customize your alerts so you can have different follow and sub alerts. Be subtle, don't overdo this but consider creating a cool tune for your special alerts so viewers who convert can see that you care. Your fans always appreciate a little celebration.

Plan Ahead of Time

If you want to succeed on Twitch or any other social media platform, there's one thing you must commit to - consistent content production. The only way to be consistent, especially as your channel and responsibilities grow, is through proper planning and scheduling. I've heard of those rare beings who can produce lots of content without a plan. Personally, I don't buy it. It's never worked for me, so I cannot endorse it. What has worked thus far is having an organized content plan and a reliable scheduling system.

When should you schedule your streams?

From the moment you plan to go live for the first time. The younger and newer you are, the more you need to plan ahead and schedule your stream. Streamers with thousands of viewers can get away with "on the fly" streaming, but if you're serious about growing your channel, a schedule is your best ally.

Think back to the days (if you're old enough) when you would have to tune in every Friday at the same to watch your favorite show. There was no binge-watching or any kind of on-demand entertainment, so if you missed it, you'd be bummed and have to wait another week. Okay, so nowadays, thanks to technology, that's not our experience of entertainment. Whether you want to watch or listen to something, everything is on-demand. But still, the habit of wanting to know when a "fresh" episode goes live so we can tune in and catch it first lingers. That's why successful YouTubers, podcasters, and bloggers always announce when they'll be releasing new content. And for streamers, announcing when you'll be going live makes it easier for people who like you enough to add you to their daily routine, so they never miss tuning in. That is the perfect way to build a consistent following and to ensure maximum views. It also makes it easier to promote on other social media channels. If you like streaming in the afternoon, people will get used to watching you on your lunch break. Do you prefer evening streaming? Great. Let your people know so they can try to catch you at night before bed.

If you have a small community, especially in the first few months, consider sending direct messages as reminders, so people get trained to show up at a certain time. For example, I like to stream in the evenings every Thursday, Friday, Saturday, and Sunday from 7:00 EST. Because I've set a specific schedule, I am able to send out reminders on Twitter, TikTok, Snapchat, and Instagram about my upcoming stream. It also helps me plan ahead. So how would you go about doing this?

Option #1: Edit the stream schedule section on your creator dashboard.

Navigate to your channel to the section indicated as "schedule." This is what we are going to edit. Click "Edit schedule" and make whatever edits you desire. Once you're done picking your days, you should see them appear under your Twitch channel's schedule section.

Option #2: Create a Twitch panel (**we talked about panels earlier**) that includes your streaming schedule.

To edit your Twitch panels:

1. Go to the about me section where the panels are located and turn the edit panels button on.
2. Create a panel that has your schedule on it, nothing fancy.
3. Just make sure it communicates the dates and times.

Pro tip: Consider putting your schedule on both the Twitch panel and on your creator dashboard to maximize the effectiveness so that everyone gets a chance to see when you'll be live.

Don't Stop Engaging

Connecting with your audience should never stop when the Livestream ends. Engaging with your community should become a top priority at this point. Why? Because success on the platform hinges on having a healthy audience size. There's no monetization on Twitch if you fail to create a highly engaged audience. That has to start at the beginning of your journey. I like to think of the 80-20 rule whereby 80% of your time as a newbie should be invested in interacting with viewers, streamers, followers, and subscribers, and 20% goes into producing epic content. So, if you plan on releasing lots of content, take into account that you'll need to make lots of time for community building to match all that content.

Contrary to what most gamers think, the gameplay is only half the equation of success. There are a thousand ways to do this. You can build up your social media and use Discord as well as any other suitable channel to ensure you're nurturing that relationship with your new fans and subscribers. Most gamers have found great success through using Discord, and if you don't know what that is, in the next section, I will walk you through how to set it up.

Making Use of Your Vod

Vod stands for Video On Demand, and it's a great way to ensure your viewers can rewatch that epic gameplay. It's also a great way to ensure your followers who may have missed the stream can still catch some of that action. However, before you can, it's essential to follow the instructions below to enable VOD for your channel.

#1: Click on your profile icon in the top right-hand corner of your Twitch and find "dashboard."

#2: Navigate to "settings" on the left-hand side and click "channel."

#3: You will see a list of headings under the heading titled "Stream Key and Preferences," and you will see a section titled "Store Past Broadcasts." Tick that small box to allow Twitch to store past broadcasts.

#4: Once you click the small box, a green check will appear, which confirms that you are allowing Twitch to save your past broadcasts, and just like that, your VOD is active and ready. If you ever want to turn it off for some reason, just uncheck that small box again.

A few things you need to remember, though, is that VODs have an expiration date. They are only saved for 14 days (two weeks) for regular streamers, but if you have Twitch Prime, Twitch Turbo, or are a Twitch partner, Twitch will save your broadcasts for 60 days (two months).

How to manually save your VODs.

If you'd like to have your VODs to reuse at a later date or for a different purpose, you can download the VOD to your computer. They do take up a lot of space, so I recommend getting an external hard drive which you can easily buy from Amazon, where you can store them.

If, however, you'd like to get creative and create a collection of your best moments so you can have that instead of the full stream, you can create highlights that showcase portions of the live stream. How?

#1: From your dashboard, navigate to the left side of the screen and scroll down till you see "videos" and click "video producer." A list of past broadcasts will appear.

#2: Locate the broadcast you want to highlight and click the "highlight" button next to it.

#3: A new tab will open up, and here you can begin to highlight different sections of your videos. Select the parts you want, then click the "create highlights" button, and your highlights are complete.

These little gems, when created properly, will provide an overview of your gameplay, show people what you do and what your channel is all about without you having to be online live streaming. It's incredible marketing and a good way to attract new viewers. There are many people casually scrolling through Twitch to look for new channels, and if they can land on your highlights, they are more likely to turn into real viewers, followers, and subs. Another reason you should consider creating highlights is that many of your subs may not want to watch the entire Livestream they missed, but they certainly would enjoy seeing your best moments. So, this works well as an update for your followers and subs. A good length to go for is 1-2minutes.

An Avenue for YouTube Content

Okay, so you have VODs that were downloaded to your computer, and you've been making epic highlights from your gameplay. Isn't there a way to repurpose this content? Yes, there is. None is better than repurposing your content on YouTube. There is a multitude of ways through which you can leverage YouTube to grow your Twitch channel. The most straightforward one is through the Twitch website. To do so, make sure you've linked the two accounts first (Twitch and Google). Find the little arrow icon (on Twitch dashboard) next to your name in the top right corner of the screen and click on Video Producer. That will take you to a list of all your Twitch videos, including your past streams. Click the three dots on the video you want to export to YouTube and click "Export." Don't forget to fill in the title, description, and tags for the video, which will determine the video's discoverability and ranking on YouTube. You can also decide whether you would like YouTube to split it into 15minute segments automatically. Hit "Start Export," and in a few minutes, your video will be live on your YouTube channel.

Should you upload your VODs directly to YouTube?

Given how long normal gameplay is, I would suggest avoiding the shortcut of uploading a full Livestream. If you think about it, there are many "boring parts" ranging from bathroom breaks to time spent reading chats, etc. These moments are fine for live viewers, but it can be a turn-off for people who tune it to watch the recording. On YouTube, especially, what I find works is uploading the highlights of your gameplay. That means creating highlights of your best moments as discussed earlier or, better still, editing the content like you would a regular video. It will ensure your YouTube viewers enjoy the content they find on your YouTube channel because it won't be an exact regurgitation of the Twitch Live stream experience. There are a few options here to consider:

The first and most recommend is to get a video editing software and edit the downloaded VOD to make it a little more in-depth than a highlight reel. Now, this might present some issues, especially if you're using a laptop or an older computer. Of course, if you have a high-end gaming/streaming computer, then you likely won't struggle with lag time or slow downloads. Rendering is also another issue you might struggle with, so I recommend using special editing software that actually makes it easy to edit longer games. A common one that works for most gamers is Flixier. It runs in your browser and uses cloud servers to render any video in 3 minutes or less. The best part is that it has a full Twitch integration, meaning you can link it to your account and import your VOD straight from the Twitch servers. Flixier also has YouTube integration capabilities which means you can set it to publish your freshly edited content as soon as it's ready.

Chapter 13: Monetizing Your Content

Although you can make money through your TikTok channel, focusing on Twitch seems to be a little easier and perhaps more fruitful in the long run. Some well-known gamers have found the formula to make good money. For example, Shroud makes about $100,000 a month from subs. And this is just one income stream. There are also sponsorships, tips, and other money-making techniques. Compared to TikTok and YouTube, the deal seems sweeter on Twitch when you consider that some of these platforms take as high as 50% commission on your total earnings. According to a poll conducted by gamer Sizzarz, Twitch viewers enjoy supporting their streamers through Gifting Subs (40.2%), Cheering Bits (28.9%), and Tipping (30.9%). So, in this chapter, we're going to walk through how you can start generating either some or all of your income from the streaming platform.

Start Being An Affiliate

Most people know affiliate marketing and, in fact, establish affiliate marketing links on many of their social platforms. The common affiliate marketing method is to sell something from Amazon that your audience might be interested in. Then you get a small commission payment from all your sales. But that's not the same as being a Twitch affiliate, which I want to help you become. As soon as you gain some momentum with your channel, you should aim to become an affiliate. It will take some work, but here is the fast track route and its benefits.

How Twitch Affiliates Make Money:

Becoming an affiliate for Twitch unlocks the "subscribe" button, which viewers can use to access your custom emotes and show support through financial investment. As you can imagine, getting someone to subscribe is a lot more challenging than getting them to follow you since money is involved. Still, if you have great content and an addictive personality, your people will ultimately want to show their support by subscribing. Although it's not easy, it's also not as hard as one might think.

Take, for example, the story of Cherry Horne, who says that she became hooked on watching Twitch streams during the pandemic season. Cherry watched seasoned dancers playing Just Dance, and since she'd purchased the game herself, she found watching these streamers quite motivational. She also learned a few moves. After a little while, she grew fond of certain streamers and decided to start "tipping" them as a token of her gratitude and ultimately subscribed to two of them. For Cherry, it's not just about getting exclusive content or "spending money" on the streamers but more about encouraging fellow creatives for the hard work they do. If she gets entertained and enjoys the content a streamer provides, she wants to tip to show her appreciation.

The bottom line is, there are lots of people waiting to fall in love with your content and get entertained. Once your subscribe button is activated, your biggest fans will likely be more than happy to naturally upgrade into subscribers as long as you remain authentic and deliver epic content regardless of category.

Twitch requirements:

You must stream for at least 500 minutes per thirty-day period and have at least seven unique broadcast days. That means over 8hours of streaming a month. And you can't just stream one long 8-hour gameplay. They have to be at least seven broadcasts within the thirty days. Then you must have an average of three or more viewers per thirty-day period and at least 50 followers on your channel. With such strict requirements, I would suggest you think about becoming a Twitch affiliate once you hit your first 100 followers. You can check to see if you qualify for the affiliate program by navigating to "Insights" > Achievements from your creator Dashboard. That's where Twitch will track your progress. Once you are eligible, all you need to do is click the button that appears on your Path to Affiliate achievement. Twitch offers a complete guideline that you should read and follow once you qualify. Visit their Affiliate Onboarding Guide page and remember to read their terms of the agreement. So, the requirements aren't so impossible, but the question is, how do you get there? Here are a few pointers:

- Be willing to put in the time.

In other words, you must commit to doing at least 500 minutes on seven separate days each month. Now, this may not sound like much if you're a teen with a lot more time in your hands, but for someone with a full-time job, family, and other obligations, this can be a lot. Keep in mind that just doing 500 minutes is the minimum that Twitch wants from you, not the amount of hours needed to build an active audience. When you're going from zero followers to the first one hundred, you'll need a lot more streaming and interaction time than a mere 500 hours.

Pro Tip: Some streamers are very strategic when it comes to hitting their monthly targets. Remember, you need the 500 hours done on seven separate days, and you also need an average of three viewers. Sometimes, streamers will turn off the stream if they have no viewers because they don't want to risk missing the monthly requirement. So, if you don't have a large following yet with lots of active viewers, be strategic about when you stream so you can have the largest number of viewers.

- Pay attention to the ideal times for streaming.

Piggybacking on the last point, it's super important to figure out the best times to have your Livestream as early as possible in your journey. That will enable you to create a schedule that makes it easier to create consistent content and for your viewers to show up on time. Nothing is more important than knowing what your audience loves and the times they are usually available.

The other key aspect is finding creative ways to attract people to join your stream. Given how many gamers are playing simultaneously, you can't just cross your fingers and hope someone will stop by to support your gameplay. You need a plan, and in the last chapter, I will give it to you so you can finally learn how to attract the right attention to your channel.

- Leverage your offline social groups.

Since it's going to be important to reach the average view target, a very simple yet highly effective tactic is to convince (sometimes bribe) roommates, family members, friends, fiancé, and anyone else who can give you some time to watch your stream while you're live. Those views will still count toward your average monthly requirement, and it's likely to draw in new viewers because humans like to gravitate toward action. More often than not, action is dictated by how many viewers are on your stream. So, someone who is just casually browsing might come across two exact games taking place at the same time, and she is likely to click on the one with more viewers. It's just our human nature. Use this to your advantage.

Next Step: Partnership

The next level up when it comes to monetization is the Twitch partnership. That requires a sizeable audience to qualify for, but you should easily scale up to partnership if you're already successful with Twitch affiliate. Here you will earn revenue by accepting subscriptions from your viewers, which are: $4.99, $9.99, $24.99, or the Prime Gaming free subscription. You can also unlock up to 50 channel emotes. Another way you can earn money is through Bits. Your viewers buy bits to cheer you on (tip you) without leaving the platform. You will, of course, share this revenue with Twitch, and you'll also get to customize your Cheermotes and Bit Badges. Lastly, as a partner, you can earn a share of the revenue generated from any ads that are played on your channel. You get to determine the length and frequency of the mid-roll advertisements through your dashboard.

Twitch Partnership requirements:

To qualify for Twitch partnerships, you need to complete the Path to Partner achievement or demonstrate a large, engaged viewership/following. Your content should conform to the platform's community guidelines which is why you must read them as soon as you launch the channel. And just in case you think this is a one-time thing, please note that Twitch expects you to consistently maintain your channel status, meaning you need to keep your audience hyperactive month over month. So, this is definitely the big leagues. You cannot just have this as a side hustle. The best-paid Twitch partners are doing it full-time.

How much can you expect to make as a Twitch partner?

On average, expert streamers can earn anywhere between $3000 and $5,000 each month by putting in about a 40-hour workweek. If you put in the time and effort to grow a sizable audience, this can become pretty lucrative. Add to that the extra revenue generated from ads ($250 for every 100 subscribers), and you can see how $10,000 becomes a realistic goal. So, if you want to earn $10K a month playing video games, it is an absolute possibility. The path is logical. Many are doing it on Twitch already, so you can too, once you develop the right work ethic.

There's More!

As mentioned earlier, there is a multitude of ways we can generate revenue from Twitch. So far, we have discussed Twitch affiliates and partnerships. I also briefly touched on Twitch ads which, according to CNBC, is $250 per 100 subscribers.

• Twitch ads

Twitch offers standard Interactive Advertising Bureau pre-roll and display ads. Streamers get paid based on the Cost Per Impression (CPM) model, which is every 1,000 views of your ads.

• Paid Livestreams and Sponsorships

Once you have a sizable audience, many opportunities become available both on and off Twitch. One great opportunity is getting sponsored by companies to market their products. That can include promoting their merch, talking about them during your live streams, and using their products on camera. For example, the famous Ninja usually promotes DXRacer chairs, which probably pays him to display them. Another form of sponsorship is a paid Livestream where game developers will pay broadcasters to live to stream their game and get in front of a new audience, hoping that some will purchase the game as well and play.

- Affiliate marketing

Affiliate or referral marketing is an excellent way for you to be able to make money on Twitch. Keep in mind that this isn't the same as being a Twitch affiliate. With this method, you provide links to the specific products you want your audience to buy. Becoming an Amazon associate is the most common option for many streamers. And as a Twitch affiliate, you can earn higher commission rates than standard referral accounts through Amazon Blacksmith (Twitch's built-in Amazon Associates tool).

Although most people only associate affiliate marketing with Amazon, you could establish relationships with the companies whose products you're already using. For example, if you love the chair you're using, you might work out a deal with the company manufacturer and get a coupon code that you could share with your followers. Anytime someone uses your coupon code to buy the chair, the company cuts you some of their profit. The more your audience grows, the more your traffic to the products will increase, and if you're getting a fair commission, this can lead to a lot of money each month. In fact, if you've got a large following, affiliate relationships can be more profitable because you get paid a commission instead of the earlier option of a sponsorship which is a fixed fee. I like affiliate marketing because you don't even need to become a Twitch partner and go through all that hoopla. As long as you have a big enough audience that loves you, money can start rolling in.

Make Use of Your Channel Analytics

Gaining an understanding of how your channel is performing is vital to your success. You need to identify what's working and what's not as early on as possible. That requires tracking, measuring, and analyzing some data. Lucky for you, Twitch comes with in-built analytics to help you constantly improve your delivery and craft.

To increase your chances of getting affiliated and partnered with Twitch, as well as to ensure you continue to plan your streams better, you need to learn how to read your channel analytics. Let's cover the channel insights, how to read and use the data Twitch will provide you with overtime.

Channel Insights

To access channel insights, go to Twitch.tv and select your icon on the top right. Find "Creator Dashboard" then "Insights" on the left sidebar. Here you will find the channel settings where all your data is stored. There are three subsections:

• Channel Analytics

That will provide a holistic view of your channel. It gives you information about average viewership, live views, follower gain, subscription gains, and revenue.

This section is great for keeping you accountable because you can see all of the streams you've done over a specific time period, and it also shows you where your views are coming from, your top clips, and more. You can break down the data by date range, and I recommend a month-to-month comparison on how you're doing to avoid being overwhelmed or getting lost in the data.

An example of when to use channel analytics:

If you're thinking about switching game genres and want to determine whether or not it was a great idea, you can run some test streams. Then use channel analytics to see how your average viewers and follower gains were affected. That will enable you to make an informed decision on how to proceed.

Another powerful way to use this tool is to check the streamers with a similar audience that you could potentially collaborate with. Find "Which channels have viewers in common with mine?" and start connecting with the people who you feel might great make partners so you can cross-pollinate and grow your communities together.

• Stream Summary

In the stream summary, you will see data from each of your previous streams. You can see stream duration, average viewers, max viewers, new follower count, total views, unique chatters, peak time, raids received, viewers by hour chat, tips, and views by source. This information is great when you're trying to grow your following so you can reach your goal of becoming an affiliate or partner. You can also use this data to figure out the best streaming times.

For example, suppose you've been streaming from Tuesdays to Saturdays from 7:00 pm to 10:00 pm for the past three months. You now have ample data to help you figure out peak time. You might see in the stream summary that, on average, your peak time for concurrents falls at 9:00 pm. You might also realize that at 8.30 pm, there's not much action, and yet by the time you're done streaming, you have double or triple the concurrents you had when you started. That data enables you to begin testing different alternatives. You could stream from 8.30 pm to 11:30 pm to see what (if any) changes would happen to your follower gain, concurrents, and overall reception.

Another thing you can do is to check your Views by Source box. This area shows where you are getting traffic to your channel. Track to see how effective you are at bringing people from your other social media accounts to Twitch. That is extremely helpful because you can learn whether your CTAs on Twitter, TikTok, and Instagram are actually working.

- Achievements

As the name suggests, this tool enables you to stay accountable and keep track of your goals. If the Twitch partnership is a big goal, then you'll want to keep an eye on your achievements data. It also helps you track things like how many hours of streaming you have under your belt, how many average viewers you have over 30 days, and so on. It takes out the guesswork and the fatigue of manually having to figure all of these things out. The best part is when you hit the desired goal for becoming a Twitch partner, that form for applying will open up for you automatically.

You can use Achievement in combination with Stream Summary and Channel Analytics to improve and change your content. Each of these subsections provides detailed information about certain items of your channel. Use them to see how your channel performed month by month but remember, don't get lost or discouraged by what the data shows, especially when you're just getting started.

SECTION 4: Growing Your Brand

Chapter 14: Engaging with the Community

The benefits of growing a successful brand on any social media channel, especially Twitch and TikTok, should now be very obvious to you. There's a lot of success to be had on the Internet. But here's the thing. Everything hinges on growing a sizable audience. The more interactive and loyal your audience, the quicker you will grow. Of course, that cannot happen unless you have the right mindset. What is the right mindset? Get into Twitch and TikTok to socialize and create connections with community members. Unless you take it as a social experience, you're going to have a hard time reaching your goals.

Some people desire fame and success on social media but hate the work needed to get there. If that's you, then this won't be the right decision for you. Unless your community becomes essential in your eyes, you will still fall short of success.

I understand it's a lot of hard work, and you already have a lot to take care of, but the fact remains - you need to engage with the community.

Instead of finding shortcuts, work on establishing a routine that enables you to have regular, personalized communications on all the platforms you enjoy socializing. More than one platform is advised because you can use that growing connection to drive traffic to your main account. For example, If you want to grow your Twitch career, having a Twitter and Instagram account is a fantastic investment as well because your fans are likely to come to watch your live streams when you send out DMs since they already know, like, and feel a connection with you.

It Goes Both Ways

Have you ever come across an account with lots of responses from people (emojis or text comments) yet no response from the account owner? How did that make you feel? Would you feel inclined to connect with that person?

Keep that thought in mind as you grow your channel. Socializing is a two-way experience, and you will need to invest time to interact with your audience, whether you have one response or one hundred. Sometimes people expect the account owner to take the initiative, so I encourage you to visit the accounts you like, whether they belong to influencers or fans, and start a conversation with them. Make sure it's appropriate and positive. Avoid self-promotion as much as possible. Just be a generous and kind human genuinely interested in making a connection. A couple of things you can do to build genuine relationships on social media include:

• Asking for advice or recommendations.

• Posing a question to your community or to an influencer's post to start up a conversation. Just make sure it's relevant.

• Send special DMs with some kind of value add, even if it's just a motivational message that will brighten their day.

Interactive content types to experiment with:

#1: Polls and Surveys

These are quick and easy to set up. As long as you craft something thoughtful, people will participate. You can use it to get feedback, audience preferences, and so much more.

#2: Contests

People on social media always love engaging in a contest, especially if there are great rewards up for grabs. Not only will a contest grow your brand awareness and engage masses on social media, but it may also help you with list-building efforts so you can grow an email list and build an internal fan base. A popular form of contest that you can try is the "enter-to-win" giveaway.

#3: Questions and Quizzes

You can create social quizzes and share the results on your social channels. It can be around the games you usually Livestream to add that touch of personalization and draw on people who already love what you do. Quizzes also allow you to capture data from the questions answered to gain insights about your audience. That will help you as you develop content and marketing ideas to grow your brand.

When creating interactive content to drive more engagement, the most important thing is to utilize all the free tools and resources available for you. For example, if you have a Facebook account, create a free, fast, and easy poll. Many social media platforms have lots of features in-built that will enable you (with a bit of creativity) to create opportunities for people to engage with you and vice versa.

Creating a Discord Server For Your Community

Discord is a social tool that gamers use to build their community within Twitch. It's free and offers voice chat channels as well as text making it super convenient for streamers. Once you create your server, you can divide it into channels to separate whichever topics your community will engage in. The server can be public or private (private servers are for closed communities and the public ones are for anyone allowing larger groups to gather and share their interests, use custom emotes, and dedicate moderators to ban unwanted members). A major benefit of setting up your server is that it allows you to interact with your viewers off-stream, which will help you grow your channel faster. You will have the ability to interact in real-time, form a genuine connection with your community and have a dedicated space for your growing audience. Think about it this way. You can only be live on Twitch during a stream, but with Discord, you can be engaging and nurturing your audience 24/7. That's how brands are built on social media.

Many streamers use Discord to do things like movie nights, off-stream game nights, and other events. It's also pretty helpful when setting up multiplayer games both on and off stream.

How to get started:

You can sign-up for free on Discord by downloading the Discord app for Desktop or from your mobile device's app store and just follow the instructions. You can choose to use your username from Twitch or change it to something new, but since you're using this to grow your channel, I suggest keeping the same name and profile picture for branding purposes. Then follow the steps below to create your first server.

One. Press the +Plus sign button on the left sidebar of the interface.

Two. Choose the "Create" option to go to a screen that will allow you to enter your server's details.

Three. Select your region and a logo for the server.

Four. Name your server.

Five. After you create your server, go into your settings and set up the verification levels and notifications settings.

Pro tip: Set it to @mentions only so that you only get notified when it's important.

Once your server is live, you can add stream integrations as well. You can use bots like Nightbot, Muxy, or whatever else you prefer to your server to help you moderate the communications. For this, you will need to open your Discord and click the User settings icon next to your name. Select "Connections" and then click on the Twitch icon. If you're logged in to Twitch on your computer, it should auto-populate your account.

How Discord can help you grow your community and some best practices:

Most people are looking for a place to hang out online with their favorite streamers and friends without having all their communication exposed on Google, and that's precisely what Discord will offer you and your fans. Because it's more controlled and private, this real-time chat nature of the platform makes the connection more intimate and genuine.

Another benefit is that by setting up your channel, you don't need a big following to be heard or build loyalty. It allows you to just hang out with the people you want to hang out with and interact with them in any way you want, whether it's through voice, text, images, video, or whatever else. With Discord, you can set up an announcement channel to promote new products or anything else you'd like to share with your audience, and everyone will get the message. So, the more people value your ideas, the easier it becomes to create affiliate marketing sales. There's no reliance on algorithms, reach, or any of those technicalities with Discord because it's an independent third party that cares more about the community and the creators.

When you set up your first server, be sure to start with a welcome channel. Also, remember to be authentic and hold the right intention. Discord is not an advertising platform. It's a hang-out spot.

You should also pick one of the bots to integrate so you can track users' activity patterns and engagement. That will help you learn about peak hours, best-performing topics, etc. With this information, you can capitalize during the right time frame to do a plethora of activities ranging from basic conversations to tournaments. Just make sure not to add too many bots or moderators. If you already have enough followers, consider assigning some roles for your community members to help you run the server. The more users join, the more you'll need some support from other members who can help with questions, concerns and even keeping the energy of the channels high. Use the same process you did with mods within Twitch by going for people who resonate with you and those that are highly engaged and active within the server.

Protecting Your Identity

Although we emphasize the importance of remaining authentic as you share your passion for gaming on social media, we must also insist on preserving your privacy. There are six things you should never share in public.

#1: Your home address

The risk involved with disclosing where you live is not worth taking. And I don't just mean because of thieves and robbers who might use this to their advantage. I am talking about trolls and sometimes even crazy obsessive fans who might make things uncomfortable for you and your family members by stalking you. Besides, if someone has your full address, it's easy to search through different databases to acquire additional information like your phone number, employment history, and other sensitive information. And by the way, if someone has enough sensitive data, they can do crazy things like open up a credit card in your name or steal money from your accounts. Never disclose where you live.

#2: Clubs or other affiliation

The more information someone has about your interests and where you like to spend your leisure time, the easier it is to launch a successful phishing scam. It can be as easy as sending you an email that appears to be from an organization that you volunteer for.

#3: Pictures of your credit cards or driving license

I know this seems obvious, but it happens more often than you might think. The first time we get a credit card or when the driving license finally arrives, that excitement can cause us to act without thinking things through. Just in case you're tempted to share with your social media fans these sensitive details, remember, anyone with access to your credit card number and expiry date can pretty much order for anything they want online on your tab!

#4: The same goes for your bank information

Isn't it great to show social proof of the money you're making now that your accounts have started monetizing? While I agree it's motivating to show fellow creators that they can do it too, remember it's unwise to give people that much back office access. Keep your financial statements to yourself unless you want to attract hackers and ill-intentioned people.

#5: Insensitive rants ranging from politics to religion and so much more.

I will not dictate what you should and shouldn't discuss on social media, but I will warn you against off-color jokes, sexism, religious and political debates. The world is already so divided when it comes to these heated topics. Do you really need to be considered misogynistic or labeled harshly by people who would otherwise be helping you build a lucrative brand? A good rule of thumb is to apply your grandma's test. If you can share that piece of content with your grandma confidently, then it passes the test. Otherwise, keep it to yourself.

#6: Sharing intimate information about your relationships

Before you post something about your parents, girlfriend, boyfriend, boss, or the bank manager that pissed you off earlier in the day, pause and think twice. While it might seem innocent at the time to bash about the institutions you work with or work for or that it's cool to share selfies of you kissing your bae, remember someone can easily use all this sensitive information against you if they land on the wrong hands. Think of this scenario. Imagine tweeting a complaint to your bank and ranting about how horrible their service was and potentially even naming the bank manager that mistreated you. It's not a stretch to imagine that if someone wants to target you, they could use this information to contact you, pretending to be the bank and creating a whole scam around it. Now, let's think of another scenario. Imagine sharing with your community intimate details about your girlfriend or boyfriend and how you surprised them at work etc. By sharing all these details, someone can literally grab that information and contact them, luring them into a scam as well under the pretense that they know you. Some might say this scenario is unlikely, but it is possible, so try to limit what you share in public no matter how tempting it is. It's always a good idea to consciously consider what kind of information the post could give away and what the consequences of that might be. Not only does it protect your identity, but it also protects your loved ones.

Chapter 15: Connecting and Expanding

Now that you understand how both TikTok and Twitch work and how to launch yourself, it's time to utilize both these platforms simultaneously. Many gamers are experiencing great success in both viewership for their streams and attracting new followers and subs. The best part is that it's easier than you think to do it.

Let's start with the fact that you already have content that can easily be edited and tweaked for the TikTok audience. Your live stream highlights can be easily edited as short clips with great trendy TikTok music and published to that audience. That can act as an excellent teaser for your Twitch channel, and it draws in viewers and followers on TikTok who love gaming.

When publishing your highlight clips, the hashtags you use matter a lot. If you want to get discovered, you will need to add #FYP so that the platform can push your content to people likely to enjoy gaming. You should also add a few more hashtags that are relevant to the game you're promoting. For example, if you're highlighting your Pokémon game, it's best to go with hashtags related to that, including #pokemon #twitch #streamer #pokemongo #pok #gaming, etc. What you should never do is attempt to be too general by going with trending hashtags that have nothing to do with your game.

What kind of strategy works best?

The correct answer is - the one that you experiment with and see great results. Many gamers apply different strategies to drive traffic from their TikTok to Twitch. Try other things, and don't be scared to think outside the box. The content you publish on TikTok doesn't need to be about gaming. It can also be silly stuff that happens before or after your live streaming. Twitch streamer OfficerStealth posted a video challenge on TikTok where he said that he would do one push up for every like. That got the community really engaged as they tried to see how many push-ups he could actually do. Although that has nothing to do with gaming, it's still getting him attention and new followers who can potentially convert to Twitch followers.

How to get more viewers to your Twitch broadcast using TikTok

Once you've grown your TikTok to about one thousand followers, a new feature will become available to you. That is the Livestream version of the platform that's pretty similar to Instagram live. You can broadcast directly from your smartphone, and when you're live, all your followers are usually alerted and invited to join the stream. This is the perfect time for you to interact with people and encourage them to come over to your Twitch stream. It's a simple strategy, and it works incredibly well, even for people with only a few thousand followers on TikTok. OfficerStealth likes to leverage this technique and usually begins a stream on TikTok before his Twitch broadcast starts to attract viewers. Then, he jumps over to Twitch and leaves the TikTok stream running while he streams his gameplay. The results have been pretty impressive as more and more people jump in and raid his Twitch from TikTok. If you are going to do this, here are a couple of things to keep in mind.

- Make sure to start the TikTok stream before the gameplay on Twitch so you can interact with them.

Don't Stop with Just Two.

If you're feeling ambitious and you're serious about becoming a superstar on Twitch, then this section of the book is for you. Chapter 11 of the book shared five tips for beginners where I encouraged you to leverage social media to boost your growth and viewership on Twitch. Most people will opt for a maximum of two social media channels, but serious streamers often have more than two social networks. That's what you're going to do as you learn to make gaming your full-time, high-paying job.

We already mentioned that YouTube, Twitter, Instagram, and Facebook are great for connecting and building an audience that can convert into traffic, but how exactly would you do this?

First, you need to set up profiles on these platforms, e.g., YouTube, Twitter, and Instagram. Then follow best practices when it comes to posting content and growing an audience. Here are a few to consider.

#1: Cross-promote; don't cross-post.

That means you should never use the exact same piece of content on any two channels because no two social platforms are identical. People shift their psychology and preference depending on the channel they're currently on. For example, the same viewer on Instagram might be more intrigued by your Instagram Stories highlights if you created the best moments of your last gameplay. They might follow your account if you usually post funny selfies of yourself before and post streaming. But while on YouTube, they might want to get a more in-depth taste of the last gameplay and actual walkthrough of the game that you specialize in. As you can see, this same viewer is expecting a different experience whenever he interacts with your content across different social networks, so to show them the same content over and over would only nauseate him.

A mistake I have seen a lot with new gamers is they will post a tweet that says, "I posted a new photo to Facebook," They will include a link that people should click. Does it ever work? Nope!

I know you might want to save some time by taking the same content and mass distributing it, but if you're going to gain new viewers and fans, you'll need to invest time and tailor your message in a way that makes sense to each particular audience.

#2: Use a customized URL that you can track when posting on social media.

It's vital to add trackable links so you can identify which social network is offering the highest and best engagement. If you don't know where the most traffic is coming from, you might end up investing your energy in the wrong place. For example, if you would like to be doing a live promo to get people to show up for your live stream, then half an hour or an hour before your Twitch stream begins, you will need to start prepping your audience on the other social platforms. Suppose you have no idea where the most traffic comes from, and you simply assume it's TikTok when it is, in fact, Instagram, then you might kill all your promo time on TikTok and ignore doing an Instagram Live, which would cost you more viewers on your Twitch stream. So don't take any chances with this. Make sure each link on your social media accounts is tracked, and you invest your time and resources where you see the most traction.

#3: Use Twitter To Test Content Ideas.

If you're going to get a Twitter account as most gamers do, consider using it to tap into potentially hot content ideas so you can produce more of what your potential viewers are likely to enjoy. Twitter is a great "content lab" for testing how well-received a piece of content is likely to be or gauge how much interest there is for a particular game. Even if you don't have a large following by simply following peers with bigger Twitter audiences and asking questions in their chats as well as reading what others are saying, you can learn a lot about what viewers want. This is especially awesome when you're thinking about starting a new game.

#4: Use your social media platforms to take followers behind the scenes.

Using Stories on Facebook and Instagram, you can easily create unique content that gives followers a different aspect of your life. There are over 800 million people engaged with Stories every single day on just Facebook and Instagram. What does that tell you? People love watching other people share their stories. You should leverage this. Share as much or as little as you like about yourself, but I've found these "behind-the-scenes" content to be highly effective for attracting new people to my Instagram and, ultimately, my Twitch channel. I like to give people an inside peek at how I prep up for my gameplays, how I choose what to play, and also who I am as a person. It creates a bond between the Instagrammers who then show up for my Twitch streams and me.

Collaborate with other Content Creators

Some streamers see their peers as competition and feel very hesitant to build collabs with already existing content creators. That is very shallow thinking because only good can come about when you collaborate with the right streamer. Your journey would be less lonely. You'd have an ally and someone you can grow with. So, if you're wondering whether collabs can help you achieve your results faster, the answer is yes. You just need to approach this relationship the right way and set clear intentions even before reaching out. Working with the right kind of people can also help you create better content that will increase your exposure to a broader audience.

I also recognize that as gamers, we tend to be more introverted, so putting ourselves out there can be scary. Rejection is a big obstacle. If you realize you need a little mindset work to help you become a better communicator and relationship builder, then find resources online that can help you do that. Once you feel ready to start reaching out to potential collaborators, begin with the social networks that most appeal to you. Here's how to go about this.

Consider looking for collabs on TikTok, YouTube, Facebook Groups, Discord Channels, and through friends.

You can join popular Discord channels where you can start to network with fellow streamers and participate in their conversations so they can see you adding value and sharing your ideas. When it comes to Discord, you can check out the StreamScheme Discord, Gaming Careers, Twitch Subreddit, and the Bait Squad. One of these Discord channels is bound to resonate with you. For Facebook Groups, you should check out Twitch.TV Streamers Community is very active and allows you to network and even promote your streams. Don't become spammy, though.

Once you've done some research and spotted a few people you like, reach out to them. Make sure you have clear criteria of the people you can collaborate with. It should be someone you feel naturally connected to so that you can leverage that chemistry while creating content. Viewers will be more attracted to good conversation and might be more engaged and interactive with your content. You should also work with someone who compliments you. That means they have certain strengths that you lack. I like this approach because it enables both parties to create content and do things together they would others struggle with. That creates unique experiences for both and more value for the audience. The last thing I want to add is you need to find someone who resonates with your style of doing things and someone who is just as serious and committed to building their channel and community as you are. Don't get into partnership with jokers because that will lead to a lot of disappointment down the road.

There are different types of partnerships that you could get into. We'll talk about that shortly. But first, let's emphasize the importance of taking your time when initiating a partnership.

Choosing the right candidates is only the first step toward building a good partnership. Most people will not be the right fit for you, so take your time and do some thorough checks before committing to something serious. You should both be willing to start slow. As with any relationship, dating is essential before marriage. Think of it the same way. So even when you reach out, start by building a friendship, commenting on their stuff, supporting them in any way possible, and building a relationship from there. As long as you remain authentic and sincere, your relationship will grow, and collaboration opportunities will become a natural by-product.

Why partner with the so-called competition?

• Mutual support.

When you build a relationship and work with someone who is on the same journey, you will enjoy this process more. It also means both of you will have the ability to get twice as much reach for less effort as you both distribute and promote your content.

• Reputation by proxy.

As a newbie, you can grow your reputation by just being associated with other high-authority figures in your niche. The more people see you with streamers they already know, like, and respect, the better they'll think of you.

- Follower cross-pollination.

The best part of collaborating with someone is that at least some of your followers will discover this person for the first time and vice versa. That means you get new viewers and followers that are more likely to become loyal fans and subscribers quickly.

Different types of partnerships to consider include:

#1: Commentary and discussion

This type of collaboration emphasizes engagement. Social media loves engagement, and when you and your peer can start a thread on your post or theirs and have a healthy discussion, even if you're not in agreement, it will attract more people and more conversations.

#2: True collaboration

This is when you come together to create content that you can both share with your audience. It could be as simple as organizing dual gameplays or entire tournaments for your communities to participate in.

#3: Cross-promoting content

This type of partnership is relatively easy because all you do is agree to post each other's content and give each other shout-outs. For example, you could receive from your partner his latest gameplay highlight and publish it on your TikTok, then start a conversation around it to invite him and his followers to engage in your post. Your partner would then do the same for you.

The Power of Networks

Networking is vital to your Twitch success regardless of how much of a social animal you consider yourself to be. And if networking has a negative connotation, think of it as relationship building. You don't have to spend all your time trying to reach out to everyone on Twitch, but you do need to have a scheduled time daily where you hang out on relevant Discord channels to find people who vibe with you. Connect with people who have similar concurrent viewer count as yourself. Experts recommend going no higher than a concurrent viewer count of 50% more than your own count.

But don't limit yourself here. You can also connect with people who have a smaller audience. What matters is that you collaborate with people who have personalities that mesh with yours and people who bring fun and entertainment to the table. Think of it this way. If you stream for 12 hours a day, you have 12 hours where no one on Twitch gets to know about your channel and the fantastic work you do. Now imagine you've surrounded yourself with a strong team of fellow streamers, and you all support each other, mention each other's channels and even talk about each other's games while streaming. In that case, even while you're not streaming, a word about your brand and channel is still circulating across Twitch, thanks to your team. That's the power of a good network.

Grow at Your Own Pace

While it is exciting to talk about big followership and earning thousands of dollars each month, I want to remind you that everyone's journey will be unique. Learn to embrace your personal journey and grow at the right pace for you. Even if you hear stories of people who went from zero to hero within six months and you look at your channel twelve months from now and realize you're still not there, don't let that discourage you. I know people who took five years to reach their ultimate goal. It took multiple years as well before my channel truly became as successful as I had envisioned. And I also know people who blew up within a matter of months. I don't know how your story will play out, but I'm confident with the right mindset, and that persistent attitude you will hit your desired target.

Conclusion:

You've made it to the end, but this is only the beginning. We covered a lot in this book, and it might require a couple of reads on some of the earlier chapters to fully grasp all that was shared. By now, you can see the potential of both TikTok and Twitch and how they work together to help you realize your dreams. These platforms have grown a lot in recent years, and experts anticipate accelerated growth in the coming years.

The opportunities are endless if you are serious about creating an online business and passive income through both of these channels. You have a basic understanding of how to set up each account and how to create content that both people and the algorithm will love. You've received detailed strategies of how to grow your audience, where to go to build your network and collaborations, and how to start monetizing your account once you've got enough momentum. I walked you through a very detailed process of identifying your niche and finding gaps that you can leverage so that people can learn to associate your brand with something specific that adds value. In all that technical education you've received, remember one thing. Nothing matters if you're not willing to consistently create beneficial, entertaining, and useful content for your ideal audience.

To become successful and rich, the main focus should never be on making money. It must always remain on building and serving your audience. Most aspiring social media influencers never succeed because they have the wrong mindset and approach their online business from a self-focused perspective. Hopefully, this book has given you insights that enable you to see how serving the Twitch community and heavily investing in build yourself as an authentic brand is the best way to create the passive income and online success you desire. None of this is easy. But if you can stick to it and follow the strategies and tactics outlined in this book, you will find yourself living a life beyond your wildest dreams sooner rather than later. Life on your own terms earning the kind of income your parents never thought possible, and, best of all, having the freedom to live, work and play wherever and whenever you want. Isn't that why you picked up this book in the first place? That kind of freedom is not within your reach. It's time to take the next step and implement. Good luck and may the Twitch and TikTok gods favor you on your journey to success online!

Resources:

P. (2020e, November 18). Social media algorithms – what they are and how they work in 2020. Retrieved April 7, 2021, from https://www.pickandmixms.co.uk/social-media-algorithms-2020/

Chaney, P. (2014, March 24). Market Through Shared Interests and Passions Using Social Media. Retrieved April 7, 2021, from https://www.clickz.com/market-through-shared-interests-and-passions-using-social-media/32524/

TechCrunch is now a part of Verizon Media. (2019, January 29). Retrieved April 7, 2021, from https://techcrunch.com/2019/01/29/its-time-to-pay-serious-attention-to-TikTok/

Ferguson, J. (2020, July 7). Using TikTok Advertising To Promote Your Business. Retrieved April 7, 2021, from https://amplitudedigital.com/social-media/using-TikTok-to-promote-your-business/

M. (2021, April 12). TikTok Hashtags: A Guide to Using Hashtags on TikTok. Retrieved April 7, 2021, from https://boosted.lightricks.com/a-guide-to-hashtags-on-TikTok/

Stroud, D. J. (2014, October 29). Understanding the Purpose and Use of Benchmarking. Retrieved April 7, 2021, from https://www.isixsigma.com/methodology/benchmarking/understanding-purpose-and-use-benchmarking/

Startisans. (n.d.). Benefits Of Having Popular Creator Badge On TikTok. Retrieved April 7, 2021, from https://startisans.net/benefits-of-having-popular-creator-badge-on-TikTok/

Southern, M. (2020b, August 14). Here's How Much Brands Are Paying for Sponsored Content on TikTok & YouTube. Retrieved April 7, 2021, from https://www.searchenginejournal.com/heres-how-much-brands-are-paying-for-sponsored-content-on-TikTok-youtube/346290/

A. (2021a, March 9). How Do Tik Tok Gifts Work. Retrieved April 7, 2021, from https://social.techjunkie.com/how-do-TikTok-gifts-work/

Yaden, J. (2021, March 16). What is Twitch? Retrieved April 7, 2021, from https://www.digitaltrends.com/gaming/what-is-twitch/

Etienne, S., & Faulkner, C. (2020, April 6). How to stream your gaming sessions. Retrieved April 7, 2021, from https://www.theverge.com/2018/7/19/17581510/how-to-stream-gaming-twitch-youtube-mixer

Painter, L. S. S. W. (2019, June 25). How to use OBS (Open Broadcaster Software). Retrieved April 7, 2021, from https://www.techadvisor.co.uk/how-to/game/use-obs-to-live-stream-3676910/

J. (2020a, October 26). Ways of Improving Your Twitch Stream (That Don't Involve Spending a Fortune). Retrieved April 7, 2021, from https://inthirdperson.com/2020/11/11/ways-of-improving-your-twitch-stream-that-dont-involve-spending-a-fortune/

CPSIA information can be obtained
at www.ICGtesting.com
Printed in the USA
BVHW060937151221
624107BV00014B/419